Life at Five Knots

The Circumnavigation of Shadowfax

by Scott McPhee

Photos can be found at
www.LifeAtFiveKnots.com

For Gretchen
All the t-shirt acquisitions and more...

Chapter 1

At the time we had no idea we would ever take it on ourselves to sail around the world. All we wanted to do was to travel a little, and somehow we arrived at the decision to try it by sailboat. People still ask me how a couple of non-boaters managed to end up battling Pacific, Atlantic and Indian Ocean storms as we made our way westward. I guess we just wanted some adventure.

My name is Scott McPhee and I was married to an adventurous wife, Gretchen, and we were lifelong Rhode Island residents. We were in our 20s and tired of cold, snow, and the short summers of New England. Our sailing experience started in Rhode Island and took 10 years to evolve into a sailing circumnavigation.

We wanted to travel and to leave Rhode Island and our first thoughts were of traveling in a more normal fashion. Grabbing one of those big motor homes and heading west was our first thought. It was Gretchen who found a calculator and started to figure out fuel costs and other real-life problems. We nixed the motor home idea before we bothered to look at one. It seems after buying the thing, we would only have enough money left to get to Connecticut before we would have to stop and get a job.

In short order we also ruled out cars and bicycles, but when we thought of traveling by power boat, we stopped and gave it some serious thought... at least for an hour or two. Again we ruled it out because of all the dollar bills we would have to stuff down the fuel tank. I don't think either one of us bothered to bring up the fact that neither one of us had any idea how to drive one.

I'm not sure which one of us said the word "sailboat" first, but it really seemed to be the answer. Gretchen and I had never looked at a sailboat up close, so the first chance we got off we went to check one out. Sure, we had seen them sailing around the bay, but seeing a big white sheet-type thing flapping around in the wind was about all that came to mind.

The first sailboat we looked at was what the salesman called a sloop. We had no idea what "sloop" meant, but it didn't matter because we were hooked. Downstairs, or below, as the guy called it, was set up like a mobile home. The boat was for sale, but we knew it was much too early to think about buying one. We went back to the apartment to think things over.

It always helps to have a plan, and I think we came up with a good one – buy a sailboat, sell everything, quit our jobs, and sail somewhere out of New England in a southerly direction. So what if we knew nothing about sailing. We reasoned that this being America, people were allowed to do all sorts of insane things.

We started to tell all our friends and relatives about our great plan, and the encouragement they gave us was less than expected – and we didn't expect much. The general opinion was that we would sink, or starve, with no other option. I knew it was inevitable, and it was my best friend who brought it up first. He looked at me kind of strangely and said, "Hey, you've never even been on a boat." Well, this wasn't exactly true. I had an eight-foot rowboat when I was ten. As that thought came to mind, I tried not to think about how many times that boat did, in fact, sink. Of course, being an adult of 25, I was pretty sure I could bail a boat quite a bit faster.

Next step, try to find a boat. In our opinion the best place to start would be near the water. Rhode Island, being called the Ocean State, had hundreds of sailboats, and they all seemed to be for sale. We were a little curious about that, but not enough to stop us from looking.

The budget allowed us fourteen thousand dollars for the boat. This would leave us enough left over to pay up our life insurance for the next nine months - just in case.

The first boat we really liked was anchored in the harbor in Newport, Rhode Island. The salesman took us out to the anchored boat in what he called a "launch," and tied up to a sleek looking forty-two foot boat. I was trying to learn as many nautical terms as I could, but when he started talking about reefing, degrees of heel and windward ability, I sort of slipped on downstairs... or "below" as they say.

What I could understand were terms like microwave, showers, diesel and standing head room. What Gretchen caught on to right away was that this had to be a lot more than fourteen thousand dollars. We approached our happy salesman about this and he said, "That's no problem. With that much money down, your payments would only be..." as soon as he mentioned that black listed word "payments," we knew we were in the wrong ballpark. When we learned that full price of that forty-two footer, we knew we were in the wrong stadium.

Our friendly salesman wasn't so friendly anymore, and he told us for that amount of money we couldn't possibly find a boat to take cruising for any distance. On the way back to shore he stopped to show us what he called a daysailer. The boat was about twenty feet long, and it tipped violently to one side as I stepped aboard. The inside was all fiberglass and only had enough room if one of us stayed home. The cost of this little baby was a cool thirteen thousand five hundred dollars. That sure seemed like a lot of money for a three-by-three-foot living area.

We went back home feeling that maybe we should buy the forty-footer we had looked at and try to pay it off. If we took out a twelve-year loan and worked hard, we could probably have paid it off in just over eleven and a half years.

Armed with a comfortable night's sleep, we decided to resume the search. As we ran all over the eastern seaboard, our friends were watching intently to see how far we would go before giving up and resuming a normal life.

Finally, we found the boat. Ironically, after covering enough real estate to be considered a voyage in itself, the boat was docked four blocks from our apartment. A guy named Sam had owned it for almost a year, but owners on neighboring boats said that after his one time out, he absolutely hated sailing. It's true that I didn't know much about sailing, but I did know the value of a motivated seller.

The boat was a twenty-seven-foot Coronado sloop (one mast) with a one cylinder inboard diesel, which in months to come I would get to know intimately. We liked the boat even though down below it seemed a little small. While looking it over I found an owner's manual that said the boat would "sleep five," and couldn't figure out where they meant to stick all those people. I let this bit of false advertising go, as all we needed to sleep were two people and our Amazon parrot (appropriately named Captain).

The next step was to find a boat appraiser – if there was such a thing – to tell us whether or not to buy it, and if so, at what price. We hated to trust a stranger with this decision, but when he arrived for the inspection all our fears were gone. He was six foot four, weighed about two hundred and fifty pounds, had a full black beard, a can of beer, and was called Captain.

After his twenty-minute appraisal and a few words about a Coronado being nothing to get excited about, he said, "A 1973 Coronado in this condition should sell for fifteen thousand bucks." Amazing! Exactly what the seller claimed his bottom-line price was. I wondered to myself how the Captain and the boat owner could be related. It really didn't matter because we knew in our hearts that this boat would be our new home.

We approached Sam the next day to see if we could make a deal. With some words about winter coming and the boat still sitting in the water, we managed to change his bottom line fifteen thousand to thirteen thousand five hundred. We bought the boat.

Chapter 2

A few things had to be done if we were to leave in June - a mere seven months away. Number one on the list was to move the boat from where we bought it in East Greenwich, RI, to a marina that had what's called "bubblers" in the water to keep the water around the boat from freezing into an ice cube in the winter. We also knew we had to take some sort of boating course, but we figured we could handle moving the boat a few miles to a different marina without any problems.

Gretchen and I armed ourselves with all the necessities for this short trip – sandwiches, warm clothes and beer – and we were ready for our solo flight. The one cylinder diesel motor didn't have a whole lot to it - a couple of levers, a starting button and a few gauges. The past owner had shown me how to start it, and I was sure I could remember.

Red battery switch on, gear lever in neutral, throttle lever halfway. Okay, now push the button. As soon as I pushed it I knew there was something I had left out. The motor turned over just fine, but refused to start. Luckily there was the manual (which I would come close to wearing out in the future) and under the heading "cold starting" I read about the priming pin. It seems they wanted me to pull the pin out, squirt oil in the hole, and shove the pin back in. The pin hole would hold about a tablespoon of oil, and the pin – or plunger – would shove the oil on to some other destination. Where it went and why this tiny motor needed it would have to be investigated in the future.

A push of the button and the little Petter diesel started right up. Gretchen untied the lines, and I shoved the gearshift into forward. I gave it some more throttle and popped open a beer. I felt like I was on my second beer before the boat started to move. I shoved the throttle all the way to the full position, but it didn't seem to make much difference. I don't think I ever knew what slow was until that day. It wasn't until weeks later that I found out the reason for, and how to cure, the situation. We needed what in the boating world is called a "bottom job." Of course that depends on who you ask. Some people seem to call it a "dreaded bottom job."

As the boat moved out into Narragansett Bay, we felt we had made the right decision. Off to the right we had the Atlantic Ocean, and to the left a beautiful lighthouse in the distance. We turned to the left, or should I say port, and headed along the shoreline – right onto a sandbar.

We looked at the boat, the sandbar, and then the lighthouse way off in the distance. They couldn't possibly want us to go all the way around that lighthouse, could they? That would add miles to the trip (not to mention hours) and maybe leave us out after dark. Not a great idea for a couple of novice sailors, or should I say novice motorers.

Well, first things first. Full reverse seemed in order. We discovered Murphy's Law also followed people to sea as the temperature gauge on the motor started to climb higher and higher. As I had it in reverse, Gretchen wasn't just sitting around watching. She was up on the deck running back and forth trying to make the boat rock. This action turned out to be one of the most important parts of learning how to sail. The boat slowly backed off the sandbar, and we were again on our way. The couple of miles out to the lighthouse took just over three hours.

Time to eat lunch, and then for the first time, use the bathroom. Understandably, a twenty-seven-foot sailboat can't have a "bathroom." What it did have was called a head. It measured three-feet by two-and-a-half-feet by five-feet in height. A sink and a toilet took up most of the room. The toilet was operated by a plunger and a valve, and the sink was operated by a lever. Takes a little getting used to.

After using the one-hand-at-a-time sink, I went back to Gretchen who was steering with the stick (soon to be called piloting with the tiller) and still heading toward the same lighthouse. I remember thinking, "What if we don't get to the marina by dark?" Not a pretty thought. We knew absolutely nothing about the technique of anchoring, but if we had to we would give it a try. It would be a lot safer than continuing after dark.

Gretchen is much better than me when it comes to organizing, and as we sailed around this rusty looking lighthouse, Gretchen said it was way past time to start a "things we need" list. As the sun began to set on this calm, clear December evening, all I could think of for the list was a shiny new heater. I wished I'd thought of it sooner.

Although Gretchen agreed with me, her foresight proved impeccable. She wrote as the first entry on the list, "massive boating instruction." We had plenty of time to add to that list as we motored up the bay toward a little place called Pawtuxet Cove.

When we finally arrived we still had a good ten minutes of sunlight left. Our designated slip (parking spot) was at the mouth of a fresh water stream, which should, with the help of the bubblers, keep the boat from being frozen into the harbor waters as full winter set in. When we tied the boat up we knew it would be months before we would leave that slip again. Lots of time... after all, we had a whole six months until we planned to sail away.

Our jobs in downtown Providence didn't make us want to stay any longer than we possibly had to. We both managed separate retail stores, and Gretchen was finishing her last year at college. With Gretchen's expert organizing, it was Power Squadron courses on Monday and Thursday, Coast Guard Auxiliary on Tuesday and Friday, Red Cross First Aid on Wednesday, and for fun, Scuba classes on Saturday. I looked over this schedule and wondered if we could possibly go snow skiing on Sundays.

The next step was to try to get our budget to allow us to continue to eat, as well as attend all these classes. Not possible. The only answer was to sell something, but our list of assets was dim. We were in a rented apartment with two large untrained dogs (no money there), two sometimes running old cars, some musty furniture, and a tree strapped to our refrigerator where the parrot lived.

We worked some overtime, sold some stuff, and made enough money to start the courses. We even managed to buy a few things we needed for the boat. One was an excellent quartz heater for those freezing cold days while working on our as yet unnamed ship.

We had heard that to change the name on a boat was supposed to bring you bad luck, but we were willing to take the chance. The boat's name was "Sassy." Fat chance I was going anywhere in a boat named Sassy.

The time we set aside to work on the boat was used well. We polished and cleaned everything and then started to move a few personal things aboard. One of the best items we put on board was a book (or should I say Bible) titled "Piloting, Seamanship and Small Boat Handling," commonly called "Chapmans." This book would be used more than the motor's manual.

As spring rolled around the snow started to melt, people began to come out of hibernation and the docks were becoming crowded with boat experts. These experts were all the other people who chose to leave their boats in the water for the winter. On weekends people would group together and talk over what they had to do to their boats, and this is where we got all the inside information on the dreaded bottom job. Our sailing courses were almost finished, so we saw no problem in hauling, sanding and painting the bottom of the boat on the following weekend.

We wanted to have a name put on while we were hauled out, so now was the time to choose one. Word was out that we needed a name and our friends wanted to help. The winning name came from our downstairs neighbor - Shadowfax. The name was from the fictional trilogy "Lord of The Rings" by J.R. Tolkien. Shadowfax was Gandalf the Wizard's horse and would always get him out of trouble. That sounded great. We needed all the help we could get.

Chapter 3

The time came for the haulout. They lifted the boat out of the water and set it down on what looked like a pile of old, rotten driftwood. This was the cradle that came with the boat. Although it didn't look very safe, it held with only a slight sag. When the painter showed up to put the name on the boat, we went underneath to paint the bottom.

As we've seen since then, most boatyards come with instructors. An instructor is somebody who stands around with apparently nothing to do, but more than willing to volunteer advice. We gratefully accepted any suggestions. Anyone who hung around boatyards must have more experience than us.

All in all, the sanding and painting went well. We realized barnacles were as sharp as razors early enough to avoid serious injury. Our instructor's advice was again heeded, and new through-hull fittings were installed along with something called a cutlass bearing and a zinc to prevent what he called electrolysis. Lots of interesting words in the sailboat world.

I also installed a holding tank for the head waste. The law demanded it. The salesman demanded two hundred bucks.

After four days of being hauled out and many sore muscles, Shadowfax was compounded, waxed, scrubbed and polished. She couldn't have looked better six years earlier when she was new. Gretchen and I had never looked worse. We were covered in bottom paint, wind-burned and smelled like turpentine.

The guys at the marina put the boat back in the water and we went to the apartment to clean up before we returned in the morning for our maiden voyage. It was April sixth; the wind was blowing at about ten knots with a brisk temperature of sixty-five degrees. I wouldn't have possibly remembered all that if Gretchen hadn't given me a log book for Christmas that year. It was an excellent gift that I used every time the boat moved.

I think everybody has friends who say they will show them how to do something, and we ran into loads of people who said they knew how to sail and would love to show us the ropes... so to speak. When the day of reckoning came around it seemed everyone was just too busy. All, that is, except David Poole, one of our best friends. The only problem was that he hadn't ever sailed either, but was willing to help us figure it out. He must have enjoyed it because in ten years he would come with us on the first part of our sail around the world.

So there we were after over a hundred hours of classroom sailing education, not to mention reading dozens of books on the subject. We thought the best approach would be to take the boat out and see if we could actually make it sail. We motored out of the marina, pointed the boat into the wind and raised the mainsail. Next step, raise the jib. So far so good. I shut off the motor and turned the boat away from the wind. That's it! Nothing to it. We were off on what's called a beam reach. We'd studied navigation and our route for the day was all planned out on the chart. No more sandbars for these pros.

We practiced tacking, jibing, anchoring and even a by-the-book-man-overboard drill. David piloted the boat for a few hours, and the smile never left his face. Gretchen and I looked at each other and I think for the first time we realized that we were about to venture where normal people never go. Maybe at this point we would have started to believe that sailing around the world would really be possible.

We knew we still had a lot left to learn before we left in two months. Two months really meant eight weekends, which in turn meant only eight more times sailing before we jumped off the edge of the world. Actually, all we were planning was to sail south along the U.S. coast until we got... somewhere else.

As our weeks were spent working and planning our weekend sails, we knew it was time to put the wheels in motion and start selling off some of our treasured junk. It turned out easier than we thought. When you don't have anything to sell, it's over before you know it. As for the dogs, we found them the best homes we could and just gave them away. Definitely the hardest thing to get rid of, but there was no way to fit a couple of German Shepherds on a tiny sailboat. I knew our Captain, our parrot, would miss the dogs too. He loved to climb down from his perch and torment them. It was his favorite pastime.

We sold one of the cars in no time, but we still needed the other one so we could get to work. Our employers were given notice and replacements were found to take our places. There was no turning back.

As time passed we ordered all the charts we would need to get us as far south as Florida, and with the sale of the car we bought scuba equipment for our new sport. After all, we needed something to replace our addiction to snow skiing that we both had. Who knows, maybe we'd find loads of treasure somewhere down there. With only three paychecks left we could have used it. In the next few weeks we managed to get rid of everything we owned and moved on to our shiny blue boat.

Shadowfax was set up like your typical small sailboat. A v-berth forward, where two people could cram themselves in and try to sleep. Just back from the v-berth on the port (left) side was the head. The dinette table was also on the port side and could comfortably sit four. Across from the dinette on the starboard side was a couch, or extra berth as they called it. Just to starboard of the companion way – which is the entrance stairway down into the boat—was the galley (to call it a galley is really reaching). A two-burner propane camp stove, a small sink and a smaller ice box. No turkey dinners would be cooked here. The aft part of the boat only had storage lockers outside.

As for the parrot's new hangout, we tied his perch onto the table. Captain was usually a well behaved bird, as far as birds go anyway, but his first reaction to his new home was to climb up the wall, sit on the railing under the window, reach down with his beak and rip up a three-inch piece of teak. I guess that was his opinion of boat life.

The last week of work started with a bang. The store I managed was broken into, and as Gretchen approached a shoplifter in her store, she caught a solid left hook. If we had any doubts about leaving, they were gone.

As the day of reckoning approached, we moved aboard the boat and stocked it with as much food and supplies as we could afford. We hoped to have enough provisions to last us for a month. With our last paychecks and the sale of the few things we had left, our cash to leave with was a grand total of seven hundred dollars. We had no idea how far that could take us. Sometimes it's best to be naïve.

Chapter 4

Finally all seemed to be in order for us to say our last goodbyes. After a few tears from relatives and some unbelieving looks from friends, we waved and then motored out the channel. When we entered the bay we opened our only bottle of (six-dollar) champagne.

We made it eleven miles that first day. That put us somewhere off Jamestown Island, still in Narragansett Bay. Neither of us cared about the fact that we didn't make it very far. We'd left home port for good and that was satisfying enough. Sitting at anchor, listening to Jimmy Buffett music and looking over the charts, we were about as relaxed as we could be.

The next day we woke early, had a breakfast of bacon, eggs and lots of coffee and took off out into the Atlantic Ocean. Winds were light, so again we didn't get very far. A total of twenty-two miles capped off the hard day's work. We didn't know where we were going, so it didn't really matter how long it took to get there.

The sail to Florida took five months and is a story in itself. We learned in a sort of trial by fire routine. The intracoastal waterway allows you to sail inside the protection of outer barrier islands, or to sail out in the Atlantic and then sail into another inlet for a comfortable night's anchorage.

On the way south we learned about fog (combination of fear and hatred), breaking inlets in heavy seas (hitting a sandbar and being lifted off with the next large wave), and how to replace a busted transmission in Portsmouth Virginia (Gretchen and I both getting jobs selling five boiled hot dogs for a buck to earn the money for a new transmission).

I think our learning experience could be a story in itself, but to get to the around-the-world thing, we ended up on the west coast of Florida on Captiva Island just off the coast of Fort Myers. Long sandy beaches and new careers kept us busy as we worked toward our sailing goal.

PART TWO
Chapter 5

Nine years later it's 1988, and we needed a vacation. Here we go again. It started with Gretchen and I trying to figure out how we could take about a month off, charter a boat and go sailing. I received a charter captain's license and had been working for a local sail charter company. I was spoiled by sailing larger boats so we sold the 27-foot Shadowfax.

We had also become domesticated: a house, two cars, a dog and about a dozen parrots. A hobby that got way out of control. Sadly, our first parrot, Captain, had died, but we had no trouble buying more.

With all this "stuff" we had huge bills to keep us tied down. No way could we afford to take off for a month and lose the income we needed to pay the bills. A typical civilized rut.

But what if we decided to sell everything, buy another boat, and go cruising for an extended time? We talked about selling everything for quite a while – about six seconds—and decided to pursue this idea and see where it would lead.

As well as working part time for the charter company, Gretchen and I were both in the real estate business and we thought we could figure out how much our house was worth against how much we owed. Good news in that department! Our house was on the island of Sanibel, just south of Captiva, and property values had really appreciated. Of course, nothing we had was worth as much as we thought— not even close—but we could still come out ahead.

The next day Gretchen brought home a listing contract to put the house up for sale, and I brought home a Cruising World Magazine to check out boats for sale. I don't think that at any time after that did we doubt we would pull this off.

So many questions we needed answers to. What kind of boat do we want? Where do we find the supplies and equipment we would need, like charts, a ham radio, a sextant and safety equipment?

We figured the first thing to do was to decide where to sail. How about around the world? Hey! Good idea. Other people have done it, so why not us? I think we decided on the round-the-world thing in the first two days of this plan. Man, all this just because we couldn't get a month off. We're dangerous.

David Poole, the friend we first took sailing years ago in Rhode Island, had since moved to Sanibel, and he was in on this crazy idea too. He was willing to sell all his belongings, and come along to help. Sure, it sounded great. We didn't know what we were doing, so we were sure we would need help doing it. He was welcome to come for as long or as far as he wanted. Besides, between the two of us we might be able to fix all the mechanical equipment aboard that was sure to break.

Gretchen took charge of organizing everything (sound familiar?) and our house started filling up with books about people who had done something like this. Mostly horror stories with titles like Adrift, Survive the Savage Sea, and Heavy Weather Sailing. These were only a few of the best sellers. Also books on learning the sextant, learning Morse code to get a ham radio operator's license, and learning advanced navigation and, of course, a catalog of all the world's charts. What a mess! What fun!

We gave ourselves a year to get everything together before we sailed off toward the horizon. Lots to do and the time started to fly. We wrote to every boat broker we could find and told them we were looking for a world cruising boat. We also told them there were a lot of brokers looking, and the hardest working broker would win.

This was pre-internet so the brochures started to pile in our mailbox. We noticed lots of boats were for sale on the east coast of Florida and almost all of them said something like "make offer." We figured that after everything was sold, and with what we had saved, we would have almost a hundred and fifty thousand dollars to spend on a boat. Boy, were we dreaming!

Time dragged on and we devoured every book we could find on any subject even remotely related to sailing. The longest passages we had taken up to that point were overnighters to the Dry Tortugas, just a hundred miles away. We had a lot to learn about everything.

Somehow I managed to learn enough Morse code to get the ham radio license, and I also absorbed enough information to get a handle on using a sextant from a great little book called Sun Sight Sailing by S.L. Seaton. From there I started hitting the heavy navigation books. Believe me, there are many. I knew I had to take the navigation more seriously than I had ever taken anything else in my life... either that or die out there. Not much of a choice.

While I was doing all this, Gretchen wasn't just hanging around. She was making lists, checking things off, making more lists, pricing supplies and, oh yeah, working two jobs full time. In between all our running around, we would sit down with the chart books and try to pick a route.

Our first thought was to head out into the Caribbean and play around there for a while, but we nixed that thought immediately. Almost every sailor did that, and many of them never made it much further. We decided we had to get as far away as possible before the money ran out (preferably into the trade winds) so we couldn't turn around and run home with our tail between our legs. We thought perhaps we should be in Australia a year from the day we left. Again we were dreaming. Try three years.

We chose to begin our route through Central America: Belize and Guatemala. Sounded like we were jumping off the edge of the world. We had only dreamed of going to places like these. We picked charts out of the catalog with names that charge the imagination with all kinds of conflicting thoughts: Panama- great canal; Galapagos – strange animals and Darwin; Bora Bora—sun drenched reefs and diving; Fiji—who knows, cannibals?; and

Australia – kangaroos and meat pies. What a terrific time we had picking out charts. It was a lot of work to try and organize literally hundreds of charts, but definitely one of the most enjoyable jobs.

The great boat search was going slowly, but it was a good thing because the house hadn't sold and, in fact, neither had either car. We'd acquired a foot-high stack of information on boats in the first six months, and we had driven over to the Miami area a couple of times to look at some of the hopefuls. No luck. Boy, were we being picky.

One of the most aggressive brokers, a guy named Blake Davis, insisted that we come and look at what he called, "The only boat on the market for us." He had sent us a brochure on this "only boat for us," and we had crossed it off immediately because we thought it had too many windows.

Even though we crossed it off our list, Blake said we needed to see it in person and drove us to a great looking house near the Miami River. We walked into the backyard and there she sat. Named Criterion, this 46-foot ketch (called a Cal 2-46) sure had lots of room. Also, lots of windows – nine of them—each about two feet by two feet. Right away I could picture waves crashing through and lots and lots of death – ours. I think I said something like, "Nice boat, but can we go now. Too many windows." Gretchen agreed and off we went. So what if Criterion had been recently reduced in price to one hundred forty thousand dollars.

The next few months were hectic. Still no house sale. Time to lower the price, maybe get a cheaper boat. That's it, a cheaper boat.

Our friends were watching our activity and listening to our talk of exotic ports, and I knew it was Rhode Island all over again. I'm sure no one thought we would pull this off. Go sailing, sure. Go around the world, not so much. I guess it did sound a bit crazy. Sure we had sailed around Florida and even down the east coast of the U.S., but around the world sounded pretty heavy. Just sailing to Belize would mean a week at sea, and that sounded crazy enough.

We were asked a lot of questions by everybody who knew we were planning this, and the one question asked most was, "How long is this gonna take?" We kept answering, "I don't know," for the first few months, but people were so persistent we finally decided to say three years. From that point on everyone had pegged it as "The Three-Year Trip." Sounded like forever at the time.

One year went past and our friends started looking at us funny. Not only hadn't the house sold, but we still didn't know which boat we wanted. Ok, drop the price of the house again. Maybe we could get a cheaper boat. That's it, a cheaper boat.

Back to Miami for the tenth time to check out the latest list of possibilities. Still no luck. Our aggressive broker showed us another boat, and after rejecting it, and before we could leave, he said, "Come on, your boat is still for sale. You better come and visit it again. I'm telling ya, it's the only boat to consider."

Actually, just about every boat we'd ever looked at was still available, so we weren't surprised to see this one still sitting right where we had seen it before. The price of one hundred forty thousand was now so far out of reach that we didn't see much benefit in looking at it again, but we were starting to like this guy. Definitely the best broker, if only he wouldn't drive so fast.

I remember when it happened. I was thinking, "You know this isn't a bad boat. It's almost all set up to go long-distance cruising." Then I was hit with the obvious. I said, "I wonder why you couldn't make storm windows to fit over these windows. Maybe make 'um outta plywood or something." Dave Poole was with us at the time, and we started to check the boat out seriously.

The Cal 2-46 was eighteen years old and was hull number one in a long line of Cal 2-46's. On the down side, this meant this was the absolute oldest one you could get, and on the up side maybe they made hull number one extra strong to help sell hull number two. Anyway, we started to like what we saw. Over the boat's eighteen-year life it had accumulated all sorts of gear. The owner didn't plan to take any of it off the boat when it sold. In fact, he planned to empty his garage into the boat for whoever bought it. Oh boy, lots of "stuff."

Anyway, we couldn't get too excited about it because of the money thing. Unless we won a lottery or something, we were down to looking at boats in the ninety-thousand range, and only if the house sold. We told Blake about our money problem and in true salesman fashion he said, "Don't worry about it. I'm telling you, you are destined to own this boat. When you're ready, just make an offer."

After the first of the year things started to happen fast. We lowered the price of the house, the cars, and the furniture and advertised a yard sale. A friend of ours, who I don't even think knew the house was for sale, said he'd buy it. Wow! Great news! We also found buyers for the cars, and the yard sale was a hit. We sold lots of things we shouldn't have, and kept a bunch of things we should have gotten rid of. Oh well, maybe next time around we'll be smarter.

One last problem - our dog. Always the hardest thing to do. We knew we couldn't bring her – she was a huge German Shepherd – and it wouldn't have been fair to confine her to a small boat. Déjà vu just like giving our pets away in Rhode Island. It was hard to give her away, but we did.

Next step, make an offer on Criterion, the Cal 2-46. How much should we offer? How could he accept it? We didn't have nearly the amount they were asking. What the hell... all they could do was to say no.

Our offer was seventy-nine thousand, subject to sea trial and an out-of-the-water survey by an expert. We were willing to accept a counter offer and go as high as ninety thousand. We would have had to leave without buying any electronics, but we figured it would be worth it. We sat down to wait for the answer. We didn't have to wait long.

Blake called the next morning and said, "You've got yourselves a boat. Let's line up the survey." Wow! What a deal! We'd have enough money left over to get radar or some other shiny thing from one of our catalogs.

We had the boat hauled out in the Miami River, and everything checked out fine. We hired an experienced appraiser – inspector – to check the boat, and he couldn't find anything to bitch about. After the inspection we shoved the boat back into the water for the sea trial.

We didn't go on any long offshore voyages for the trial, but we did sail around enough to know everything was mostly okay. A few things needed fixing up or throwing out. The seller told us Criterion had been hit by lightning so most of the electronics were acting wacky. The autopilot, the loran, the radar and the batteries were also shot. None of this really worried us because we thought that with a trip like we were planning, new electronics wouldn't be a bad idea.

The big day came, and we parted with most of our money, and the seller parted with the boat. Arthur, the seller, actually got a little misty-eyed during the transaction, which we took for a good sign that the boat wasn't a lemon. That night we stayed on the boat tied to his dock and became friends with Arthur and his wife... not to mention getting slightly plastered.

We were excited. Criterion was quite a boat. We had sailed on lots of different boats with the charter company but nothing like this. This was the biggest forty-six foot boat we had ever seen. The v-berth was three times as big as the old Shadowfax, with bookshelves lining both sides. Room for a couple hundred books. Just aft from the v-berth, a head and shower were to starboard, and a hanging locker was opposite to port. From here going aft you came to a huge main salon/galley area. Before we closed on the boat Arthur told us that when they went sailing in the company of other boats, they would have dinner on one of the boats, drinks on another and come back to Criterion to dance. Definitely a roomy boat.

The salon was surrounded by the nine big windows (six could be opened) which let in tons of light and ventilation. On the port side, an L-shaped settee wrapped around a five-foot-long table. On the starboard side, a double sink, an oven/stove, and a huge freezer-refrigerator. The stove was electric, but we figured we could sell it and get a propane one. Not much electricity where we were going. A microwave was built in, and there were huge areas for storage under and behind everything.

Still going aft, a walk-thru to the aft cabin was to starboard, and the walk-thru contained the navigation station with all the navigation equipment... or at least it would when we bought some. Opposite the nav-station was a walk-in engine room that even had a little work shop to fix everything that was sure to break. The motor was a Perkins 85hp diesel and there was also an Onan 7.5 KW diesel generator. Every wall of the engine room was covered with strange looking gadgets. It was going to take a while to figure this place out.

Continuing back through the walkway was the aft cabin. A double berth to port (well, a small double) and a single to starboard. The larger of the two heads was also to port in this cabin. More bookshelves and storage under and behind everything. We would be able to carry lots of "stuff."

Even further aft, the outside lazarette on the very stern of the boat was large enough to start a smuggling business. Although we didn't plan to smuggle anything, we did have a pile of scuba equipment and, of course, more general "stuff" to bring.

What a boat! The outside had just as much room as the inside, and the center cockpit was large enough for guests to hang around comfortably. The boat was a ketch (two masts) which we thought would give us more of a selection of sail arrangements for most kinds of weather. We couldn't have been happier. We even had a bit of money left.

After selling everything and paying for the boat (owning the boat free and clear was the key to this whole thing) we still had enough left to put ten thousand in electronics and supplies, and fifteen thousand left to leave with. Man! A huge amount of money like that should last forever, shouldn't it?

David, Gretchen and I sailed the boat back to Sanibel from Miami and tied up with all the charter boats at Fort Myers Yacht Charters, the company that David helped to run. We gave ourselves two months to get everything together and leave.

We ordered charts and cruising guides all the way to Australia ($1000), a bottom-of-the-line radar ($1000), a bottom-of-the-line SatNav device ($1,000), A few fairly important items in the category of "food" ($3,000), medical equipment ($400), ham radio ($550 - should have bought a better one of those), Sextant ($400), stove and propane system ($800), miscellaneous repairs (autopilot, rigging, etc. $1,400), haul-out and bottom paint ($600). Sure went quick. We'd never spent money like that in our lives. Exciting and scary all at the same time.

As you can see, insurance isn't anywhere on that list. After we bought the boat we found that we couldn't get insurance on such an old boat to sail around the world. We had more than one friend say they were sorry that we couldn't go on the trip because of lack of insurance. Fat chance. We were willing to put it all on the line and go for it. So what if we lost it all, at least we'd give it a try.

Can't forget guns. There is a controversy in the sailing community about whether to carry guns on a passage or not. We thought it over and talked about it and our decision was to buy them and keep them hidden but accessible. I had no doubt in my mind that I would use them to protect everyone aboard. Lots of wars going on out there in the big ol' world. We had to be our own police, doctors, mechanics and navigators. Being naïve wasn't the answer.

One more important thing was the boat's name. We didn't like the name "Criterion," so we had our friends try to come up with something. After a while the choice was clear. By the time the haulout was over, we slid the boat back into the water with a crack of a champagne bottle over the bow and the new name proudly written on the stern. Shadowfax. Not Shadowfax 2, just Shadowfax. She grew up, that's all.

We were finally ready. The only thing left to sell was the nineteen-foot power boat that I used to sell out-island real estate. One of the reasons I liked selling real estate was I didn't sell anything you could drive to. Just out island properties you needed a boat to get to. A friend of ours said she was interested in the power boat, so I just turned over the payment book and told her to enjoy. This move would come back to haunt us in about four-thousand miles.

A dozen or so goodbye parties and we waved farewell as we untied the lines from 'Tween Waters Marina on Captiva Island. What a weird feeling. I'm sure no one really thought we were actually leaving for anything more than an extended vacation, but I don't think any one of the three of us doubted that we would make it all the way around the world.

Shadowfax was looking good. We had all the signal flags flying, and the white hull was buffed out to the point where you could see yourself. We motored out a small pass called Redfish Pass to the north of Captiva and shut off the motor. Could we really be on our way? If we were, it would be a slow trip. The wind was down to almost zero, but we were determined to wait for the wind and not to start the motor (at least I was).

About an hour later the wind came up and there was no looking back. April 17th, 1989, the last time we would be on the mainland United States for almost five years.

Chapter 6

Our first stop was the Dry Tortugas off the Florida Keys. It only took about twenty-four hours to sail the hundred and fifteen miles—a piece of cake. We'd made this trip about a half dozen times on charter boats (the longest trip we had ever made), and with Shadowfax, it was ten times easier. Our first experience with an autopilot, and we liked it. Just point the boat, turn it on and walk away. Also, we never had this many navigational electronics before. The radar was still too new for any of us to understand all that it did, but the Loran (long range navigation through land-based towers) and Sat-Nav (pre-GPS but still using satellite technology) were incredible. Either one would tell your position, speed and direction. How hard could this sailing around the world be with all these conveniences?

We stayed almost ten days at the Tortugas to finish up projects on the boat that we couldn't get to before we left (because of all the parties) and also to prepare ourselves mentally for the "jump" seven hundred and thirty miles to some strange land called Belize. Should be about five or six nights at sea. Man!! It sounded wild.

We couldn't put it off any longer so off we went with clear weather and a deep breath. We triple-checked all the hatches - David called it "water-tight integrity" and it certainly sounded good to me. Keep the water on the correct side of the hull and all that.

We worked out a schedule of two-and-a-half hours on watch for each of us, which would give us each five hours off in between watches. The watches consisted of not much more than just keeping your eyes open for other ships, whales, flying saucers, dinosaurs or whatever the hell else happens out there. At night we wore safety harnesses clipped to the boat to make it harder to fall over... also harder to move around. Try jumping up and running down below for a cup of coffee while forgetting you're clipped in (for almost five years).

Our first couple of nights went well. Almost a full moon, fair winds - a good training trip. We tried to stay out of trouble and to keep things from breaking, but despite trying to do no harm, the loran antenna broke at the top of the mizzen mast. On the second day out around noon, I decided to go up to the top of the mast to try to fix it.

To this day I don't know why I wanted to fix it. Loran doesn't work outside of U.S. waters. Up I went in the boson chair with David and Gretchen cranking on the winch to get me to the top of the mizzen mast. Even though it seemed like calm waters down on deck, the motion at the top was something like Space Mountain at Disney World. Once at the top I had to hang on with both hands as tight as I could. This left me my teeth to work on the antenna, so no luck fixing it. But what a view and what a ride!

The next afternoon we were off the coast of Cuba with no wind, so we decided to stop for a swim in five thousand feet of water. Talk about an eerie feeling. We had lots of little fish to swim with, and looking down we cold see at least a hundred feet into the incredibly clear water.

A few hours later the wind came up and we decided to put some distance between us and the Cuban coastline. We weren't sure how close we could safely sail off the coast of Cuba before we would get in trouble. We had read horror stories about the Cuban Coast Guard pulling in unsuspecting Americans who sailed to close to their country.

Just a few days out and we were getting used to this strange lifestyle. The weather was being kind to this poor crew of novices, and Shadowfax kept sliding through the water. At least until about halfway to Belize when we thought we were going to get run over.

It was my watch around midnight, and clouds covered the moon, so "dark" pretty much sums it up. It didn't make sense, but I was sure I heard motors behind us, and they were getting louder. I stood up in the cockpit to try and get a better handle on the situation and see if I could distinguish anything. Nothing. But the noise was getting louder and coming right up on our stern. I was sure we didn't want to get crunched this early in the trip so I went below to wake Gretchen up and to turn on the radar to see what was going on. The radar takes a minute to warm up before it comes on (eats too much power to leave on all the time), so I ran back on deck to see how close the boat was while Gretchen started calling on the radio. Dave was lucky—he slept through this.

"Sailing vessel Shadowfax calling the ship on our stern. Please reply. Repeat. This is the American sailing vessel Shadowfax to the unlit ship, please come in." Gretchen said this so calmly, and there I was just about to get the guns out while thinking thoughts of pirates. The reply was immediate and the approaching ship lit up like a Christmas tree, "This is the U.S. Coast Guard Cutter number 906. State your destination please and your last port of call." Pretty sneaky of these guys.

The radio calls kept going back and forth trying to satisfy whatever it was these guys wanted. They were part of the "Drug Net" which was trying to stop, or at least slow, the incoming traffic of drugs. Hey, we can agree with that. No problem. We just wished they wouldn't sneak up on us like that. Our heart rates would stay in the triple numbers for a while.

The conversation went on and on until we were sure we were going to be boarded. All the stories about boats being torn up and holes drilled while looking for drugs went through my mind, but there wasn't a whole lot we could do about it. Then luck came in the form of a powerboat heading north. The Coast Guard called him and found out his last port of call was Panama and his next port was the U.S., which made him a lot more likely to be in the smuggling business. It's obvious more drugs get smuggled into the states than out, so off they went to sneak up on that poor guy.

Our reprieve only lasted until three the next afternoon when ol' number 906 came over the horizon again. Not only did this remind us of just how slow a sailboat is, this time they would board. Within minutes of catching up to us they launched an inflatable dinghy and raced over with a boarding party.

Four Coast Guard men and one woman climbed aboard wearing bullet-proof jackets, guns and carrying briefcases. They looked more like drug smugglers than we did.

It was a two-hour search that included the use of fiber optics (you know, one of those things doctors stick in various places to look at your insides). They stuck this thing in all the tight spots as they looked for the mother load. It only took about fifteen minutes for them to figure out we weren't the "Sanibel Connection," and the mood lightened up tremendously. They played with the sextant and looked through the ship's logs (navigation and radio logs). All in all, I think everyone had a good time. At one point one of the guys found a dozen gallon wine bottles filled with flour under our floor and said, "This is either a couple dollars worth of flour or millions in cocaine. Do you mind if I check it?" I wonder what he would have done if I had said yes.

Anyway, he determined it was harmless flour and they all started to gather up their things to jump back in their inflatable. That was the last time I ever saw one my light list navigation books. A mistake I'm sure, unless USCG Cutter 906 really, really needed one. All this time we maintained course and speed, so we really enjoyed the break in the routine and we didn't lose any miles. These were just a bunch of folks doing their job.

Just as they were leaving they asked if they could do anything for us, so we asked them for a compass light as ours had burned out the night before. We had enough spares aboard to rebuild almost anything on the boat, including all the running lights, but who thought of a little thing like a compass light? The head of the boarding party radioed back and guess what, they didn't have one either.

For all I knew, a modern ship like theirs might not even use a compass.

So off they went and now it was Mother Nature's turn to show us her meaner side. She was about to throw our first gale at us. My entry in the logbook for 12:34pm reads, "eight-foot seas, moving like a freight train at nine and a half knots." The entry for 1:30 says, "Gale, fifteen foot seas, put on harnesses." Green water was breaking from the tops of the waves and smashing into the side of Shadowfax which would shudder and vibrate like a rock concert.

One wave was so large that it picked Shadowfax up and dropped her with such force that the diesel generator ripped from its bolts and slid a foot to starboard. Dave was the hero and managed to get it secured before we ended up with a hole in the hull. It got so rough that for forty hours all we could eat were Fruit Loops (no milk) and cookies. When the cockpit filled with water after one particularly big wave, Dave asked us how much we were going to sell the boat for in Belize. Not a chance.

With a double-reefed mainsail and a tiny jib we flew the last two hundred miles and slid behind the protection of one of Belize's great reefs. We arrived at night, and the channel entrance wasn't lit so we just kind of "hung out" until daylight. Too deep to anchor, so we just took turns watching the radar and drifting around the entrance. Boring stuff after the two previous days of gale force winds.

When the sun came up and we could find our way into the channel, we sailed to Belize City to clear Customs, Immigration, Health and whatever else was needed. We anchored just off the city, and even though the cruising books said to wait for immigration officials, we soon discovered that if we waited forever nothing was going to happen. No choice but to go to shore and call somebody.

Gretchen and I took the inflatable dingy ashore, and Dave stayed aboard to keep an eye on the boat. The first thing we ran into was a ten-year-old kid standing in our way saying, "One dollar charge to pass." Nice try, Kid.

The city was run down with poverty screaming from all the buildings, and we had quite a time trying to find anybody who knew anything about yachts clearing in. Finally, we called the airport and found that if we would pay for the taxi, someone would come out to see us. Fair enough.

Two customs agents, a health inspector and an immigration officer showed up about an hour later and said they had to come out to the boat to look around... at least that's what we think they wanted. Our Spanish was just as bad as their English. They had no way to get to the boat, and it was too rough to bring the boat to the dock, so we offered our dinghy. One customs officer and the health guy were the only ones to take us up on our offer. The other two took one look at how small the dinghy was and decided to stamp our passports on the dock and call it good. The fact that it took ten pulls of the starting cord to get the tiny outboard going didn't help any. The motor was a British Seagull. I'll tell you about that disaster of a motor later.

We made it out to the boat and they looked around for about five seconds. Then they sat down to play with the paperwork and drink our coffee. Really nice guys. They seemed glad to be out of the airport and relaxing on a boat. We took our time and practiced our Spanish (which was almost non-existent) with everything going well until I told them about the guns. I wanted to play it straight and not hide anything, but apparently that's not what they wanted. They would have been a whole lot happier if I hadn't mentioned them.

They talked about it between themselves for a long time trying to figure out how to get out of all this extra paperwork. Finally one of the guys asked if there was someplace on the boat we could lock the guns up, either that or he would have to take them until we left. I asked if they took them and we sailed down the coast and left the country from the southern end, how would we get them back? We were told in broken English "Don't know." So we found a place to lock them up (the spear gun too), and they put a custom seal on the lock and everyone was happy.

Once we got rid of the customs people, we took off to explore. Belize, which was once called British Honduras, is just about the same size as Massachusetts. 8,867 sq. miles, with a population of around 195,000. Half live in Belize City. The boarders of Belize touch Mexico to the north and Guatemala to the west, with the longest border touching the Caribbean Sea to the east. Belize is definitely most famous to us Yanks for its barrier reef and scuba diving fame. After a short time in Belize City—very short—we sailed away to check out the rest of the country.

We sailed south down the protected waters on the inside of the reef, which extends the entire length of the country, and found secluded, protected anchorages every night.

One of our favorite places was the Sapodilla Lagoon. The entrance was so difficult and hidden that we felt we might be the only ones to ever anchor there. Rain forest all around and hundreds of birds screaming at us. I could just picture pirates hiding there years ago. Maybe even weeks ago.

Gretchen and I launched the dinghy, and with Dave again staying on guard aboard Shadowfax, we left to explore our way up the Sapodilla River which drained into the lagoon. Just like going back in time—flowers, cactus, freshwater, and parrots in all the trees. We returned hours later just at sunset (the fault of the Seagull outboard) and locked ourselves in Shadowfax for the night. We slept until noon the next day.

Father down the coast we found the little village of Placentia. Lots of deserted beaches and the road was a narrow little walkway that stretched for a couple of miles through hundreds of palm trees. We met people from two other boats there – a power boat called Dixie Gig and a sailboat named October—who were both from the U.S. In fact they had both been to Captiva many times, and we had common friends.

We sailed side-by-side with October for a day and headed out to Laughing Bird Bay to check out the diving. Clear, warm water greeted us with lots of sea life—huge schools of tarpon, manta rays and barracuda. The only problem was that the trade winds were blowing at a strength that kept us out of the deep waters. This meant that we just snorkeled in twenty feet instead of breaking out the scuba gear. Still, it's hard to complain about a tropical day in paradise.

On the way back, Ken, on October, wanted to help us out with our fishing skills (or lack of). We told him about our fishing record—we had dragged two lines for five hundred miles and caught nothing. He gave us one of his special "guaranteed" lures and we sailed fifty feet from October, at the same speed, with the same lure out to the same length. At the end of the day the fishing score was October 3, Shadowfax 0.

Oh well, back to Placentia for a week to relax in a hammock and recover from our embarrassment.

Can't stay forever, no matter how comfortable the hammock was. Up anchor and sail south, picking out quiet, protected anchorages as we headed toward the port of Punta Gorda.

Punta Gorda is at the southerly end of Belize, and this is the port we needed in order to check out of the country. It was another windy, open anchorage and, again, nobody wanted to come out to the boat. We found an immigration officer in a small office looking very lonely. He charged us five bucks and stamped our passports. I asked him if it was okay to take the lock off the guns, and it was obvious he didn't care one way or the other.

So off to Guatemala. Not far... only twenty-five miles of no wind, no seas and again no fish. We were aiming for the mouth of the Rio Dulce, a freshwater river. Everyone we'd met while in Belize told us not to miss it. If we could get in, that is. Shadowfax needs five-and-a-half feet of water to float (probably closer to six, loaded down like we were), and the mouth of the river has a huge sandbar extending across the entrance of an unknown but shallow depth. We were also told that sailboats would sometimes hire one of the local boats to drag them over the sandbar. Not really something we wanted to do.

Chapter 7

Guatemala is 42,043 square miles in size, and a population of almost ten million people. Since 1944 Guatemala has been under a long line of military dictators and even today war and violence seem to be common practice. With the average wage per person equal to less than one thousand U.S. dollars per year, it looked like things weren't about to change very soon.

On the up side, the country is beautiful. Mountains, volcanoes (some still active) and near-perfect weather make it a great place to visit. Most of the locals were as friendly as they could be and seemed disinterested in their country's politics.

We arrived at the river entrance during the highest tide of the day and slowly approached the shallows. We could see it plainly because of the change in water color, and it sure looked shallow. We saw two local boats aground just outside of the middle channel.

Just as we motored toward the shallows, the transmission shift cable decided to break. It was stuck in forward until Dave could go into the engine room and shift it by hand. From then on I had to yell orders down to him like, "Five seconds of forward, okay, ten more seconds, reverse, three seconds," as we inched forward. Our depth sounder said we should be aground as we crossed, but somehow we never touched. Within seconds we over the shallows and approaching the main town of Livingston where we needed to clear customs.

The minute we anchored off the town we were approached by a dugout canoe (called a cayucos) with five officials aboard (only one wore a shirt even resembling a uniform) who climbed aboard without asking. In less than ten minutes they had looked in all our lockers, filled out lots of papers, taken the guns, and given us a three-month cruising permit. Very efficient.

The sun was just starting to set, but we wanted to get part way up the river before we anchored for the night. What a beautiful place that river is. The Rio Dulce is a couple hundred feet wide with two-hundred-foot sheer cliffs on both sides which were covered in thick jungle growth. Parrots flew overhead, and we had been told if we anchored too close to the edge we'd have monkeys in the rigging by morning. All this time, motoring up the river, we kept alert in case Dave had to jump down to the engine room for a quick switch to neutral or reverse.

The river increased to eighty feet in depth so we had a little trouble finding a good place to drop the hook. We found a place in fifty-five feet of water and we circled a couple of times to pick the best spot. Once the anchor was down I jumped in and swam a line ashore to tie the stern to a palm tree. Even after making it all the way around the world, this one anchorage is way up on the "most beautiful" list. Once we were secure, the three of us couldn't get enough of swimming in all that fresh water. It was way after dark by the time we swam back to the boat to sleep.

When morning came we noticed that our stern line was tied to a tree that was near a small palm-thatched hut with a large family staring at this 46-foot boat in their front yard. Our Spanish still wasn't all that great, so we just smiled and passed out balloons to all the kids. The balloons turned out to be a hit everywhere in the world. Break the ice with the parents by using the children... perfect.

As we sailed farther up the river the scenery continued to impress: jungle, mountains, tiki huts and waterfalls. The river made sharp turns until it finally opened up into a large lake. Not much wind this far up the river, so we motored across the lake until the river again narrowed to a few hundred feet. Our destination was a place called Manana Marina – another place we were told not to miss.

What a lost sort of place for a marina. You can't drive there, no roads, also no electricity, no food, no supplies and the strangest thing, no dockage. Not very normal for a marina. What they did have was a lot of visiting yachts and a small generator so they could show movies. Every Sunday was potluck dinner night when everyone brought in a food dish to share. For drinks you just wrote down your boat's name and then paid manana (later). The reason this place gets all these boats visiting is because word is out that this is a safe (and cheap) place to spend hurricane season. Many of the people who sail around the Caribbean in the winter hot-foot it up to Manana Marina every year when spring (and hurricane season) rolls around.

Once we had Shadowfax securely anchored in the cluster of boats already there, people started coming over to introduce themselves and give us the rundown on the area. We were made welcome in true "yachtie" style.

Dave wanted to go to the capital, Guatemala City, 180 miles away to check the place out and to make some phone calls and to find a replacement shift cable. It was about a half-hour dinghy trip to get Dave to some sort of highway where he could catch a bus. After sending Dave on his way, Gretchen and I just sort of relaxed and got into the "manana" attitude.

While Dave was on his way to the city, Gretchen and I were invited with two others to take a ride to see Tikal, the largest Mayan ruins ever discovered. Wow, what a deal, sure we'd go.

Conrad, the guy who invited the four of us, was an adventurous sort, and he knew that between us and Tikal 120 miles away all we had were mountains and a road made from "organized rocks." Also, the fact that this route was infested with most of the guerrilla activity in the country (Guatemala being almost in a civil war) guaranteed to make this an adventure. We planned on a six to ten hour ride each way depending on mud slides.

Conrad kept an ancient, huge Buick buried in the jungle near a small town that we could dinghy to. When we first saw it we had to laugh. It looked like it had already fallen off a couple of cliffs. It started right up, so we all climbed in.

Conrad took off at a steady fifteen mph driving over some of the worst roads we had ever seen. One of the first things we noticed was that we were the only people in sight who didn't have either a gun or a machete.

We were stopped and thoroughly searched five times on the way to Tikal and six times on the way back. Every small village we drove through had bunkers made out of mud on the side of the road. People were standing around the bunkers with automatic weapons. In one village we were rushed by five of these people as they stopped the car. We were told to get out, and I was put up against the car and searched by a fifteen-year-old kid with an Uzi machine gun to my back. Conrad told me not to worry about it because they probably didn't have any bullets. Just the same, I couldn't help but think of Barney Fife on the TV show Mayberry R. F. D. who always had the one bullet in his top pocket.

The entire time we were being searched, Conrad kept a light humor and intimidated everyone who, as he said, "bothered us." Conrad stood six-three and weighed about two-fifty. With a voice like General Patton, we could tell nobody wanted the job of searching him. Along the way Conrad also tried to explain the situation to us. He said, "It's hard to know all the players without a program: Blue shirts – Federales; Green shirts – Police; Camouflage shirts – Military; No shirt – don't' stop!!"

We finally made it to Tikal and it was fascinating. An eight-square-mile city with temples up to 200 feet high which were built as long as 2,500 years ago. A large portion of the city has yet to be excavated, and being so remote, it didn't look like there was anyone hurrying to do it. The dense Peten Rain Forest surrounds Tikal so you could get a great view just by looking up. We saw a family of monkeys swinging through the trees while the baby monkey kept trying to catch the toucans and parrots who were flying by. Definitely worth all the trouble getting there.

Once back at Manana marina, we just loafed around for two weeks as we worked on boat projects. Even a short passage left us with lots of stuff to fix. Speaking of broken things, when Dave came back from the city he had with him a new shifting cable. I guess he didn't like his new job as engine-room shifter. He found the same brand cable as you would find in the U.S. but at half the price. Are they getting a deal or are Americans getting ripped off?

The time came for us to say goodbye to everyone at the Manana. We wanted to take our time sailing back out of the river and enjoy our last blast in all that fresh water. We drifted around the lakes and the river for another week or so, trading balloons for blue crabs with the locals and generally enjoying the scenery. At one spot along the river we were able to anchor the boat fifty feet away from the river's edge where a sulfur hot spring bubbled away. We spent many hours just sitting in the spring and watching the world go by. So far, sailing around the world was agreeing with us.

Off we went back to Livingston to clear out and get the guns. Not much problem except for one of the rifles being in tough shape. It had obviously been shot and not been cleaned. That along with it having a rusty tinge made me rethink turning over our guns to shady officials. I was just hoping they didn't kill anyone with it. We also provisioned as much as we could in the little town to prepare for the trip to Panama, with a short stop on the island of Roatan in Honduras.

Honduras is an even bigger country than its neighbor Guatemala. It covers 43,238 square miles but only has about half the population of Guatemala.

We had only planned on short stops as we sailed toward Panama and we had no idea how much we were going to like all the places we visited. We were starting to realize that every place we would visit would take much more time than planned.

Even though we enjoyed Guatemala we had to pay a high price to get out. Guatemala is right in a corner (shaped like an armpit) where all the wind in the world blows straight in, and the only way out is to sail hard on the wind for days. My entry in the log reads, "Very rough passage, strong trade winds of 40 plus knots." Heart and Stone's cruising guide to the Caribbean states, "Plan to live on sandwiches when underway as cooking may be physically impossible," and if that's not bad enough, "Strong trade winds and one-way currents, the sheer discomfort and futility of trying to beat your way against them cannot be overemphasized." What the hell, we had no choice.

By the time we arrived at the island of Roatan, not only hadn't we been cooking, we also hadn't slept in two nights. I was actually hallucinating when we were coming in to anchor. Not a good sign when the captain is seeing things. None of us was used to sleeping in that kind of weather with the boat lurching so violently. Believe it or not, I've learned to sleep in any kind of weather since then, well, almost any kind.

We stayed anchored at a place called Coxon Hole at the foot of the Roatan airport for a week while a tropical storm passed nearby keeping the winds at fifty knots. Luckily, we'd anchored a day before the storm hit. We anchored just off the end of the runway and I think the jets used our mast to line up their approach. The thought "any port in a storm" came to mind.

Roatan is an island just north of the Honduran coast and measures about 26 miles east to west by two miles north to south. About 2,000 people live there. The island is one of three islands – Utilia, Roatan and Guanaja called "The Bay Islands." Like Belize, Roatan is famous for its reefs and diving and usually does a brisk tourist business. Of course, our whole time there it blew like stink so we never even got in the water. We did manage to get on a bus and check out the island a little – lots of small shops and homes built along the shore and bays. The roads were mostly paved but narrow with straight drop-offs without a guardrail in sight.

We never stayed away from the boat for very long because of all the wind, but happily, every time we came back she was in the same spot. Sitting at anchor and looking over the charts, we added the nearby island of Guanaja to our list of places to stop. Since Guanaja was only fifty miles away, it would break up the horrible sail against all that wind. We figured we would stop and enjoy a good night's sleep before we headed on toward Panama.

When the wind dropped to a manageable thirty knots we pulled up the anchor and motored out into the seas. After a full day of sailing hard and giving it everything we had, we were seventeen miles from where we started. Sailing against the wind and current was tough. We tacked back to the eastern end of Roatan and pulled into a protected little cove for the night. Guanaja was becoming a quest.

Early the next morning we headed out again. The log book says, "Long tack, seas building, squalls and rain." Not fun, but we made it. Guanaja materialized out of the rain, and we ducked in out of the wind and found a lost civilization. With a population of about 3,000 people, and the size slightly smaller than Roatan, we noticed something right away. These people had a perfectly good island with mountains and waterfalls but just about nobody lived there.

Chapter 8

Almost everyone lived in "The Key." A city of stilt houses built in shallow water one mile from shore. The homes were connected by small wooden walkways that joined the small shops at one end to the "Country, Western, Spanish Disco" at the other end. All the homes were leaning one way or another, and I remember trying to find customs and immigration and thinking, "This place is crazy." When we asked someone where we should go, we were given four pounds of lobster tails and introduced to the port captain who said, "Enjoy your stay," and walked away. Over the next thirty days we really got to know the place.

After meeting the port captain we took our lobster and moved the boat to a small cove near the west end of the island. We weren't anchored more than a couple of hours before one of the locals rowed out to introduce himself and invite us to come and tie up to his bar. A bar sounded like a funny place to tie up to, but we told him maybe we would come over in the morning to check it out. "Great," he said, and also told us he had plenty of fresh water if we needed any. That's an offer that we could never refuse.

Bright and early the next day (around noon) we raised anchor and motored over to Bradley's bar, The Blue Horizon. The bar was built on stilts away from any land, and it was also away from the main "Key" by about a mile. Being only one small room with a small bar, there wasn't a whole lot to it. When Shadowfax tied to the dock along the front of the building, we took up the whole thing. True to his word, Bradley gave us a hose and told us to use as much as we needed. He had a pipeline going underwater all the way from the island to his bar and told us that more water falls down from the mountains and into the sea every day than the whole state of Florida could use. I don't know if his statistics are right, but Gretchen and I did see an awful lot of water falling into the sea.

Once full of water we said our thanks and told him we didn't want to take up his whole dock when he started to get busy. He just laughed and told us to stay at least for the night and meet some of his friends (Bradly spoke perfect English). "Why not stay for the night?" we asked ourselves. We could always leave in a day or so for Panama.

As it turned out "friends" were all who ever came to The Blue Horizon. Apparently tourists didn't usually visit "The Key" or any part of this area of the island. A couple of dive resorts are located on the main island, but we were told later by one of the resort managers that tourists were mostly afraid to come to The Key. I guess it did look a little scary with all those leaning houses. Well, that was their loss because these were some of the nicest people living in one of the coolest places we'd ever been. Even after we were there for a month it was still hard to drag ourselves away.

During our second week tied to The Blue Horizon, we decided to sail over to the other side of the island to check out the scuba diving. Everybody had been raving about how great it was so off we went. It was just a half day's sail around the island, but we'll never forget it. We caught our first fish! It was a huge king mackerel. Actually, I think it was a huge king mackerel. By the time we got it to the boat, something else had eaten the mackerel, and all we had left were the lips. Nice try though, and it was only a few minutes later that we caught a barracuda. We thought he might have been the one that ate the mackerel, so we ate him.

As we sailed past the dock one of the workers at the dive resort (Bayman Bay Club Resort) yelled for us to tie up at the dock instead of anchoring. After we docked they told us they just wanted to see the boat, and since sailboats never seem to come to the area they had plenty of room at their dock. So why not stay? No charge. Even after a week of diving with them, they wouldn't let us pay for going out in their dive boat or our scuba tank air fills. We held a few "Open Houses" on the boat for their guest s to look around, and I think they appreciated it.

As for the diving, it was fabulous! After diving in as many places as we could around the world, we found Guanaja to be the number two dive location (stay tuned for number one). You could dive every day for weeks and never dive the same reef twice. Huge fish, caves and colorful reefs circle the entire island. If it was too windy on one side, just dive the other. Plenty of shallows for snorkeling also.

After sailing back to The Blue Horizon the Fourth of July had rolled around and so did a great fourth party – hot dogs, hundreds of U.S. flags and a terrific time. It was nice of them to celebrate another nation's holiday. This place was full of surprises.

After 37 days we had to go. We had stayed too long and hurricane season was almost in full swing. We weren't far enough south to be considered safe. Not even close. We gotta go.

One of the hardest parts of sailing around the world is always saying goodbye to new friends, but we were starting to get used to it. Off we went on our way to Panama, maybe a seven or eight day trip with good weather. We sure take our time. It took us 17 days.

Once we left Guanaja, the wind wasn't so nasty and we made good time. We had been told horror stories about sailboats that had sailed to close to "The pirates of Nicaragua," so we made it a point to stay at least a hundred miles offshore. We didn't want any nasty government officials (pirates) confiscating the boat, or worse. We had heard talk of everything from kidnapping to the murder of passing sailors.

Except for repairing a large rip in our jib we had an uneventful sail for a couple of days, and it was the third day out when we sighted a military ship approaching us from the port side. The closer it got, the more rust streaks we saw dripping down its side and the huge billows of smoke coming out of the exhaust. Lots of people were looking over the rails at us with only a couple of them being in uniform. I don't think they had a radio because despite our attempts to call them, they had to get close enough to be able to yell to us. As they approached, Gretchen spotted a small ripped Honduran flag flying off the stern. Much better than a Nicaraguan flag. After questions and answers were yelled back and forth we must have passed inspection because they motored away in a puff of diesel smoke.

Our next stop was an island not shown on any of our charts. Our chart showed a depth of 96 feet where we found this island. True it only had a couple of trees on it, and it was only about fifty feet by fifty feet, but we had to check it out. The area we were in was covered in reefs, so we had to sail as carefully as possible with Gretchen on the bow directing me which way to turn to avoid the shallowest areas. The waters were so clear it was hard to tell the depth. Quite a challenge to get close enough to this island to anchor.

We found a good spot and dropped two anchors. I put on my mask and snorkel and jumped in to be sure the anchors were set. With all the reefs around, this would be no place to drag anchor. In our lazy way of heading to Panama we decided to spend the night. I sketched a chart of the area and the way out through the reefs in case we had to leave in the middle of the night because of storms, pirates or whale attacks. I'm glad we didn't have to try it.

Safely at anchor, Dave and I fell asleep only to be awakened by Gretchen in about an hour. She said, "There's a small boat coming with about thirty people on it, I think you'd better get up." It was still daylight and when the boat got close we counted at least forty people. They were dressed in rags and staring at us from the side of the boat. I don't know what kept it from tipping over. We didn't take the guns on deck, but we were definitely on our guard.

Gretchen stayed below and Dave and I went topside to see what we had gotten into this time. They didn't speak English very well, but after a while we got the picture. These were Mesquite Indians out lobster-diving the reefs, and they would gladly exchange lobster for a bag of coffee and sugar. These were a bunch of shy, polite guys. Things are rarely ever what they first appear. We gave them a jar of coffee and sugar and also a big bag of old clothes we had for just such an occasion. We gladly accepted a big bag of fresh lobster.

We spent a couple of days anchored off our private little island and managed to spear lots of grouper for the freezer. One time while swimming under the boat looking for fish, I looked down at a pile of fish parts we had laid on the bottom to attract more fish to spear, and two huge sharks swam up to check it out. Gretchen was in the water with me and when she saw them she screamed underwater loud enough to scare these sharks all the way back to Florida. They were gone like lightning, and I'll bet they're still moving. Who knew you could scream like that underwater.

Can't stay forever, so off we went to Columbia... kinda. The Quita Sueno Bank is a huge (28 miles north to south and 7 miles east to west) reef lying in the middle of the Caribbean on the way towards Panama that Colombia claims to own. The fact that there is nothing above water doesn't seem to make a difference. We couldn't resist anchoring behind this cool reef for a little diving and fishing. We were definitely much better at fishing as long as we had a speargun. In true Shadowfax fashion, we stayed five days.

During our stay we took some time to fix more things that had broken since leaving Guanaja. I better start telling you about things that break or else you'll think we just played all the time. The freshwater foot pump had broken (new when we left); the radar stopped working (new when we left); propane safety switch self-destructed (also new); and, of course, the Loran antenna was still broken.

Between the three of us we managed to fix everything; even the radar (after spending a full day up the mizzen mast). It's surprising the things that can be hammered back together if you put your mind to it.

After a pleasant visit to this Columbian reef we found ourselves in the first week of August – dead center in the middle of hurricane season. We were now far enough south that the chances of getting a hurricane were a little slim, but not non-existent. We finally left for the three-day sail to Panama.

We spotted a few large ships on the way and found that if we called them on the radio they all wanted to talk. These were bored guys who would do almost anything for you: weather reports, make phone calls, and even drop fuel to you if you needed it. We didn't need any fuel, but our requests for ice cream never did get filled. I don't blame them. I wouldn't give away the ice cream either.

Chapter 9

Being the gateway to the Pacific Ocean, Panama was one of the milestones of the trip. The country is about the size of South Carolina (30,193 square miles) with a population of about two and a half million people. As we approached we knew it would be a little it exciting. What we had to look forward to was the famous canal, the entrance to the Pacific Ocean, and the drug smuggling dictator Manuel Noriega in charge of a country about to go to war against the United States.

Once we made it through the canal and into the Pacific, there was definitely no coming back. Our plan was to get through as fast as we could since a war with General Noriega was said to be only weeks or days away. That was what we told ourselves, but by now we knew better. We always seemed to stay places a little longer than planned and we stayed in Panama for almost a month.

We were excited when we arrived at Cristobal on the Atlantic side of the Panama Canal. We tied up at The Panama Yacht Club across from a large Russian ship. Within minutes we were being boarded by a herd of people who were all connected with the canal in one way or another. We were folded, stapled and mutilated until a pile of papers had been filled out. When I told them about the guns I was told by the official, "Give me $20.00 and you don't have any guns. Give the guns to me and you'll never see them again." We could see a pattern forming with these guns. Nobody wanted to know about them. This was when I decided to keep them hidden and never mention them again. So much for following ALL the rules.

After all these people were through with us and our $20.00 was paid, we still hadn't checked in. We had to go to four different offices outside of the fenced-in Canal Zone to be cleared.

We were told we probably wouldn't make it if we didn't hire a bodyguard to get us there. After talking to other yachts waiting to get through the canal, we found this to be totally true. Three of them had been robbed. It seems the U.S. Army was confined to its base in a P.L.M. (personal limitation movement) so the only police for the whole city were Noriega's troops, the biggest crooks of all. The guard we hired for five bucks was just a normal guy (huge) with a chain slung over his shoulder. I shoved a can of Mace in my pocket and off we went.

All the offices we had to go to were nowhere near each other so we got to see a little bit of this crazy city. Every bank we passed had two plain clothes people outside with automatic weapons guarding the place, and we definitely didn't see any tourists. Cristobal was a good-size city in deep trouble. Almost all the time we could hear windows breaking somewhere in the distance. Just imagine New York City if you took all the police away.

Once back inside the fenced "Canal Zone," things were as safe as could be. The "Zone" was like a U.S. territory. The world couldn't afford to lose this canal to a guy like Noriega, so the U.S. was guarding it like Fort Knox.

Another area equally under protection was an area called "The Free Zone." The Free Zone was like a small city filled with hundreds of duty-free stores for people from the canal ships to go shopping. The Russian-made Lada taxi we took to get us there was searched for bombs by a private security team before we were allowed to enter the "Zone." They sold everything in there. A terrific place to get some provisions for the boat, but leaving the duty-free zone we found we had to pay a bribe to the guards. Oh well, it was still worth it.

The taxi ride back took us past three demonstrations of rock-throwing students and screaming adults. Our taxi driver said that he didn't drink, but once America got rid of "that guy" he planned to celebrate and get very drunk. This was the opinion of every local we met.

Back at the yacht club we made friends with a retired US army sergeant, Pete, and he was able to give us a great tour of Fort Davis, the local army base. We stopped to watch the elite Jumping Ambassadors practice skydiving from Black Hawk helicopters and when they saw us watching they turned up the action and put on an incredible show. These people were really focused. I guess with war right around the corner they had to be.

We were scheduled to transit the canal on Tuesday, August 15th. Small boats could only go through the canal on Tuesdays and Thursdays and our transit happened to be the 75th anniversary of the first transit through the canal in 1914. We left the yacht club and motored south up to Gatun Lock (the first of the locks) at noon... just in time for all the locks and ships to sound their horns for thirty seconds to celebrate the anniversary.

On board we had a few extra people. The canal transit authority insists you have four line handlers, a captain and a canal pilot aboard before they will let you cross. There were professional line handlers that you could call to help, but we just put the word out on the military base and used U.S. Marines. Can't get much safer than that. For the canal pilot we were sent a nice guy who seemed to know what he was doing. He wasn't a bad tour guide along the way either.

The Gatun Lock is actually three locks which would raise us eighty-five feet into the freshwater Gatun Lake. Each lock measures 110 feet wide by 1,000 feet long and works by gravity with no motors to flood or empty the lock. Many of the larger ships we saw going through the canal were built with the maximum size in mind and only cleared the sides by inches.

Two other sailboats were to enter with us, Aberlady, a 44 foot Oyster sloop from Britain with Jeff and Sheila aboard, and Aquarius, a 32-foot homemade sloop from Bulgaria with Vladimir and Jorjet aboard. The three of us would cross half the Pacific together and become good friends. Vladimir was actually on a slow escape from communist Bulgaria. More on that incredible story later.

To enter the lock and get floated up, we were told to tie (raft) our boat with Aberlady. This made it easier on us, as we only had two lines out to one side of the lock, and Aberlady had to deal with the other side as the two boats floated in the center of the lock. Aquarius got lucky - all they had to do was raft to a large tugboat that raised snug against the side of the lock. Vladimir just relaxed and took the pictures for the rest of us.

Once we left the lock we motored twenty-one miles into Gatun Lake to an anchorage where we were to stay for the night. Our pilot was taken ashore once we anchored and planned to return at eight in the morning.

We had a good night's sleep (after a small party with the marines) and were up and ready to go at eight. The pilot showed up right on time and off we went nine miles north (the Panama Canal runs north to south, not east to west as most people think) to Gaillard Cut, a ditch cut into solid rock and shale. Lots of people died cutting this trench, and it's pretty spectacular. At the end of the cut you come to Hold Hill (Elev. 662 feet) on the left and Contractors Hill on the right. This is the location of many devastating landslides during and after the construction of the canal. What a marvel of engineering and guts it took to dig this route between the two oceans.

Our next lock was the Pedro Miguel which lowered us 31 feet (again rafted to Aberlady) and the turbulence is ten times greater going down than it was going up. You couldn't screw up or the boat could be left hanging by its lines against the lock wall. We motored the mile to the next lock still rafted to Aberlady (like a catamaran). The Miraflores Lock was to lower us two steps to the waters of the Pacific Ocean. Throughout all these locks we could hear the rapid fire of the U.S. artillery practicing a couple of miles in the distance. We knew the war could only be a few more days away.

The cost to transit the canal for us and other boats varies greatly. The largest fee ever charged was $99,865.10 which was paid by the ship Marina Ace in 1987. The lowest was 36 cents paid by Richard Halliburton in 1928. He swam.

Shadowfax paid $120.00 which included the pilot. An incredible deal considering the alternative is to go around South America and Cape Horn.

Once we entered the Pacific Ocean we had something to deal with that we never had before... tides of up to 18 feet. No more anchoring at high tide in ten feet of water.

We motored under the 5,428 foot long Thatcher Ferry Bridge (also called the Bridge of Americas) that connects North America to South America and dropped our pilot and line handlers off. We went to anchor for our first night in the Pacific. A bottle of Moet capped off by a full lunar eclipse helped us to celebrate the occasion.

Next stop - Balboa Yacht Club near Panama City. To call it a yacht club is definitely giving it the benefit of the doubt. You could see where it used to be one stately mansion, but if there was anybody in Panama who condemned buildings, this one would be the first to go. We tied to one of their deep water moorings and went in to investigate the city. My log book sums it up best, "Panama City great! Machine gun bunkers, casinos and mail."

The up and coming war was never more present than it was here. I'll try to describe the situation. The U.S. and Panama were once friends (not that long ago) so the officer's base was built in a giant U-shape with the Panamanians on one side, U.S. on the other, with Noriega's office (looked like Scarlet's house, Tara, in Gone with the Wind) at the bottom of the "U". In the middle – filling up the U—was an 18-hole golf course.

Picture this - a line was drawn exactly down the middle of the golf course. Half to the U.S. and half to Noriega. Noriega's half was waist-high with weeds and piles of dirt everywhere. Machine guns were pointing at the U.S. side with Panamanian troops everywhere. Now the U.S. side - immaculate, plush and green. American Generals were playing golf without a care in the world. People with cars in their yards being washed, houses in great shape. Pretty comical actually. When we asked one of the officers why they didn't seem to care, he said, "When the time comes, they can pick their teeth with those machine guns. We'll be gone while artillery and jets take care of these guys. I give 'em fifteen minutes and it's over." He also said, "It's embarrassing to think the U.S. trained these guys. They should know better."

When the time came to check out of Panama we had to wade through a ton of paperwork. I believe it would be easier for a Panamanian to become a U.S. Citizen than it was for us to leave. We were a little sorry that we were going to miss this little war, but we would definitely be safer out of the country.

The Gulf of the Panama contained enough islands to keep us busy for another week while we worked up the nerve to head out into the big ocean. One of the smaller islands, Pedro Gonzalez, showed a secure cove on the chart so we sailed over to check it out. We didn't have the anchor down ten minutes before a little kid, maybe ten years old, rowed out from the small village on shore. The first thing he said (in English) was "Buy cocaine?" Our reply was, "No, thanks. Do you think you can get us a lobster?" He said, "Why are you here?" We told him it looked like a nice place and repeated our request for lobster. He rowed away but came back in an hour and said, "Hey, you no want cocaine, you go." And he rowed back to the village where we saw a small group of people staring at us from the shore. We had definitely sailed into the wrong little island.

We can take a hint. We definitely didn't want to be attacked while we were sleeping so off we go to find a more friendly place. Panama sure was exciting. I guess wars, drugs, machine guns and a dictator can do that to a country.

We all decided we weren't ready to leave, so we sailed to Contadora Island for a last dinner at a resort before we headed out. On the way we caught a Dorado (a.k.a mahi mahi). Broiled with lemon it was fantastic! We had run out of store-bought lures so we caught this one on a lure

Gretchen made out of a Joy Detergent cap and some dental floss. I think she was on to something.

We found Vladimir and Jorget (Aquarius) anchored off Contadora, and it was while walking around the resort watching deer drink out of the swimming pool that we heard Vladimir's story.

Vladimir was born in Bulgaria under the strict communist rule, but he wanted out without endangering his family. He decided to build a sailboat. Not knowing anything about how to do that he studied different ways to work with fiberglass, and his first attempt to build a hull fell apart. When he finally got it right and had a sailable boat, seven years had passed.

He then went to a government official and explained that it would prove to the world that Bulgaria was a great and free country if they would let him compete in a trans-Atlantic race while videotaping it for Bulgarian TV. They went for it and gave him a visa to travel while keeping his family in Bulgaria for security. Well, Vladimir videoed enough stuff to really impress his government and convince them it was great PR to keep him sailing and sending video back to Bulgarian TV. Vladimir wrote them and asked for his wife to be sent to Cuba where he could pick her up. The government agreed, as they still had his daughter for security.

Before Vladimir picked up his wife, he sailed to the U.S. and got a job with a sailmaker so he could make himself a new set of sails (his were made of cotton) as well as learn to be a capitalist and save some money. He liked the U.S. a lot and somehow worked out how to stay for almost a year. I regret not asking how he pulled that off.

So by the time we met Vladimir in Panama, he had convinced his government (with lots of video tapes) that he was a good little communist, and they should send his daughter to Tahiti to be with her mother. After all, they still had his parents for security. I was left with no doubt that given time he would get them out too. To make things more of a challenge, Jorget was pregnant from the great reunion they had in Cuba.

Again we couldn't stay forever, so we finally decided to take off for the Galapagos 1,050 miles away. No reefs to duck behind this time, just open ocean. We set up a schedule on the ham radio to keep in contact with Vladimir.

Chapter 10

The entire sail to Galapagos was upwind with Shadowfax heeling 20 to 30 degrees. You get a little tired of walking on the walls after a while. The third day out our jib ripped again, and it took Gretchen six hours to sew it back together. The sail was starting to look like a Frankenstein creation.

We made good time, but we used the motor more than we should have. Vladimir headed almost directly south from Panama until he hit the trade winds near the equator and then headed west while we headed directly southwest. Even though he lengthened his trip by many miles, he had a much more comfortable sail. Apparently we could learn a lot from this guy.

The closer we came to the Galapagos (which is directly on the equator) something strange started to happen. It was getting incredibly cold! We even dug out our long underwear and ski hats (no we didn't carry skis). The reason for the cold weather is the Humboldt Current bringing up cold water and air from South America.

Another strange thing that happened as Shadowfax sailed closer to the Galapagos Islands was that we were sort of attacked by Swallowtail Gulls, the only nocturnal gulls in the world. Actually, the attack was on our mast top VHF antenna. I don't know why. Maybe they just wanted to sit on the mast or maybe it was some kind of gull game. Weird creatures in this part of the world.

The night before we arrived we crossed the equator into the southern hemisphere. Now summer was winter and winter was summer and hurricanes would spin clockwise (opposite from the north.) This would take some getting used to.

The Galapagos Islands consist of 13 major islands and 20 smaller ones which are claimed by the country of Ecuador. The famous explorer Charles Darwin estimated the number of extinct volcanoes on the islands to be around 2,000.

There is also a strange local weather phenomenon known as "garua" which results in the islands disappearing from view after being plainly visible.

We read that the officials would not let yachts cruise any of the islands unless a permit is applied for at least a year in advance telling the dates you would be there, what kind of boat, how many people, etc. Since we didn't even own a boat the year before, never mind know when we would arrive, we had nothing close to a permit. Chances were we wouldn't be back to this area for a long, long time, so we wanted to convince the officials to let us stay.

We made landfall at Wreck Bay on San Cristobal Island after nine days at sea... tired, cold, but happy. We cleaned the boat so everything would be shipshape when customs officials boarded us. Ah well, it seems they don't do that there. We launched the dinghy and went to find an official. Easy, they said they would give us a three-day permit, but by saying please and being as polite as possible, we turned the three-day permit into a five-day permit with permission to also sail to the island of Santa Cruz. We were never asked about the guns, so we didn't mention them.

The Galapagos sure had the strangest animals all gathered together on a few small islands. Blue-footed Booby Birds, saltwater iguanas and fairly tame sea lions to name just a few. The locals were more than happy to throw us in the back of a pickup truck, take our money, and give us a tour of the island. One place we were taken was one of the active volcanoes, but the mist was so thick (garua) we couldn't see our feet... never mind the volcano. But we were told after the two-hour ride that the volcano was, in fact, close by and we were getting our money's worth.

The meals were cheap all over the island and a full dinner would cost something like 2,000 sucres ($4.00) and usually consisted of rice, chicken and salad. Not much of a menu but it tasted great. We also wanted to buy diesel fuel while we were there, and it turned into a hassle.

First we were told we could have diesel delivered to the dock by truck in the early evening. Once we showed up, the military was there saying that we could get fuel only from them, not the locals. Sure, why not. We sent the truck away and then we motored over to the military base, and the situation got crazier. The pumps were locked up, but these military guys picked the locks and handed us a hose with no attachment on the end and told me to put it in our diesel fill hole. The fuel started to come out so fast and so hard that twice as much was going in the water as in the boat. This was nuts and we made them stop immediately. They got pissed. We kept telling them that the Galapagos Islands were special and you can't just dump fuel in the water like that. They kept telling us it was okay and just kept getting madder. Here we were arguing to save the Galapagos Island against people who actually lived there. We untied and went back to anchor.

It turns out these guys were stealing the fuel and planning to pocket the money. The next day we found this out by going back by dinghy to see if we could find a nozzle for the hose and sure enough, no problem, and nobody knew a thing about selling fuel at night. After all this, it was only $.50 a gallon. All around the world we found local officials to be the real pirates of the planet.

Once full of fuel we left for the 45 mile sail to Santa Cruz Island. When we arrived we were boarded right away by some guy demanding money. We were getting a little tired of the corruption in this country. Everybody we met from the government wanted money for no apparent reason. We are fast learners - we just said no and he went away.

Santa Cruz is the main island with a population of about 4,000 and lots and lots of tourist shops. The Charles Darwin Research Center was there along with an intensive effort to protect the endangered tortoise population. It was kind of nice to see that someone cared.

We were told we could stay for a couple of days only to visit the Research Center, and since the anchorage was subject to a large and uncomfortable ocean swell we didn't want to stay much longer anyway. Aquarius was in the anchorage with us and we decided to tour the island with them and then try and sail together as long as we could for the next passage.

When the time came to clear out, the officials wanted $65.00 from each boat. We argued them down to $5.00 (actually Gretchen did). A couple of other boats in the anchorage wanted to borrow Gretchen for a while so they could get their bribes reduced too.

Our next passage was "The Big One," 3,050 miles to the west with absolutely nothing in between except lots of deep water. What a scary thought. The place we were aiming for was the Marquesas Islands of French Polynesia. Six large and six small islands with mountains reaching a height of 4,000 feet. The whole area of French Polynesia sounded fantastic.

The French Polynesian territory extends over a Pacific area the size of Europe, but the land area is just slightly larger than Rhode Island. The 130 islands hold a population of about 205,000 people with over half living on their capital island of Tahiti.

French Polynesia is one place we really looked forward to visiting. Not only was it at the end of a very long passage, it was the first of the many tropical South Pacific Islands that everyone has dreamed about. We knew we had nothing but white sandy beaches, warm waters and coral reefs to look forward to. Lots of time to read all about it over the next three weeks at sea.

We also read all about the boats that had been hit by whales along our route. This sounded a lot worse than a little corruption in Ecuador. David had read somewhere that if you kept a depth sounder on, the sonic noise might alert the whales that you're there, and then they would get out of your way. Since hitting them as they sleep on the surface was the biggest danger, we decided to try it. I guess maybe it was like a whale alarm clock. On the ninth day at sea we spotted a huge whale in the distance. Definitely something to be aware of - these guys wouldn't have any problem sinking a little boat like Shadowfax.

We set up a schedule on the ham radio with Vladimir for noon every day, and it's funny how we all came to look forward to it. We could talk about the weather, sail changes, nothing, everything. It proved someone else was out there somewhere. We could also talk about all the things on board as they broke. We sure had our share.

It's hard to explain three weeks at sea on a small boat, but I guess you could relate it to a short prison term without a recreation yard. Luckily, the wind blew from behind us for the whole trip at between twenty to thirty knots. Absolutely perfect for Shadowfax. Sometimes we went days without touching a sail. Sailors refer to this passage as "the milk run" because of the steady trade winds pushing you along.

For watch duty we were doing two and a half hours on and five off. After a while you get used to this schedule and maybe even enjoy it a little. A clear night with a full moon was actually something to look forward to.

My watch was always noisier than everyone else because I had to feed Gandalf, and he was always hungry. No, we hadn't picked up a pet. Gandalf was the name we gave our electric autopilot, a very important crewmember. In exchange for his steering the boat perfectly in any weather, he ate a bunch of electricity which came out of our batteries. During my watch I would run the Onan Generator for an hour to replace all this Gandalf food. Noisy but worth it.... nobody wants to steer. I could also run the fridge and freezer while the generator was running.

The fourth day out we put up our mizzen staysail (like a small spinnaker but flown from the mizzen – far aft mast). The sail, along with the jib sail, pushed us along for our best run of the trip—177 miles in 24 hours. I know you can drive that far in no time, but we tried not to think of that.

One night while Dave was on watch and Gretchen and I were sleeping, we were awakened by a loud "ping." We went topside and it happened again. We think we were "pinged" by a submarine. It sounded exactly like those subs on TV that run around pinging the enemy in all those old war movies. They probably picked up our depth sounder coming from a boat without a motor running and wanted to check us out. Maybe they were just having target practice, and we'd just been practice nuked. If they contacted us we could have explained our "keep the whales away" depth sounder witchcraft. Everyone needs a laugh.

Seven days out Gandalf (autopilot) got sick and died. He just "took a left" and wouldn't turn back. Mmm, not good. After a full day, the log book sums it up in four words, "No autopilot – everyone tired." What a bitch steering is in ten foot waves while heading downwind. We shortened our watches to two hours each and tried not to complain. Dave and I took Gandalf apart for a little open heart surgery.

It's true we were fair at fixing mechanical things, but when it came to circuit boards and logic centers, we were like Dorothy in Oz – lost. Just to get the thing out to work on it was a project in itself. The autopilot actually had three separate computers to run it – the compass, the control panel and the thirty-pound motor. This was definitely a serious type autopilot. Dave and I manhandled the thing out (Gandalf's motor lived in the engine room) while Gretchen steered (or surfed) Shadowfax down the waves. After one particularly big wave sent me into the engine room wall, I probably should have had stitches put in a three-inch gash in my arm. Luckily a few butterfly bandages did the trick. I was getting mad at ol' Gandalf.

We opened up the autopilot and saw at least six circuit boards staring back at us. Boy, did we hate steering, but fixing the autopilot looked hopeless. Day four of Gandalf's death, we decided to take a day off and drift while we got some rest... maybe just drift all the way to Polynesia. I got out the calculator and figured out how long we would have to drift on the current – 67.7 days! A little too long.

Meanwhile, on our twelve o'clock talks with Vladimir, he tried not to rub it in but "I told you so" fit pretty well. What incredibly experienced Vladimir told us back in Panama was, "Never leave with just one autopilot. Someday it will break. Everything does."

Day five of steering and I'm injecting 12 volts into various circuits and resistors trying to make Gandalf suffer like we were – and all of a sudden he started to click. I figured clicking must be good. It was better than not clicking. We stuffed his innards back in the appropriate place (we hoped), installed it without any serious injury, and we all looked at each other. Nobody really wanted to try it. It would either be a huge downer or maybe the best day of our lives. We were just at the halfway point of the passage. I flipped the on switch - Gandalf lives!

We were we happy campers. Gretchen dragged out the spinnaker and off we went at nine knots sipping a cold Gatorade, resting and checking out the sunset(s). All good things must come to an end, and after a couple of days it was time for something else to break. The forestay.

This is the wire that connects the top of the mast to the bow of the boat, and this is also what the jib sail flies from. The wire broke at the top so rather than going up the mast in ten foot seas, we could only use halyards (lines that raise the sails) to jury-rig a new forestay. Luckily we were sailing downwind at the time as this put pressure on the backstay, which kept the mast from snapping off.

Our jib was what's called a "rolling furling" which rolls and unrolls from the forestay – like a roll of toilet paper—so no way could we use the sail. No problem... we still had the mainsail and the mizzen.

The next morning Gretchen woke me to show me a small rip in the main. As I was looking at it a gust of wind came up, and it ripped front to back... just like a zipper. This little project took all day to fix. I started the generator and Gretchen took one of her sewing machines (she had two aboard) into the cockpit. With Dave pulling and me pushing, the sail finally fit through the machine and was fixed. All day long we sailed with just the mizzen sail. The boat sure was squirrelly with only one sail up on the back of the boat. Gandalf had to work his tail off. Serves him right.

Day 20 and we saw our first ship (although I don't think he saw us). We figured we must be getting close to something. Actually we knew exactly where we were. I was using the sextant a few times a day to make sure I knew our position, and we also had the sat-nav that gave our position a few times a day. It was temperamental and didn't spit out our position very often, but on a long distance passage like this it really didn't matter. The sextant was more interesting to use than the sat-nav and it usually produced a position I could put on the chart. The hardest part of using the sextant was to find various spots on the boat where I could hang on tight, use the sextant to find the sun's declination, as well as look at my watch to get the exact time of the site - usually I had to count "one-one-thousand, two-one-thousand..." until I looked at the time, and then I would subtract however many seconds it took for me to look at my watch. It sounds more difficult than it actually is. After taking thousands of sights it gets easier and easier. To get sights using the stars or planets it's actually easier and involves less math to get the result.

By the way, as far as our fishing went on the passage, it was great... great for the fish that is. We dragged two lures behind the boat every day (except when Gandalf the autopilot was broken) and only caught one Bonita, which none of us liked. We promised ourselves to keep trying.

Chapter 11

October 9th, 1989, 6:00 a.m. after the 23 days at sea (we were getting a little goofy), Land Ho! We smelled the flowers well before seeing any land. Hiva Oa in the Marquesas Islands of French Polynesia, truly paradise. To this day we're not sure if it was being at sea for so long that made this place seem so incredibly beautiful, or if that's just the way it is. My money is on "that's just the way it is."

Foliage so green and flowers so colorful covering the mountains, it was hard to believe this place could be so beautiful. Bananas, oranges, mangos, papayas, breadfruit and limes free for the asking. Vladimir and Jorget were already there (they passed us after our forestay broke). Jeff and Sheila on Aberlady were also there. A breakfast was prepared and waiting for us onboard Aberlady, and it sure felt strange to get off of Shadowfax and actually see other people.

We had to walk to the small town of Atuona (population 1,500) three miles away to clear customs. Lots of locals stopped to pick us up, but after 23 days at sea we really needed the walk. Once we found the officials we knew what to expect. They wanted money... lots of money.

To sail the waters of French Polynesia, each person must put up the price of airfare home (in case you're a bum) as a bond which you get back when you leave – for us it was six months later. The three of us went to the local back to hand over our $2,400, and we had a funny experience.

We were invited into an office in a small wooden bank building by a very polite Marquesan who took our money, opened a drawer of the desk and lifted out a folder stuffed with money. She put this folder on the desk and then left the room to get us a receipt. What was this, some kind of Marquesan honesty test? She came back after a couple of minutes with our receipt and then left the room again. I'm not kidding when I say there had to be thousands of dollars sitting on that desk staring at us. We could get used to a place that can exist with honesty and trust like that.

So we gave them almost all the money we had and went to check out this beautiful little town. Beautiful but expensive. True, the stuff on the trees was free, but eggs were $5.00 a dozen. Lettuce was almost $5.00 a head. We definitely had to stay out of the stores.

The very next day while we were at anchor one of the local fishermen came out of nowhere and invited us to his house for pig roast. Great! We asked if Aberlady and Aquarius could come (we thought it would be like a picnic) and the man, Hosan, said sure. When we arrived their dining room table was set beautifully with coconuts and flowers. What a feast! Hosan and his wife, Tahia, told us that about once a year they invite a "yachtie" to their home to hear news of the outside world and also to listen to sea stories. No problem. We could handle that.

A couple of days later Hosan came by in his boat, threw some fish at us, and said he shot another pig so come on over. Another great feast. This one he cooked buried in the ground covered with banana leaves and local spices. We had printed up a pile of Shadowfax t-shirts and passed them out to Hosan and his family (more later about how the hell we printed t-shirts on a sailboat) along with a Jimmy Buffett tape. We introduced Jimmy Buffett music to lots of locals all around the world. Our Buffett tape collection diminished but we made lots of new friends.

Hosan's house was on the mountainside and overlooked the graves of painter Paul Gauguin and French singer Jacques Brel. Hosan introduced us to quite a few of his friends, so now we had lots of people to say farewell to when the time came... still the hardest part of sailing

The anchorage filled with a few more boats while we were there. French, Swiss, and a Chilean boat joined our ranks, and people from every boat joined in the fixing process of our broken forestay. We had to drop the long rod-type jib furling gear, get it to shore (it took five dinghies) and try to straighten it without breaking it. With a multi-national team like that working on it we got it fixed in a record two days. Once fixed we could leave whenever we wanted to, but in our laid back style we figured a stay of at least two weeks was in order.

After two weeks of climbing mountains and meeting locals we dragged ourselves away. Just yank in the anchor (actually with an electric windless), climb on the trade winds, head downwind and there's no coming back. You really get some exciting sails around this part of the world with a constant 20 to 30 knots of wind blowing you toward the west. The whole world should be like that.

We didn't sail all that far from Hiva Oa; in fact, a day sail of 20 miles brought us to a perfect horseshoe shaped cove called Hana Moe Noe Bay on the Island of Tahuata.

Immediately upon anchoring a small dugout canoe came out with three natives who were covered in tattoos and looking strong enough to break Shadowfax in half. When they pulled alongside they gave us the biggest smiles possible and said in broken English, "My name is Aka, these two are Tieki and Joe, and we want to welcome you to the Hana Moe Noe Yacht Club." We were then presented with two fish and told to come ashore once we got settled in.

The only building on shore was an open hut with a tiki thatch roof. These three lived here and farmed the land behind their "yacht club" for a few things to sell in the main town over the mountain.

All we had to do to secure our lifetime membership in the club was to sign their small book, which was already full of yachts that had sailed through in previous years. Lots of famous sailors we had read about had signed so we were honored to put our names with theirs. About the only benefit of joining the yacht club (besides making three new friends and relaxing in their hammock) was to get a stalk of bananas to hang in the rigging to eat as they ripen—which they would do all at once.

Our membership secure, off we sailed to an island with the strange name Ua Pu, 85 miles away. The anchorage had a slight sea swell, but the village was worth the inconvenience. The inconvenience wasn't so much living with the swell rocking the boat as it was trying to get on shore. By the time this "swell" reached the concrete dock that we had to dinghy to, it was more like surfing waves. Your timing had to be perfect riding the backside of a wave or else you would be flipped end over end. We never got flipped but we did have one wave break over us and fill the dinghy. The fault of our Seagull motor, not us.

Ok, time to talk about this dinghy motor from hell. I think the only moving part is the person pulling the starting cord. The thing came with the boat and it seemed to start every time before we bought the boat. Once we owned the boat, not so much. The system to start the motor went something like this; Take the syringe that we always kept in the dinghy (lots of funny looks because of this), suck up some fuel out of the tank and inject it into the carburetor, start pulling the cord. Your chances are about fifty-fifty that it would start. If it doesn't, start over with the syringe. If the second syringe attempt failed, you had to take the sparkplug out and heat it up with a lighter. Once you get the motor started your chances are still low that you will make it to shore with the thing still running. We never, ever, left without the oars. We were definitely on the hunt for a new motor.

Once we crashed onto the shore of Ua Pu we were in for a treat and a shock. The shock was that we found a bunch of kids sitting along the shore eating fish they had just caught. The fish were raw, and the children were eating it like corn on the cob. They were digging out the fish eyes with their fingers and popping them in their mouths. Not really what were used to, but they sure were having a fun time sitting there covered in fish slime.

The treat was that Gretchen found a Frenchman who let her walk through his terrace garden and shop like a supermarket. Talk about fresh vegetables. What a beautiful place overlooking the harbor. He told us he had given up the hectic life in France and had been on Ua Pu working on his garden for about five years. What a great life. He grew just about everything you could possibly want as well as a few things you didn't want, or even recognize.

For all the free wild foods – bananas, papayas, coconuts and breadfruit, we thought we should pay our respects to the island chief before we took any. We always wanted to meet a tribal chief anyway, so Gretchen and I, along with Vladimir, walked along the tree-lined street looking for the little house where the locals directed us.

The house wasn't anything like what you would think a chief would live in. No tiki thatch, no dirt floor, it was almost like a house in the suburbs. A wooden structure with a small porch out front and a shingled roof. We found the chief inside watching TV and within 15 minutes of meeting him, Vladimir and I found ourselves working on the Chief's Peugeot automobile. Times seem to have changed.

The chief was very fat (as all chiefs should be), and he just sat, watched and ate as Vladimir and I worked. There wasn't a whole lot wrong with the car except that it had been many, many years since it had a tune up. We explained to him that the car didn't have any spark, and he shook his head and said very seriously, 'The devil must have taken it." Maybe times haven't changed so much after all.

We left the island ahead of Aquarius and Aberlady for the short 30 mile sail to the main island of the Marquesas, Nuka Hiva. We anchored in Haka Pehi Bay off a large village in a picture perfect setting. Before going ashore we just relaxed and enjoyed the scenery. We had our VHF radio on since Vladimir wasn't there yet and we figured he might call us with questions about entering the anchorage. When our radio came to life it was Vladimir and Jeff (Aberlady) supplying some entertainment.

Vladimir called Jeff on the radio and told him he had bought a pig weighing about 20 kilos (44lbs.) before he left, and he was having trouble tying it down in the cockpit. As he sailed closer we started to hear stories about the pig getting loose, destroying the boat and finally falling overboard while Vladimir still had hold of his tail. These guys should receive an Academy Award for their acting. No pig, no tail, very entertaining though. With no TV we just made shit up.

While at anchor we noticed an old steel sailboat rusting away a short distance from us. No big deal really except that on its stern we spotted an Aries self-steering wind vane. This thing could steer a boat over long distances without electricity. The Aries wind vane had the "Vladimir seal of approval." He used one, he swore by it. We needed something like that so we decided to try and track down the owner. Not much of a problem… such a small island everybody knew everybody. We found the owner and managed to talk him out of it for not much money. He also said the vane had steered a boat around the world twice before and just might have enough life left in it for one more time. Not to be outdone, our favorite ex-communist, Vladimir, talked him out of the boat's depth sounder. All in all this Aries steering gear was a score for us. Not having to feed battery power to an electric autopilot sounded fantastic.

We loaded the wind vane on the boat and figured we could install it when we got to the French Polynesia's big city – Tahiti.

After sailing out of the main harbor on Nuka Hiva our next stop was Daniel's Bay, also on the island of Nuka Hiva. What a tough bay to get to. You head the boat downwind (in 30 knots of wind) right toward a cliff with breaking waves. At the last minute you have to slam the wheel over to the right and slip into the calm waters of a small extremely protected bay. Only one small hut could be seen on the beach and this, of course, was owned and lived in by Daniel.

We rowed in (the Seagull motor had taken the day off) and met Daniel, a very nice man with lots of grandchildren running around. He invited us into his hut to talk and eat some of his fruit. He picked some mangos from his garden as we walked toward his house, and he told us of a hidden 4,000 foot waterfall deep in the mountains. He said it would be possible for us to get to if we didn't mind a long walk. After our visit with Daniel we decided to take the next day and find this waterfall.

What a walk! We had to follow markers in the form of small carefully laid rock piles. I think we crossed three rivers, two mountains and a valley. Just when we thought we were lost, we would see a pile of rocks on the side of a hill marking the way. When we finally reached the waterfall it was everything Daniel said it was. Cold (I mean very cold), clear, freshwater crashing against the rocks. Exactly the kind of thing you would expect to find in Polynesia. I know it couldn't be, but the walk back seemed twice as long. We were sure we wouldn't have any trouble sleeping that night.

Back on the boat after the sun had set, an unlit ship of about 100 feet navigated the treacherous entrance pass. He went to the back side of the bay, stayed for about an hour, and then left. Definitely some sort of smuggling operation. Things in French Polynesia are so expensive that this ship could have been smuggling anything from alcohol to stereos. We'll never know what they were doing, but the captain sure was brave, and a little nuts, to get that boat in that tiny entrance.

Before we knew it five days had gone by, and we were stuffed with bananas and planning our next passage. The bananas given to us in Tahuata had ripened all at once along with the stalk Aberlady had hanging in their rigging. We ate bananas in every way you could imagine. We made a rule where anybody going on deck for any reason had to eat at least one banana. Daniel had given us another stalk of unripe bananas to replace the ones we were eating, so we could see bananas in our future for a very long time.

On our way again... this time 450 miles to the southwest to Manihi Island in a large group of islands called The

Tuamotus. The 76 islands stretch for over 1,000 miles across the Pacific and have a population of less than 6,000 people. All of the Tuamotu Islands are completely opposite from the Marquesas Islands. Instead of lush and mountainous, they are flat - mostly palm tree and sand covered islands forming a circle with a deep lagoon in the center.

The passage wasn't one of our favorites – strong winds, rain squalls and even a little lightning followed us the entire way. At times during the four-day trip the wind would die completely, which would leave us with a huge beam sea to roll around in. Shadowfax was like a ride at Disney World – anything not put away would find itself on the floor. Probably broken.

We'd been told the island of Manihi was off limits and yachts weren't allowed to stop there, but we found that a little hard to believe. How do you close an island? Still, we didn't plan to stop there unless our timing was wrong. If we couldn't get to the island beyond Manihi before dark, we wanted to stop there. The guide books and charts agree that the Tuamoto Islands all have deadly entrances, and there was no way to safely sail in after dark. As the winds died it became clear that Manihi was the only island we could reach without staying out an extra night. We changed course toward the "off limits" island to see if it was really closed to us poor tired yachties.

We approached the inlet to the lagoon and we could see lots of sharp coral heads lurking just under the surface. Most of the lagoon was over a hundred feet deep, but the coral could grow to within inches of the surface. This meant dangerous sailing, but it meant incredible diving. Gretchen and Dave kept watch on the bow and yelled back directions as I steered Shadowfax through the sharp maze of reefs. As we were weaving our way along we noticed one of the locals in a small skiff with an outboard coming our way. Our first thought was that maybe this place was closed, and we were about to be evicted.

The villagers had seen our American flag and sent a guide to get us safely past the reef and into the anchorage. So much for the island being off limits. Later we discovered the people of Manihi had spread the off limits rumors themselves because of their extensive pearl farming. Almost the entire lagoon was covered in the nets used for growing the black pearls, and they didn't want visiting boats tearing them up – or stealing them. As far as letting us stay, no problem. We stayed a week. In fact, they insisted we take time to come and tour this strange pearl farm business.

In the anchorage we found one other yacht that ignored the rumors. The Chilean ketch Patagonia that helped us with repairing our forestay in Hiva Oa. Jose, Erica and their children, Luca (4) and Natalia (7) were worth getting to know. After all, how many sailing yachts do you ever meet from Chile? Their story was a little like ours... they had never sailed before leaving Chile a few months earlier. They had a friend who was familiar with sailing come with them on the long sail to the Marquesas Islands and they paid attention and learned everything they could during that passage. Once there, their friend left and they were on their own. A tough way to learn but it worked.

As for the pearl farm, it was more complicated than we thought. Black pearls are grown by surgically implanting a small plastic ball inside the oyster and then hanging the oysters in long stings from a net under the water. The pearls take years to grow, and after the pearl is grown it still might be imperfect and worthless. The odds were good though, because the whole lagoon was covered in nets representing thousands and thousands of growing pearls. If we had the money this would have been a great opportunity to get rich. Black pearls would never be cheaper - ever.

We really liked these atoll islands. Walking around on shore was like walking on an endless beach. When you get thirsty or hungry, just drink a coconut and grab a mango and sit in the shade of a palm for a while. The underwater world was even more spectacular. Every reef was different, and diving in the entrance pass was incredible. The current flies through so fast that all you have to do while underwater is just look. You fly past everything without even one stroke... just like watching a move.

Time to move on - up anchor and out the pass with Patagonia right behind. Our sights were set on Ahi Island only 25 miles away. We wanted to visit more of these fantastic atoll islands.

It seems all the boats we met since the Marquesas were anchored in the cramped little Ahi anchorage. Aberlady-Britain, Aquarius-Bulgaria, Izaura-France, Patagonia-Chile and, of course, Shadowfax-U.S.A. Quite a multi-national group.

Ahi was a little smaller than Manihi, but the entrance was almost exactly the same. With Gretchen and Dave on the bow "reef spotting" we were getting good at these unmarked and confusing entrances. We had to take it seriously because you don't want to bump into of these coral heads. They would puncture any hull in a second. Even after anchoring I would dive on the anchor to be sure it was set, and then swam around the boat to be sure we wouldn't swing into any rough hunks of coral. We tried to be anchored secure enough for a gale. When bad weather showed up it always seemed to be at four in the morning, so it was much better to think about it in the daylight.

When we were finally secure at anchor we found everyone in a deep debate. Vladimir had found a skinny little pig on shore that he wanted us to kill and eat (this time a real pig, not just a story). All the men from the boats came over to Shadowfax to discuss the fate of this poor little thing. This summit meeting of five countries came to be known as "The Male Chauvinist Pig Council" (maybe you've heard of it). We argued for a while, but when the vote was finally taken, it was four countries to Bulgaria that we have a fish fry and invite the pig to dine with us. We had a great time roasting fish on the beach, and I'm sure the pig had a better time too.

Before we knew it, another seven days had gone by with everyone diving, spearing fish and generally goofing off. But when it came time to leave we had to wait for a couple more days while a storm blew through. No problem. This cruising laidback lifestyle was agreeing with us. After the storm passed we decided to make it a convoy and sail to the next island together.

Our last stop in the Tuamotus was to be the island of Rangiroa. Rangiroa is a small bit of civilization in the middle of all those tiny circular atolls. Rangiroa had a store, a bar and even a small airport. The island had two entrance passes to choose from and lots of room to anchor. The lagoon is almost 45 miles from side to side, which meant plenty of anchorages all around the rim of the lagoon. The only problem was that if the wind changed and started blowing across the lagoon, the seas could build and make for an uncomfortable stay.

Once in and anchored we loved the place. We couldn't get enough of the drift diving through the pass and spear fishing for our dinner. It's true that dragging lines behind the boat didn't seem to do us much good, but at anchor with a spear gun we always ate well. There were so many fish, and the water so clear, it was like having a menu in front of you.

Since some reef fish are poisonous we always asked the locals which ones were safe and it's amazing what we were told. Locals on one island would tell us, "Don't eat the spotted grouper or the big barracuda," while an atoll 25 miles away would say, "Only eat the biggest barracuda and the spotted grouper." We always did what we were told, but I think it must have been a roll of the dice whether we would get sick or not. Who knows, but none of us ever got sick.

While hanging around Rangiroa, Jeff on Aberlady told us that when they arrived in Tahiti they would have to fly back to England for a couple of months and asked Dave if he would boat-sit for them. What a bachelor pad! His own yacht tied to the pier in Tahiti. Of course he said, "sure, no problem" Gretchen and I planned to stay in Rangiroa for a while longer, so Dave jumped ship and sailed with Aberlady to Tahiti.

During our 17-day stay we saw just about everything. Underwater we saw the largest sharks we had ever seen and above the water we experienced a nasty storm that blew across the wide lagoon.

The locals had large fish traps in the passes (about the size of a screened porch) that were built like a maze. When fish swam in they would have trouble finding their way out, and it was in this maze where we saw lots of sharks. We could swim right up next to the wire fence and stare at these sharks as they tried to smash their way out to get at us. A little dangerous, but definitely exciting.

A few days before we left, a 30-foot sloop sailed in the pass and dropped anchor just to our port. It was flying a Japanese flag and had Yashi Maru in large letters along the side. We had never met any Japanese sailors before, so off we went in the dinghy to introduce ourselves - just like Welcome Wagon.

We found Masa and Yuka aboard and doing what everyone else was doing... just sailing around checking out as many islands as they could. Masa couldn't speak English very well (and our Japanese consisted of the word sushi) but Yuka saved the day with perfect English. She told us that Masa was in computer sales in Japan, but the way the Japanese culture was he would probably be blackballed from getting a job like that again since he quit to go sailing. She told us that Japanese work ethic didn't allow for extended vacation like they were taking. They didn't care though, they were out to see a little of the world and do some diving. Just like us. Every time we dove with them and looked at Masa underwater, he would bow to us. These guys were great. We knew we would become good friends.

Chapter 12

Gretchen and I finally sailed out for the island of Tahiti -
202 miles and our first long passage alone without Dave.
Right away we noticed how much more work it involved.
We changed our watches to 3 hours on and 3 off, but it took
a little getting used to. The weather was full of squalls and
light winds, so we were kept busy with sail changes and all
the things that break as you sail along. Almost all the other
boats we had met made do with only two people, and even
though Shadowfax was a little bigger, we were sure we
could too.

Tahiti. We didn't know what to expect (we never did) and
we were surprised at our first sight. It sure looked like a
crowded and busy place. The main city, Papeete, is the
capitol of all French Polynesia, and it showed. Hundreds of
cars moving slowly along the road with horns blowing and
people yelling. Another hundred or so boats were tied to the
famous concrete wall along the shore which is inches from
the main four-lane road that runs along the shore. There
were so many boats that the only way for everyone to tie up
was to drop a bow anchor and back up to the concrete wall
to tie up your stern. Just like sardines in a can. Very
different from the Polynesia we had seen so far.

Tahiti is actually two islands – Tahiti Nui (big) and Tahiti
Iti (small), which are connected by a land bridge. The
distance around both islands is just under 200 miles. I
don't want to knock Tahiti completely. If you stand back
and ignore the city buildings and the huge amount of cars,
the island is fantastically beautiful. Mountains with
waterfalls in all directions. You can still picture what it must
have been like for the first settlers. Plenty of shelter from
the storms and enough fresh water to last forever.

We tied our stern to the wall and then joined the mad
rush of people trying to get things done. This was the first
place we'd been since Panama where we could re-provision
in a real supermarket and also the first place in four months

where we could receive mail. I guess cities are good for something (even though it drove us nuts).

Tahiti is also a little on the expensive side. One night Gretchen and I decided to splurge and go to one of the nightclubs along the strip, at least until we found out the prices. The average cost of the cover charge in most of the clubs was $20.00 U.S. each, and then once inside an average mixed drink cost $17.50! We decided to go back to the boat and have our own party with a $5.00 bottle of rum from Panama. We invited all our new friends and had a terrific time.

Three weeks later we were still there, and we hadn't accomplished anything. We were too low on money to do any real provisioning, and we couldn't seem to master the French language enough to get by. We had become fair at speaking Polynesian but that didn't do us any good in Tahiti. Before we knew it Christmas rolled around, so we decided to stay and enjoy it.

Gretchen decorated the boat with flowers, a tree made from cut branches, and lights everywhere. The lights could only be used when we ran the generator because the voltage was different (the rest of the world lives on 240 volts compared to the U.S. 120 volts). Gretchen's boat decorations looked good enough that a Tahitian newspaper reporter came down to take pictures and do a story about us.

One of our more memorable times in Tahiti was when Gretchen heard singing in the street and we went to check it out. We found ten Tahitian taxi drivers waiting around for customers and singing until a fare came along. These guys were really good. We sat and listened and talked to them for a few hours (it seems taxi drivers speak English pretty well), and then they invited us to a party they were having that evening. Of course we said yes - we never refused a good (or bad) party.

We met at a small bar and noticed we were the only non-Tahitians there. Everyone grabbed an instrument of some kind and they played their hearts out. They made us feel at home and never let our drinks become more than half empty. The next day my head hurt horribly, but I was told I had a great time.

All our friends had their boats tied along the wall when New Years rolled around, so we all went over to spend it on Aberlady. Dave was still boat-sitting Aberlady for Jeff and Sheila, and as far as we could tell he was having a great time. At midnight all the boats in the harbor shot off flares, turned on spotlights and hit their horns to welcome in the New Year. Vladimir brought out a huge Russian flare rocket. It looked impressive, but the only way it would be useful in a rescue would be to throw it against a rescue boat and hope they noticed. It was a dud.

While all this was going on, Vladimir's wife Jorget was sitting around very, very pregnant. She was due in a couple of weeks and they decided to have it while in Tahiti. Since the best hospital was on Tahiti, this was a good idea. Apparently this would be the first Tahitian-born Bulgarian ever. What a rare event. Even the local media got involved. All hospital bills would be taken care of, and she would even come out of it with $1,000 from the local Women's League. Around this time their other daughter (12) was given permission to leave Bulgaria and fly to Tahiti to join them. This was gonna be one crowded Bulgarian boat. Vladamir's "Great Escape" was progressing nicely.

We finally gave up trying to get anything done in Papeete and decided to leave, but even leaving appeared to be hard to accomplish. Strikes were so common around French Polynesia that you had to be lucky to have everything go your way. Tourists on vacation had to deal with airport strikes, taxi strikes, ferry strikes and hotel worker strikes. We were lucky. All we had to deal with were customs and immigration strikes. Even though we weren't checking in or out of French Polynesia, they still insisted that we go through all the bureaucracy. The strikes made office hours so undependable that it took us three days to clear out of three offices. For the third office, Gretchen found the port captain outside of his office on strike and drinking a beer. She talked him into stamping our papers as long as we promised not to tell anybody. What a mess.

Dave was still boat-sitting in Papeete and planned to catch up later. But again, one of the strikes altered our plans. The day we were leaving the ferries decided to strike, which left tons of tourists stranded on Tahiti. We met a German couple who were trying to get to Moorea Island (our next stop) and a Canadian couple trying to get to Raiatea island (our second stop). We felt bad for them, so we loaded them aboard Shadowfax and off we sailed to Moorea 20 miles away.

A short easy trip and we were anchored in Cook's Bay on Moorea Island. Moorea isn't a city like Papeete, but by being so close it was crowded just by osmosis. A few resorts dotted the shoreline and a couple of small cruise ships cluttered the bay. Still, it was beautiful. We were surrounded by tall jagged mountains with a local legend attached to each one.

After checking out the island and dropping off our two German passengers, we motored out toward the mouth of the bay to relax a little and dive on the reef that surrounds the island. Our two new friends from Canada were enjoying the Shadowfax ferry ride, so they didn't mind spending a couple of days hanging around Moorea.

Our second night at Moorea we were boarded by the French Coast Guard. Two young guys came aboard from their patrol ship, and right away we noticed the difference between these guys and the U.S. Coast Guard. All they cared about was paperwork. Not one lifejacket or fire extinguisher was checked. Since our paperwork was in order, they were gone in 30 minutes.

The overnight sail of 106 miles to Raiatea was a good one with strong trade winds and a large rolling sea. Since it was an overnight sail, our two passengers insisted that we let them take a night watch to help out, but we decided we better keep an eye on them. Gretchen and I predicted the future and we were right - an hour into their watch and they were both sound asleep. Good help is hard to find.

Arriving at Raiatea we said goodbye and dropped off our Canadian guests at the main dock where they found a taxi. I bet we were a memorable part of their vacation.

Raiatea was more like it - no crowds, lots of Polynesians and miles and miles of colorful reefs. Raiatea is the largest of the four main leeward islands (Raiatea, Huahine, Tahaa and Bora Bora) measuring 12 miles north to south and 8 miles east to west. Mountains run the full length of the island, and two of them reached more than 3,000 feet. Raiatea's largest export was said to be empty beer bottles.

Checking out the chart we found a small navigable river on the island and decided to check it out. The Aoppoman River being called "navigable" was probably giving it too much credit. Using the dinghy was the only possible way to enter it, and we could only go about a half mile before we ran out of deep water. Still it was worth it: lots of jungle, flowers and wildlife along the way. We decided to row instead of motor so we wouldn't chase away any of the birds. Rowing was easier than dealing with the Seagull outboard anyway.

When we sailed to Raiatea to drop off our guests we had to sail past one of the other leeward islands, Huahine, so we decided to go back. Huahine Island is only about 13 miles long, and on the chart it looked like two islands connected by a short land bridge. Legend says that the God Hiro split the island in two while paddling his canoe. Apparently he was rowing along and couldn't stop in time before cutting through the island. Must have been one big guy.

The entrance pass was like the rest of them in the area—narrow and deep with reefs on both sides. Not much problem getting in as long as you could find it. We found the entrance to Huahine, but our main diesel motor decided not to start when we got there. The entrance was upwind and we tacked as close as we could to it, but once we got close to the pass the island sheltered us from any wind, which left us unable to sail in.

We could see our friends on Patagonia from Chile anchored inside and we gave them a call on the radio. Jose agreed to come out in his dinghy and give us a little tow. The wind was so light his little inflatable did the trick. We tied his dinghy to our side like a tugboat, put his motor in forward and took right off at about a half knot. Once we were anchored I found the problem to be in the fuel pump. Some duct tape and Superglue and we were ready to go again. It's embarrassing to admit how much duct tape is used in world cruising.

Huahine's anchorages were so beautiful it was hard to drag ourselves away to go to the next one. The locals were shy until we managed to strike up a conversation with them. Even though our Polynesian was extremely limited, and not too many people we met spoke English, we still managed to hold abbreviated conversations. We used lots of hand gestures and sometimes resorted to drawing pictures. Almost everyone wanted to be friendly, so the rest was easy.

Huahine was also the place we saw the best Polynesian dance show. At the Relais Mahana Hotel the dancers were all amateurs who won a local talent contest. It was obvious they weren't doing it for the money. You could tell they really loved to dance.

After four days had slipped by, we again headed back toward Raiatea. Well, not exactly Raiatea but Tahaa Island, which is right next to Raiatea. The two are almost connected and are surrounded by the same circular reef system. Since it was only a trip of 25 miles we decided to tow the dinghy instead of putting it on deck (for the first time). What could go wrong?

We should have known better. Never trust the weather. As soon as we left Huahine storm clouds started to build on the horizon and the sun disappeared. The wind was behind us, and it started to build rapidly. We only had a small piece of the jib sail up and it blew out in a violent gust of wind that came out of nowhere. We kept looking at the dinghy trailing on a long line and skipping along behind us. Every time we surfed down one of the waves it would turn sideways and almost flip. If that happened we would have had to cut it free, turn Shadowfax into the seas, try to retrieve it, and flip it back over again. Dream on.

We couldn't afford to lose the dinghy so we decided to slow the boat and get the dinghy aboard before anything really bad happened. We thought it was rough and windy when we were sailing downwind, but it became incredibly rough when we stopped. We turned Shadowfax into the wind, and the seas crashed over the whole length of the boat.

The bow was starting to look a little like a submarine. It would go under a wave and wouldn't come back up until the wave reached all the way back to the cockpit. It was much too wild to get the dinghy back aboard so all we could do was adjust the dinghy lines to tow better and hope for the best.

Since the entrance pass was on the windward side of Raiatea Island we were happy to not see the waves breaking clear across the narrow inlet, but the seas were indeed huge as they rolled through. We hung on, surfed in with reefs close on both sides, and rounded up into the calm peaceful lagoon of Tahaa. What a difference - from 20-foot seas to flat calm in less than 10 seconds.

Tahaa is about 6 miles long, but finding an anchorage in that area wasn't all that easy. The waters inside the reef were up to 100 feet deep almost everywhere... way too deep to drop the hook safely. We finally found a restaurant inside a cove that had put moorings down in front for boats to tie to. Heavy sigh of relief.

After that sail, and our entrance through the pass, we thought a nice dinner ashore would be in order. Since we were using their mooring it's only fair to eat their food. The restaurant, The Hibiscus, was a small wooden building with good (but expensive) food. The most memorable thing about the place was La La, the restaurant's 200 lb. pet pig that had the run of the place. We were told that if La La was under your table and then got up to walk away, he would probably carry your table with him. I don't think the U.S. health codes would let you get away with having a La La-type animal hanging around under your table. It seems there are lots of pigs and pig stories in Polynesia.

Tahaa was worth the visit just like all the other Polynesian islands - mountainous, green and waterfalls around every corner. We walked for hours along the dirt road that cut across the island. Small churches and lots of tiki thatch homes around each corner. After meeting a local along the way we were invited on a short tour of a vanilla plantation - Tahaa's main industry. What a fun business, and the smell of fresh vanilla is fantastic! We hung vanilla beans inside the boat for months.

After a couple of days waiting for a weather front to pass it was time to say goodbye to La La and head to probably the most beautiful island in the world.

Another short sail of 25 miles away - the island of Bora Bora. Almost circular and only 5 miles long, the island is mountainous with the famous "twin peaks" reaching a height of 2,100 feet. Sheer cliffs drop into a turquoise lagoon which is completely surrounded by coral reef. This place would be our home base for the next three months.

We sailed into the only entrance pass and headed toward shore to try and figure out where to anchor. This lagoon was also too deep to anchor in most places, so we looked for other sailboats to see where they were anchored. What we found was a small resort on shore with ten moorings anchored in 80 feet of water and a sign on the dock saying "Hotel Oa Oa, Yachts Welcome." Our kind of place.

We tied to a mooring and went ashore to check the place out. The owner, Greg, was an ex-bank vice president from California who had sailed to Bora Bora years before and never left. By the time we arrived, Greg was burned out on the whole situation. It's hard to imagine, but I guess even a place like Bora Bora can get old.

For a small island, Bora Bora sure was popular. Every week at least three cruise ships pulled in loaded with tourists. They never seemed to stay more than a few hours, so we kind of enjoyed the action once in a while. One of the ships that sailed in each week was the 440 foot computerized sailing vessel Windsong, and every week we would try to get aboard for a tour - but with no luck.

Finally we decided to go over the captain's head and went right to the help. We made friends with the people at the "back door" who were running the sports concession – jet skis, water skiing and scuba trips. It makes sense to make friends with the people guarding the door. Before we knew it we were aboard, shaking hands with the captain and checking the place out. Luxury rooms and an incredibly beautiful sail design made this ship incredible. The ship's main computer was supposed to run the entire ship. When the wind hit a certain strength, its masts would automatically roll up some of the sail without any guidance. It sure looked impressive, but we were informed it hardly ever worked. It wasn't working the day we were there either. Nice ship anyway.

Another one of the cruise ships that came in was the Maxim Gorky from the U.S.S.R. (the U.S.S.R. still existed at the time), and we invited a couple of the crew members aboard Shadowfax to look around. They talked it over for awhile, thinking that they would get into trouble if they came out to Shadowfax. They had never seen a private yacht, and we could tell they really wanted to. Their curiosity won, and they climbed in our dinghy.

Kirkov and Viktor were like two kids in a candy store. Everything they looked at they asked, "How much?" We didn't know how much in rubles anything cost, so we told them prices in dollars. We asked them what they thought of Gorbachev's reforms, and we were told they didn't like him because he was moving too slowly. They wanted to be able to buy a yacht like Shadowfax then, not in five years or even in one year. They were amazed at what a little capitalism could get you. We sent them home with a couple of Shadowfax t-shirts, pictures, and a Newsweek magazine with "Gorby" on the cover.

The Oa Oa was a great place to hang out and see the island. You could bicycle around the island in only a couple of hours, which made it easy to fall in love with the place. To make Bora Bora even more enjoyable Greg let us use his bikes, phone, mailing address and everything else. We also made a deal with him that I would dive on all his moorings to check out their condition in exchange for drinks and meals at the motel. His boat moorings were a bit strange as they were all bits of junk the US military dumped in the water after WW2. Sort of like a short history lesson underwater.

We considered Bora to be a great place to wait out the southern hemisphere cyclone season until it ended in April, and this was the perfect place to call home. Cyclones very rarely come to this area of the Pacific, so we felt safe... at least until Cyclone Penny formed a few hundred miles to the northeast.

Chapter 13

The forecast for Cyclone Penny was for it to head west and pass to the north of us, but we still prepared for the worst. We cleared the decks of everything we could and moved the boat to the most secure mooring, which happened to be a huge WW2 half-track tank half buried in the sand. I put on a scuba tank and swam down to hook up six of our strongest lines and a chain to this huge piece of WW2 junk. Of course, as these things go, the storm turned in our direction and slowed down in forward speed. Two days later we had winds of over 100 knots.

Shadowfax would heel over 40 degrees in the gusts and when we had to go on deck to check the mooring lines we had to hang on tight and wear a diving mask to see through the pelting rain. We were in the lee of the huge twin peak mountain, which kept us sheltered from the waves, but the wind seemed to keep building. The wind screeching through the rigging became so loud that Gretchen and I had to yell to be heard. A sailboat from a local charter company was tied to the mooring behind us, and they had made the mistake of leaving their dinghy in the water. Maybe they thought they would use it to get ashore if the cyclone became too dangerous. The wind picked up their dinghy (with a 25hp motor on it) and spun it all day like a propeller until it disintegrated.

The storm moved so slowly that we thought it would never end. We could see the Oa Oa motel in between rain squalls (about 300 feet away), and we could see that it was completely flooded.

Sleeping was just about out of the question, but after the first night we took turns keeping watch while one of us tried to get some rest. One of us always had to be alert in case the mooring lines snapped. Every few hours someone would have to go on deck to check. Not a whole lot of fun.

When the storm was to the northwest we thought it was going to continue on the same course when Penny turned directly south. This meant trouble. Even though it looked like the storm wouldn't hit us directly, it would pass close and the wind direction would change, giving us a lee shore as the waves built and came right through the pass and over the surrounding reef.

The mooring was holding great so far, and we had no choice but to stay put and see how bad it was going to get. For two more days that storm battered us. The seas built to a point where we decided twice to try and leave, but then the wind would calm a little so we put it off. Our "halftrack" mooring never budged during the storm, but two of the six lines we had attached to it snapped. The Oa Oa didn't fare as well. When the wind switched the waves crashed over the shore and into all the Oa Oa cottages and filled the sunken bar with water. His motel guests looked a little traumatized – we could relate.

Cyclone Penny was definitely an enlightening situation. We decided that we would try to avoid these things like the plague. We couldn't imagine what if would be like out in the open seas in one of those things in a tiny little plastic sailboat. We'd read all the books about what to do in a serious storm at sea, and it would definitely be intense.

Meanwhile we heard by ham radio that back on Tahiti (even though they were another 100 miles from the storm) many boats were damaged as lines broke and the seas surged into the harbor. The computerized sailing cruise ship Windsong was stuck by a huge wave as they tried to leave Moorea Island and sail the 20 miles to Tahiti. They were slammed broadside by a 40-foot wave and apparently broke almost every dish aboard, as well as throwing TVs and tourists to the floor. So much for spending cyclone season in a country that rarely gets serious storms.

As soon as the storm ended we dropped the mooring to sail back toward Huahine to meet friends who were flying in to visit us, but we were stopped at the pass. Even though the storm was over, Bora Bora was effectively "closed" to boats. We sailed up to the pass and saw huge waves breaking across the entire length. We poked our nose out one side and tried to time our exit in between the breakers. Then we tried the other side and found the same situation. Oh well, back to the mooring to wait. Greg needed help bailing out the bar anyway.

After a couple of days we finally got out of there and met our friends. We gave them a tour of every place we'd been - again, and again, and again. We could have become tour guides for these islands. Even La La the pig got to know us. These islands are definitely some of the prettiest real estate in the world.

It was right around this time that our first year anniversary of leaving Florida passed by. It was almost the same day we ran out of our closely guarded money. We still had the bond money that the French government was keeping, so we figured we were still in fair shape. The down side was that we wouldn't get it back until we left Polynesia. Until then we could live on French bread (35 cents a loaf) and whatever fish we could spear.

Cyclone season was coming to an end and the other boats we were sailing with were starting to show up at Bora Bora to get ready to leave French Polynesia. David decided to catch up to us by taking the ferry from Tahiti to Raiatea, so we sailed upwind to pick him up. After making it back to Raiatea to wait for Dave's ferry, we decided to do a little scuba diving on a wreck we had heard about.

The weather was perfect and underwater visibility was at least 60 feet. We entered 80 degree water and dove to the wreck which was just under 100 feet deep. The 200 foot schooner, St. Michael, looked like a ghost when it came into view. She sank from bashing into a reef in 1879 and looked to be in excellent condition (except, of course, for the huge hole in her hull). She was on her side with the huge masts along the sea floor stretching off into the distance. The old anchor was still on the bow secured to its chocks. Maybe things happened too fast for the crew to drop it. Halfway along her hull we entered through the large hole.

Gretchen and I stayed close together in case one of us had any problem with our equipment. At 100 feet everything takes on a grayish tinge and looks a little eerie. Being inside a ghost ship adds a lot to the strange feelings we had. We couldn't help wondering if anyone had gone down with her.

We didn't find any treasure, but as we swam into the hull of the ship we broke the surface into an air pocket. We cautiously took the regulators out of our mouths to try breathing the air. It tasted a little funny but seemed okay. So there we were, 100 feet down inside a century old wreck, leaning against the hull and holding a conversation. That's what I call an interesting dive. I wish I could have left a note for future divers to find – or maybe a treasure map leading to the Oa Oa and Greg's bar.

The next day Dave arrived and we discovered he had fallen deeply in love in Tahiti, and he wanted to do something about it. We also found out that Shadowfax's engine was full of saltwater.

The engine was easier to fix than Dave's problem. We drained and filled the oil four times to clean out the motor. The problem was a leaky oil cooler and we fixed it with tough love - we threw it out. Shadowfax ran just fine without it. After Shadowfax was in working order, we got all the facts about Dave and what he wanted to do.

He had met a beautiful Japanese gal named Yuki who worked in Tahiti in the travel business. She had five months left on her contract before she could think about leaving. Our visas were almost up, so Dave couldn't stay. We definitely could see a problem forming. She was welcome to join us if she wanted to, but it looked like there was nothing any of us could do for at least five months.

Chapter 14

Once back on Bora Bora, we started getting ready to leave. We had been carrying the old Aries steering vane since we bought it in the Marquesas Islands, so we decided to try to figure out how to bolt it to our stern. Once it was installed we had to connect the vane by lines to the steering wheel in our center cockpit. It wouldn't have been much of a problem except that the closest hardware store was 120 miles away in Tahiti.

Luckily Vladimir sailed in and he had a good handle on these steering vane things. He had two vanes (one for a spare) aboard his boat... both made by him from borrowing someone else's and copying it. After we got it bolted to our stern we managed to figure out how to make the thing work. Long lines ran from the vane up through three sets of pulleys until securing to a homemade device on the steering wheel. A great little gadget that worked perfectly on our first test. Sailing around the Bora Bora lagoon it worked on the first try – what a great device!

Besides helping us with the steering wind vane, Vladimir had his hands full. Jorjet had a baby boy while in Tahiti, and their daughter Denitza had flown in from Bulgaria to join them. If that wasn't enough, communism was disintegrating around the world, which made Vladimir about as happy as a guy could get. He was celebrating everything. It looked like his country would at last be free.

The last to sail to join us for the sail west were Jeff and Sheila aboard Aberlady. Already in the anchorage were Yashi Maru, Patagonia, Aquarius and us. We were all just about ready... only a couple hundred more projects left to do.

Just after Aberlady sailed in and tied to one of the moorings, it was time for another little storm. Not too bad... only about 50 knots of wind, but it did create a small disaster. In one of the stronger gusts, Aberlady broke her mooring line and started to drift down on Shadowfax. Jeff started his motor to keep from hitting us, but just as he moved out of our way what was left of his mooring line wrapped around his propeller. Somehow this mooring line, coming from his bow cleat, was also wrapped around his anchors making it impossible for him to drop them.

Aberlady was drifting toward a reef. Gretchen and I jumped into our dinghy and caught up with them as they kept drifting. I yelled for Jeff to hand me his scuba tank and a knife, and I jumped in. I didn't have time to put the gear on so I had the tank under one arm and held on to Aberlady's propeller with the other.

Meanwhile, Gretchen and Jeff were each in a dinghy trying to push Aberlady with enough force to keep her off the reef and give me time to cut the line away. The seagull motor was (for once) working, pushing on the port side, and Jeff's dinghy was pushing to starboard. As I held on to the line around Aberlady's propeller, both dinghy propellers were just feet away from me and turning at full throttle. Good incentive to get to work.

What I had to do was to let the scuba tank drop and just hang on to it by the regulator in my mouth. This gave me a free hand to start cutting. As I started to cut it seemed like miles of line were wrapped around the propeller. If I needed more reason to work fast, the weight of the scuba tank felt like it was going to pull my teeth out.

A barracuda watched me from a few feet away which was slightly distracting. It seemed that all the sailboats had a barracuda living in the shade of the boat whenever we anchored. This one must have been Aberlady's. He definitely wanted to know what the hell I was doing to his boat.

The line was finally cut and removed and Aberlady was saved from crashing onto the reef, and I was happy to climb aboard without being eaten by Jeff's dinghy propeller, the Seagull or the barracuda. About this time I realized all this had happened before I had my first cup of coffee of the day. Jeff gave me one... more than half of it was brandy.

A couple of other things happened before we left Bora Bora, and none of them were very good. Our last year of work back in the real world (actually only January to April) along with the sale of the house meant that we owed the I.R.S money. Not a whole lot... just about the exact amount the French were holding as our bond. Mmm, not good.

Another problem came in the form of a letter (3 months old) from the gal we had turned our power boat over to with the payment book. The letter she wrote us said, "Sorry I owe too much money so I can't keep the boat. It's at the marina with the payment book in the glovebox." In the same batch of mail came a letter from the bank. To paraphrase, it said something like, "Hey buddy, send boat payments now. Three months please." And yet another letter – this one from the marina, "What's with this boat? Send money now, 3 month's dockage, $375.00." Not a good mail day.

If we thought we had it bad, poor Vladimir had news that was hard to believe. On the up side the Bulgarian government had been overthrown which made Vladimir extremely happy, but on the down side he received a letter saying he was a traitor for working with the communist government. He was being accused of stealing government property – the stupid camera he was using to send video back to Bulgarian TV. The letter informed him that he should come back and stand trial, which made Vladimir very unhappy. The letter said that since he had been working for the state-owned TV station and sending back videos, he must be a communist, and apparently they didn't like those people anymore.

We all sat down with Vladimir and helped him compose a letter to the Bulgarian government. Thirty pages later we thought it sounded great. He had actually performed one of the greatest escapes in history and had also managed to get his family out too - real TV mini-series stuff. He sent it off and decided not to worry about it. Time to go sailing.

As for us, when we got our bond money back we sent it all to the I.R.S., the bank, and the marina, and we were just about even (also very broke). We called everybody we could think of to see if we could sell the damn boat again. All we wanted was to get out of the payments, which we finally managed to do. We also had to give up our health insurance which we somehow managed to keep current until then. We kept repeating to ourselves - It's better to be on a yacht in the South Pacific dreaming of a hot bath than to be in a hot bath dreaming of a yacht in the South Pacific.

Finally time to leave, or as Gretchen said, sail west in search of a paycheck. I guess having a vacation for a whole year wasn't too bad. We knew we would have to get back to work sometime.

Even though Bora Bora was the last official French Polynesian Island with any real officials, there were still two smaller French islands on the sail west. Maupiti was the first one which was only 25 miles away. Most yachts didn't seem to visit there because of the reputation of the entrance pass. To quote the sailing directions from the U.S. Defense Mapping Agency, "The pass is narrow and tortuous, and is available to vessels with local knowledge." We decided it wouldn't hurt to get close and take a look. We didn't have to go in if it looked too scary.

As we approached the pass we could see large rolling breakers everywhere along the shore. The entrance was on the windward side of the island which made it look like it would be a great place for surfers. There was one area of somewhat calmer water that could have been the entrance pass, but it sure looked narrow. When faced with a situation like this the old sailing adage, "When in doubt, stay out" comes to mind. Then, of course, being red blooded Americans, there's the more popular adage, "No guts, no glory." We headed in.

Gretchen was on the bow "hanging ten" looking for the break in the reef while I tried to hold Shadowfax on course in the whirlpools and strong outgoing current. This was the most exciting entrance yet. No markers marked the pass and when we were on the crest of a wave we could line up the boat with what we thought was the pass. When we were down in the trough of a wave we couldn't see a thing - we just crossed our fingers and I watched the compass. Once we surfed into the calm waters behind the reef a line of markers showed the way toward the small village. After we were safely anchored we were told by locals that two trading ships had gone on the reef while trying to enter, one with a loss of 15 lives. Our pulse rates had to be over 100 for the rest of the day.

Maupiti is just about four miles east to west and the same north to south. The highest point is Mt. Teurafaatui which was visible all the way back to Bora Bora on a clear day. The population was only 700, and from what we saw, the majority were under 10 years old. The locals were Polynesian and spoke no English or French.

We only stayed three days, but the swimming and snorkeling in the lagoon was great, and their picturesque little village made it worth the stop. The one street through the village was paved, with small homes and shops lining both sides of the street. People were everywhere... just sort of lounging around.

At the far end of town we found the only modern thing in the village - a bread-making machine. It was huge and capable of making hundreds of loaves at a time to feed the island. We loaded up on French bread for the last time and stuffed the freezer full before we left. Great stuff!

Leaving Maupiti wasn't half as hard as entering. We could easily see the pass between the breakers. As we approached, we hardly had a second to worry. The current was going out so swiftly that it spit us out at warp speed.

The current on these reef-enclosed islands was constantly outgoing. The reason for this being that the water was always breaking over the reef on the windward side of the island filling the lagoon. This makes the pass a huge drain for the water to blast out like a fire hose. The rise and fall of the tide seemed to make no difference in the direction or speed of the current.

After an overnight passage of 103 miles downwind we were at the entrance of Mauphiaa Island. To quote a passage from Marcia Davock's cruising Guide to French Polynesia, she states, "If you didn't want to enter Maupiti's pass, you'll never enter this one." Again we figured we could get close and take a look.

Mauphiaa's entrance pass was on the leeward side of the island away from the wind and breakers as opposed to Maupiti's windward side. We didn't have any problems entering, but this pass was tougher after we were safely in the lagoon. The channel was just about as wide as the boat and it was hard to follow. It was a confusing route and as usual Gretchen was on the bow pointing the way through the reefs until we finally made it to the calm and protected anchorage. Like Bora Bora, this place belongs on the "One of the nicest places on earth" list.

Mauphiaa is a circular coral reef with a central lagoon measuring 3 ½ miles north to south and 2 miles east to west. There are no mountains and very little land. The east side of the reef has a narrow stretch of land with a few thousand palm trees. This is where all the 30 residents lived.

We didn't have the anchor set before we were met by a couple of the natives who paddled out in their small boat. We were given 5 lobsters, 2 grouper and asked to please take down our French courtesy flag. (Every foreign country you enter, you must fly their flag from the starboard side spreader). Most Polynesians we met wanted independence from the French, and this little island had already declared theirs. No problem. We dropped the flag and our new friends left as quickly as they came.

We probably spent more time swimming around this lagoon than we did on the boat, but we didn't bother spearing any fish. Every day a couple of locals would row out from shore with a selection of fish and lobster for us to choose from. Our freezer was full. We would always choose one of our favorites – the grouper - which would make them burst out laughing. We didn't find out for a few days that they didn't eat grouper; they just caught it for their dogs. Their favorite was parrot fish. Yuck! To each his own....

Every time we went ashore we were amazed at the simple lifestyle these people had. No roads, no stores, no electricity, and everyone extremely happy. The homes were all wooden with tiki thatch roofs. For a job these people cut copra (coconut) and caught lobster to sell to the once-a-month boat that brought supplies.

One day while Gretchen and I were hanging around shore, one of the copra workers, Janet, called Gretchen aside and gave her a huge pearl she found that morning inside an oyster. She then showed us a small box filled with pearls of every shape and size that she had found in the lagoon. What a hobby! I guess if you want to collect something, pearls are a good choice.

Two days later I asked if we could go fishing with them and help them catch the fish they needed for their village. They talked it over and finally agreed to let us come along. Fourteen of them jumped into our 9-foot inflatable dinghy and told us to follow their other boat.

Gretchen and I grabbed spearguns and they guided us toward the entrance pass. We jumped into the water along with 20 of the natives (the entire male population) into a fish supermarket – hundreds and hundreds of fish of every type and size. They guided us to a colorful valley with live reefs all around. As far as we could see were hills of coral absolutely covered with fish. Also, under every coral ledge was a shark - some were at least twelve feet long.

I called one of the guys (who spoke fair to terrible English) over and asked him what was up with all these sharks. Were we about to die or what? He said, "Don't worry about them. They hardly ever bite anyone." We would have felt a lot better if he had said "never." We were also told that if any of the bigger ones got too close, "Just bop them on the nose and they'll go away."

Gretchen and I looked at each other and then stuck our faces underwater so we could watch for a while to see what happens. We were definitely a little nervous, but apparently this fishing expedition with the sharks had been acted out almost every day for a couple thousand years. Everyone knew their parts perfectly. The locals would swim around spearing fish and then throw the fish into their dinghy as fast as they could. When they missed and just injured a fish, the sharks would take over. The closest shark would streak out like lightning, scoop up the fish, and then go back under his ledge to wait for the next one. No feeding frenzy or anything... just grabbing lunch in a long-practiced dance.

Gretchen and I finally joined the routine and had an exciting time. Twice that day I found myself swimming along underwater only to turn around and find myself face to face with a smiling shark. Scary as hell! After a while I found that if you pushed a shark on his side, he would go immediately back to his ledge just as if he had been trained. I know this is hard to believe, but I bet even today as you read this the residents of Mauphiaa are out in their little boats spearing fish and ignoring sharks. Amazing.

After swimming and spearing fish for most of the day, we caught well over 100 fish (quite a few grouper for the dog too) and made our way back to the village. They told us this was enough fish for the village for a day and a half, and then they would go and do it again. Without any refrigeration they had to eat it right away, salt it, or dry it out in the sun.

A few of our friends we'd met in other ports sailed in during the two weeks we stayed at Mauphiaa, so again we started planning our departure as a group effort.

Out we went like a rocket with the outgoing current and we were on our way (again downwind) 426 miles southwest to the island of Rarotonga in the Cook Island chain.

Chapter 15

Rarotaonga is the capital of the 15 Cook Islands, an independent country in free association with New Zealand. It is an almost circular island with a 20-mile-long road running around the perimeter. From a distance the island looked like one big mountain (reaching a height of 2,140 feet). The population was just under 9,000.

After a four-day sail, which gave us an assortment of strong trade winds, calms, and thunderstorms, we sailed into Avitau Harbor, the one and only harbor on Rarotonga.

It sure was a small harbor. Large trading ships were tied to the east side along a bulkhead and all other boats had to make do anchoring and running stern lines to shore. It would have been too rough for a little sailboat to tie along the wall anyway. The harbor entrance is wide open to the sea and if the wind decided to come from that direction, the harbor would close and everyone would have to leave with little or no notice. Even without the wind there was always a swell rolling through the anchorage.

We anchored Shadowfax near the entrance and ran three lines to the shore to keep our bow facing the sea. This way we were bow into the swell which made it a little less like living in a washing machine.

Roratonga is a great place. A tourist economy seemed to hold the place together as the island appeared to be a favorite spot for New Zealanders to vacation. The New Zealand Government also subsidized just about everything we saw on the island (including beer), so prices were reasonable. You could even go see a new-release movie for $.75. We were just about broke, but apparently we could still afford to go see the latest Hollywood sensation.

We could also rent a small motorcycle for $12.00 for an entire day to tour the island, so we figured why not. The US territory of American Samoa was only a couple of stops away, and we were sure we could work there legally and make some cruising money.

Driving around Roratonga we saw there were two roads parallel to each other that circled the island. The one along the water was paved and modern, and the other one was slightly inland and dirt. The one made of dirt cut through the jungle and was built from coral and lava rock in approximately 1,000 A.D. The island was so small we drove both roads, but we enjoyed the ancient "Kings Road" the most. Lots of things to see and a lot of history to go with it. Even with almost no money we still managed to stay 11 days and enjoy the Roratonga lifestyle.

Our next planned stop was the Cook Island of Aitutaki 100 miles to the north. The day we left we heard that a small ship had sunk in their entrance pass effectively closing the island. They never got the thing out of the way before we arrived, so we had to keep sailing north to our next choice. Oh well, you can't go everywhere.

Our next landfall was the Cook island of Suvarrow 525 miles to the north-northwest and the third night out we got hammered. That's a term for saying we sailed into a big-ass storm.

My first entry in the log reads, "Full jib, reefed main, 100% cloud cover, falling barometer, speed 5 knots and all's ok." It went downhill from there. By dusk the winds were up to 45 knots, and we kept putting sail away until we reached a more comfortable ride. Gretchen and I went below to try and get some sleep while Dave was on watch.

I woke up to what sounded like an explosion. The wind had come up so fast and so strong that it blew right through our poor mainsail and shredded it. The jib wasn't quite so bad but it did have a rip at the top. I decided to drop all sails and "lie a hull," as they call it, until the storm ended. We had hundreds of miles in any direction before hitting land, so we were in no danger of being blown ashore. All three of us stayed awake, kept watch for other ships and just waited. The wind roaring through the rigging sounded like a freight train.

Lightning crashed constantly all around us and the heavy rains were blowing horizontal. We were being blown along at almost six knots in the wrong direction, but it was amazing how comfortable it was down below in the boat. The wind pressure on the rigging was like having a storm sail up, which kept us from rolling violently.

The lightning was nerve wracking, and it's hard to figure why we never were hit. With that much electricity in the air, and Shadowfax having two tall metal masts sticking up, it seems hard to believe we didn't get struck. There was nothing to do but wait and hope it didn't get any worse. It seems each ocean threw a good-size storm at us, and this was the Pacific's turn.

The one thing I've noticed about weather – either good or bad—is that it doesn't last forever. The next morning the sun came out, the sky was clear, and the wind was down to zero. Not a breath. Three days later we hobbled into Suvarrow to lick our wounds, fix the sails and recuperate.

The low-lying atoll of Suvarrow is a circular coral reef with a central lagoon measuring 5 miles by 5 miles with a small island in the center. For a pleasant change the entrance channel was wide enough for a battleship, or maybe a large police boat (I'll get to the police boat in a minute).

The total population of the island was one. He had been put on as caretaker since the island was a National Park of the Cook Islands. Suvarrow was made famous in 1952 by New Zealander Tom Neale who stayed by himself on the island for three years and wrote the book, "An Island to Oneself." The caretaker was there to see that this didn't happen again. Apparently the Cook Islanders didn't care for homesteaders. Caretaker of a tropical island... where do I sign up?

When we sailed in we saw that some of our friends, Yashi Maru and Patagonia, were already at anchor. This meant we outnumbered the locals ten to one.

Since the island was a preserve we had a few rules to follow as far as diving and fishing, but we were allowed to spearfish in the pass. The pass was so huge and deep it was like a coral Grand Canyon... as colorful as a rainbow and packed full of fish.

While snorkeling in the pass Gretchen tapped me on the shoulder and pointed out two huge manta rays. Each had a wingspan of about 12 feet. I swam up to hitch a ride on one of them, like I've seen people do on TV, but I guess this manta never saw that show. I swam up behind him and grabbed onto the forward side of his wings and it was like I hit him with 1,000 volts. He sort of went nuts, took off like a shot and disappeared over the next ledge. Mental note: must remember never to sneak up on the fish.

We also noticed the always-present sharks were of the "large" breed, and they seemed more aggressive than usual. Near the entrance to the pass I saw a 12-foot gray reef shark, but we had become somewhat used to seeing sharks by now. And diving with our friends back on Mauphiaa taught us that it was possible to swim with the things without getting eaten. Well, this shark had never been to Mauphiaa and he (she?) came off the bottom awfully fast and headed right at me. Gretchen was above me in the dinghy when she saw me coming. I flew to the surface like a balloon and landed in the dinghy without even touching the sides. I know the guys on Mauphiaa would have just "bopped him on the nose," but I really didn't want to hurt the poor thing.

On our ninth day at anchor a military-looking ship entered the lagoon to check out the "yachties." I don't know at what point we all started to be known as yachties, but that term stuck all the way around the world. Like gypsies of the sea I guess. Even though the word "yacht" brings up thoughts of the rich and famous, it can also bring up thoughts of stapled sails and lots of duct tape repairs.

We knew Suvarrow Island was a National Park when we were in Rarotonga, so we asked for and received permission to stop. All our papers were checked and everything was in order, except for form number 28-B… or something like that. Whatever it was that the police wanted, we didn't have it. Nobody had it. Oops. They were friendly enough, but we were all told to "Be gone by dawn." Oh well, we'd been there for ten days anyway, so it was time to move on. I don't think I've ever been kicked out of a nicer place.

Bright and early the next morning we all motored out the pass and into light winds and clear skies. Good sailing weather. As soon as we rounded the island and pointed the bow west we raised our spinnaker and set the self-steering windvane. For three days and 450 miles we didn't touch a thing. We usually don't like to sail with the spinnaker up at night, but we had a full moon and a fair weather forecast and we've rarely had a better sail. Only a couple of things broke, and we made good speed toward our next port, American Samoa.

As we approached Tutuila Island, the capitol of the seven islands of American Samoa, we were hoping all we had heard about pollution and corruption weren't true.

Chapter 16

Pago Pago (pronounced Pahngo Pahngo) Harbor on Tutuila Island is located 2,300 miles southwest of Hawaii and is the only American territory below the equator (along with the six other American Samoan Islands). Tutuila Island is 16 miles from east to west and 8 miles north to south. The island is mountainous with the highest point being Mt. Matafao at 2, 142 feet. The population was around 50,000 with the locals being U.S. nationals, not citizens.

As we entered the harbor we thought everything we had heard about the place was a lie. The harbor was surrounded by mountains, and it looked like a great place to stop and work for a while. We even had a rainbow leading us in.

Thirty minutes later, as we tied to the customs pier, we had a different opinion. The harbor had two inches of diesel fuel on it along with what looked like tar. Plastic bags and other garbage floated by and were too numerous to count.

Two large tuna canneries operated on the edge of the harbor, and the smell was incredible. If you put a dozen fish in your garage in the summer, forget about them for a couple weeks, then went back in and took a sniff, that would probably come close to duplicating the odor. Whew!

Next, there was the electric generating plant for this part of the island. It was on the harbor just a short distance from the tuna factories. It sounded like a hundred cars without mufflers getting ready for a race. We needed money and we had to stay for a while, but this place was going to be hard to enjoy.

Clearing customs was easy. Lots of yachts were at anchor in the harbor with the same idea we had – a place to make some money before moving on. I guess we weren't the only broke yachties.

In fact, it did turn out to be an easy place to get a job. As we were tying to the pier one of the people helping us asked how long we would be staying. I told him we wanted to stay for a while and work, and he said, "Can you start tomorrow morning? I'll give you $10.00 an hour and lots of hours."

The job sounded interesting. The guy who hired me, Steve, had been contracted to insulate the generator room down below in one of the StarKist tuna boats. Not only would I make some money, but I would get to check out a big tuna boat. This huge boat even had a helicopter on the deck.

Trying to get settled in that first night was a little tough. There was dockage for about a dozen boats along the shore, but it looked like someone had to die before you could get a slip. Our next and only choice was to anchor in the harbor with the 50 other boats already there.

We normally don't mind anchoring, and even prefer it most of the time, but this harbor was a little different. Going back and forth all the time by dinghy through a tar and oil-filled harbor didn't sound like much fun. Whenever it was a little windy, you were sure to get splashed from this goop.

Getting the anchor to stick was another problem. The bottom of the harbor was so fouled with plastic bags and old line, it took us four tries before the anchor stuck. What a mess.

I have to admit that once you got away from the harbor and went inland you left all the nasty stuff behind. Friendly locals, waterfalls, and small villages... probably not much different than 100 years ago.

The villages communicate with each other once or twice a month through meetings of the chiefs (matai). Each village had a matai, and every three or four villages had a paramount chief. All of the chiefs had a "speaking" chief to talk for them at the meetings.

Only Samoans could own land on the island, which helped to keep out the large tourist resorts and hotels—although the smelly tuna factories would accomplish the same thing.

My first day on the tuna boat job I showed up at seven in the morning ready to go. I had never been aboard one of these big net boats before, and I was impressed with what I saw. The bridge was equipped with all the latest navigation equipment and the crews' quarters could have been on a cruise ship. The sleek-looking helicopter on the back deck was used to spot the schools of tuna.

When lunchtime rolled around I found we were welcome to come into the lunch room and eat with the crew. The lunch consisted of prime rib, potatoes, corn and a full gallon of wine on each table. Not too shabby.

That first week I watched them unload 1,500 tons of fish, and I'm happy to say that I saw no dolphin. Lots of shark, dorado and assorted smaller fish, but no "Flipper." But I can't let the tuna companies off that easy though.

The Samoans working in the frozen bilges were working in some inhuman and dangerous conditions. They were paid less than $3.00 per hour and I watched them eat the raw fish from the bilges for lunch. As they arrived in the morning they would each pick out a fish or two and put them in a corner hoping they would defrost enough by lunch to be able to eat them. They took turns working in the freezers - wearing socks on their hands and towels wrapped around their feet to keep from freezing.

I also noticed a large hose running over the side of the ship and into the water. I asked one of the crewmembers about it and he said, "It's a game that all the boats play." He explained that they weight the end of the hose to keep it underwater and then pump out all the sludge from where the fish were kept. He said they would get a big fine if they got caught. When I asked if any of the boats were ever caught since they all did this, he replied, "Maybe one a year." Sounds to me like someone was being paid to look the other way. This also explained most of the sludge floating around the harbor.

My job on the ship was a bit harder than I thought. There were just the two of us, and it looked like the job could turn into a career if we didn't get some help. Vladimir to the rescue. He had sailed in about a week after we did, and with his whole family on board, he really needed some extra money. Actually he was like us, and none of the money he made was "extra."

I remember one day after one of our huge lunches aboard the ship, Vladimir and I went back to work and he said, "It's times like this that I miss communism." I thought that was a hell of a statement, so I asked him what he meant and he said, "Well, after a big lunch like that, wouldn't you like to take a nap? A good communist would lie right down and take one." I laughed about that one for a week.

While I was running around doing all this work, Gretchen wasn't just playing the boat wife. She started almost right away as a work-center manager for the local Goodwill Center. The Center was a learning facility, and they put Gretchen in charge of new projects. Gretchen had designed and made lots of her own clothes as well as selling originals, so she started teaching the local people to design outfits as well as market them. Pago Harbor might be a mess, but we sure were finding it easy to make a bit of money.

Even Dave was hard at it. He found a bowling alley that needed someone to help with the maintenance of the place. His world was changing and his main goal in life was to wait for Yuki to quit her job in Tahiti and fly in to meet him. He hadn't had much fun, or enjoyed the trip since he had to leave her back in Tahiti. He was one happy sailor when she finally flew in.

The guy I worked for had a connection with the Harbor Board (nothing happened in Samoa unless you had a connection) and we were able to get Shadowfax tied to one of the dock slips by the time Yuki arrived. This made things a lot easier with the three of us coming and going at different times. Yuki moved on the boat with us, but it was soon obvious that she wasn't interested in sailing. We knew this lifestyle wasn't for everybody, so the only question was what would she do and would Dave do it with her.

Yep, they both decided to take off on one of those big airplane things and head for Hawaii and try to find work.

Oh well, we would miss Dave, but we knew he wouldn't be happy unless he went with her. At least this proves that it is possible to fall in love in the South Pacific and sail (or fly, as the case may be) off into the sunset. Just like a romance novel.

So now what? Dave was getting ready to leave, and my job aboard the tuna boat was finished. Gretchen was still working at the Goodwill Center, but I had to find something else to do. I had done some basic silk-screening on t-shirts in the past, so we thought why not try that here. I could also slide into Dave's job at the bowling alley until I could find something with a little better pay.

I silkscreened a small sign that said, "Your yacht on a T-Shirt, see Shadowfax," and nailed it to the showers that the yachties used. Even a few orders would help. We could get all the supplies locally, and the blank t-shirts were good quality. We could get just about any color tee for $1.50 retail each. Cheap. For the screen cutting I could do it on the boat with an Xacto blade. Just like high school silk-screening 101.

While I waited for the first t-shirt order I kept showing up every day at the bowling alley, and that will probably be one of the weirdest jobs I'll ever have. The place was broke, so there was absolutely no money available to do anything. If a light bulb burned out I would have to steal one from someplace in the building that wasn't as important as the one that burned out. It was starting to get dark in there.

One of their projects for me was to build a box to put propane tanks in for the kitchen. The first thing I had to do was to find a small wall to knock down for the lumber (bathroom partition). A week after the box was finished, I was told to take it apart because the lumber was needed for another project of more importance. I still wonder if that lumber is still being passed from job to job.

Our silk screen sign was nailed to the showers for only a couple days and we got our first order. Six shirts (our minimum order) with a picture of the owner's sloop on the front and the name of the boat on the top. Neither Gretchen nor I were artists, so the first thing we had to do was to get a photograph of the boat and have it blown up on a copy machine. Even though I can't draw, I can trace with the best of 'um. We discovered getting the picture was easy - just like asking grandparents if they have any pictures of their grandkids. Everyone always had dozens of pictures of their boat from about every angle possible. For any lettering we needed we bought a large book of fonts that I could trace from.

From the time we started a t-shirt order we could have it completely finished by the next day. Cutting the screen took the most time, but the actual printing (using a wooden frame and a squeegee) took hardly any time at all. It would be just as easy to do 100 shirts as it was to do 6. Well, almost.

They liked their 6 shirts a lot, paid us and went out to show them off. That night they came back and ordered a dozen more and brought another yachtie who wanted a couple dozen Ts with his boat on the front. The next day three more orders came along, and we could see we were on to something big.

Our price was $15.00 to cut the screen and $6.00 per finished shirt. Having a cool product and being cheap caught everyone's attention. We only made about $4.50 per shirt, but our overhead sure was low.

One day while Gretchen and I were sitting around the Pago Pago Yacht Club (an old wooden building with no docks and a definite lean to starboard) the manager asked if we were "those t-shirt people." We told him we were, and he showed us a great picture of a tall ship under sail and asked if we could put that on a shirt for their 25th anniversary party. I looked it over and didn't see any problem, so we took the order. Four hundred shirts, assorted colors and sizes. Definitely time to quit my day job.

The t-shirt thing kept getting better, and we even came up with a few designs to put in the local shops. We were on to something. I guess that's why t-shirt shops are such a success and are found on every street corner in America.

And to expand this business, Gretchen broke out her sewing machines (two!) and started sewing courtesy flags to sell. Every yacht arriving at a new country has to fly a small flag of that country on her starboard side, and what better place to get them than from another yachtie! Every yacht had a dozen countries in its future and we were there to help! Gretchen was a master at sewing and could whip up a pile of flags in no time. We could silk screen the flag design over and over on a sheet-size piece of cloth and then Gretchen would cut and sew them into great looking flags. She would even color in appropriate areas of the flag with textile ink. We put together a price list with over 20 flags to choose from.

If that wasn't enough, Gretchen would also make comfortable "cruising dresses" for the ladies. She was making most of her own stuff and this fit right into our flag and t-shirt selling speech. Not bad for a couple of Florida Realtors.

While we were raking in all this dough we were also saying goodbye to our sailing friends. Not everybody needed a "money fix," and the harbor was so disgusting nobody wanted to stay. Jose and Erica on Patagonia from Chile were the first to go. They were in a little bit of a hurry to get to Australia. Erica was originally from Australia and she told us, "Jose knocked the cocky off its perch, mate," and she wanted to be in Australia with her parents as soon as possible. To interpret this from Australian to English, it meant she was pregnant. Talking to her on the ham radio after she left she told us that being pregnant gave new meaning to the term "seasick."

Next to leave were Jeff and Sheila aboard Aberlady from Britain, followed by Vladimir and Jorget aboard Aquarius from Bulgaria. Masa and Yuka aboard Yashimaru from Japan were the last to leave, which left us all alone (except for about 100 other yachties who we didn't know) and a little sad. These people had been like a family to us. We had laughed, played, and bailed each other out of various boat problems since Panama. We didn't want to stay in Samoa either, so we couldn't blame them for leaving. We needed the money. We really had no choice but to stay... or did we? Could we silk screen from port to port? Had to give that one some thought.

Since we were to be stuck for awhile, we decided to try and enjoy the place by getting away from the harbor whenever we could. One thing we noticed when we went sightseeing was a strange tradition called "Sa."

Sa was an island-wide ceremony that took place three or more times a day. Sa started when locals ring bells to warn everybody that they only have a few minutes until Sa begins. The first thing I noticed was that the bells were actually made out of acetylene welding cylinders with the bottoms cut out. The cylinders were hung from trees and then hit with a stick. After the warning bell is rung the second time, all life stops. If you are driving through the village, you must halt. If you are walking, you must sit. If you are talking you have to shut up. When I tried to find out the reason for the Sa - either religion, tradition or just to play with the bells - it took me a while before I found someone to explain it.

The best answer came from a young Samoan who was studying the ancient history of his islands. He told me, "The Sa means 'sacred' and the 10am Sa and the 6pm Sa are a moment of silence in respect for the dead and hope for the living. The 10pm Sa is the same, but also acts like a neighborhood watch." During every Sa, "guards" are put into the streets to enforce the custom. These guards, called aumaga, watch for crime while also "guarding the Sa," as they call it.

The guards will let you pass to go to your home, but you need a good reason if you're out (choir practice, your job or school). I was told that Sa is so serious that the year before someone was killed by one of the guards for starting trouble. Definitely better to follow the rules. Other Sas could be held without notice for church meetings, chief councils or even political reasons.

Besides working and trying to stay out of trouble, we tried to plan our escape. We first intended to stay through the next cyclone season and keep working, but it didn't look like we were going to do that. I know I keep saying how dirty the harbor was, but man, it was terrible. We wanted out. With this silk-screening idea we didn't see any reason why it wouldn't work in any anchorage that had cruising boats in it. We could easily carry hundreds of shirts, along with everything else we needed. Why stay?

To be fair to American Samoa, I must say we returned years later and found a clean harbor and enforced environmental laws. A welcome change since this is one of the best and safest harbors in the South Pacific.

Almost four months from the day we arrived, we untied the lines from the dock and left. Actually we untied the lines from the boat and left them for the next guy so he wouldn't have to ruin his. Our lines were full of oil and tar from touching the water. We had made enough money to buy four truckloads of food, t-shirts, textile ink, and a pile of new parts for the boat. We even had a little money left over.

Chapter 17

We sailed away with perfect weather – 10 to 15 knots of wind with smooth seas. Our destination was the Kingdom of Tonga about 250 miles to the southwest... our first long passage with just the two of us.

We changed our watches to two and a half hour shifts, which took a little getting used to. You just start to get to sleep and then it's time to wake up again and go back on watch. Luckily, it was an easy trip. No bad weather and nothing in our way until we got there. Our first stop in Tonga was to be the island of Niuatoputapu. Work on it, it can be pronounced.

Tonga consists of 170 islands with 134 being uninhabited and the total population was approximately 96,000 people. The islands stretch from north to south for a distance of 500 miles, but the total land area is less than 300 square miles. Archaeological sites indicate that the Tongan Islands have been inhabited since about 500 B.C. The industry was mainly the farming of Copra (coconuts), bananas and tomatoes.

The men also continue the whaling tradition by going out in small boats with hand spears. Upon their return, they fly a black flag if their quest has been successful. The women are famous for making the finest tapa cloth (made from pounding the coconut bark) in the world. Tonga was the last Polynesian Kingdom in the Pacific.

The island of Niuatoputapu—according to most of the books we read—was not a check-in port. A couple of books even said there wasn't an anchorage, but we had the inside information along with a secret mimeographed chart of the entrance channel. A yachtie who was sailing through Samoa had been there and had the inside info on how to get there. These are the best islands to visit. Definitely no crowds.

The second morning the sun rose and showed us the island of Niuatoputapu 15 miles off our bow. Its sister island next to it, Tafahi, reached a height of 2,000 feet.

Definitely no anchorage there, but what a great marker to help find Niuatoputapu.

At 9am we dropped the sails and motored through the pass. No real disasters along the way other than the satellite navigation computer breaking.

It was somewhere around this point that we lost 24 hours. We weren't quite to the 180 degree longitude line, but the dateline that follows it takes a jog to the east to include all the islands of Tonga. Today was officially tomorrow, except when using the sextant today was still yesterday. Right? It made sense as long as you didn't think about it very hard.

As we entered, Gretchen was on the bow pointing the way through the reefs and shallows. She could see the bottom so well that twice she called back to me to get a depth reading. The water appeared shallow but the depth sounder read a steady 30 feet. The snorkeling would be fantastic.

We anchored Shadowfax in 35 feet of crystal clear water in what seemed to be a very protected lagoon. Gretchen raised our Q (quarantine) flag to show any local officials that we needed to clear with customs, immigration and agriculture. In just a few minutes some official-looking people on shore were waving for us to come in and get them. Not enough yachts visited for customs to bother getting their own boat.

Clearing was easy. Really no more than a couple of papers and a long speech of welcome from the customs officer. We were also told that the next day was the first island-wide festival of the year, and we were invited. Perfect timing on our part.

Once we were cleared, we jumped in the inflatable dinghy and went ashore. Gretchen tied the dinghy to a stone pier and we walked straight into a time warp. The village was nothing like we'd seen before. We felt like we lost over 100 years instead of 24 hours.

The first thing we saw were over a dozen tiny grass huts with just as many horses running free. Baby pigs were playfully chasing each other around. Women were sitting outside their huts weaving mats and baskets. Men in straw hats were sitting and talking under the grass huts waiting for the heat of the day to pass. Everyone was wearing a woven shirt called a "valva," which is worn ankle-length by women and knee-length by men. Dozens of children were playing in the narrow dirt road (they're a mess).

When everyone sees us walking toward the village, life stopped for a split second. The children ran to greet us, and the men sent a representative over to welcome us. The man told us proudly that their three-square-mile island had 1,200 people, three cars and one bus. He also told us that the "Palangi" (people of European descent), us, were always welcome on Niuatoputapu and that they had many things to trade if we wished.

Gretchen had brought in a huge bag of popcorn and the kids, as well as the adults, couldn't get enough. I had my usual supply of animal-making balloons, but I was running out fast. We said goodbye to our new fan club so we could take a walk. No luck... every place we went the crowd got bigger. Nobody wanted anything except to keep us company.

The next day we went ashore and started walking to the island festival about a mile away. On the way we were joined by 15-year-old Sutita. Her English was fair, and she asked if she could join us and explain the ceremonies and dances. The feast was to celebrate the opening of a new church. This tiny island already had six.

When we arrived the festival grounds were empty except for a large U-shaped covering made of tapa cloth with a vacant field in the center of the U. The food would go under the covering, and the dances would be performed in the courtyard in the center.

After a few minutes we heard screaming in the distance. Fourteen men were carrying a fifteen-foot-long, three-level-high table of food called a "pola."

Walking behind them were 20 or 30 people dancing and screaming in celebration. Everyone was dressed in their most colorful grass skirts and headdresses. This process was repeated over and over until 20 of these polas were in place. Tons of food! The entire population of the island showed up along with 100 people from their sister island, Tafahi.

We felt privileged to be invited. The pola where we sat was displayed beautifully. I counted 13 whole pigs, dozens of bananas, chickens, cakes, apples, pears and more lobsters than we could count. These were the things we recognized. There were other things that we couldn't guess what they might be. Bowls of white stuff, blue stuff and even green stuff.

After everyone ate, the dancers and singers arrived. It must have taken many hours of practice to get this right. One dance was choreographed perfectly to be a simulated combat fought with sticks and poles. If anyone had missed a beat, serious injury would have occurred.

After a fantastic day of festivities we were invited to an island singing fest the next night. If seems we showed up on Niuatoputapu just in time for all the parties. Pretty lucky Palangis.

The singing lasted most of the next night and again the whole population showed up; in fact, the whole island participated. What an incredible time! You don't get this kind of stuff by going to Club Med!

After recuperating from all the festivals we were invited spearfishing with Offisie, one of the locals. Offisie planned to spear the fish and then string them from his belt as he continued to fish, a real no-no in the spearfishing world. I pointed out to him that this was a dangerous thing to do because a shark or barracuda could see the fish hanging there, then swim in to grab them away - taking a good part of his leg in the process. He responded by telling a legend that took 20 minutes to relate. I'll try to shorten it and still get the message across.

In the old days, before iron and before arrows, there was a man named Satorie. Everyone on the island was afraid of him. He was the biggest, meanest, orneriest guy around. He would take advantage of everyone. He also had to have at least six of the island's virgins in his hut at all times.

The islanders were very upset with Satorie, but they were too afraid to do anything about it. The people approached Satorie's brother (Offisie couldn't remember his name) and asked him to please kill Satorie for them. He couldn't believe that his brother was doing anything wrong, so the islanders brought him to Satorie's hut and made him look in through one of the holes (island huts have many holes).

Satorie's brother was furious at what he saw, so he agreed to kill Satorie. He cut a spear from a fo'ui tree, crept into his brother's hut and stabbed him through the heart. Satori jumped up and yelled, "Brother, why have you done this to me? Why have you killed me?" His brother told him how he had let his village down and that was why he must die.

At the last moment Satorie saw the error of his ways. He wanted to know what he could do to make it up to his people. His brother came up with an idea and told him what he must do (now we get back to the sharks).

After Satorie died they threw his body into the sea where he turned into the biggest, meanest, orneriest fish around. Satorie swore to protect the villagers from all sharks and any other sea creatures that may be around. And they all lived happily... well, you know the rest.

So there we were after hearing that terrific story, ready to jump in the water without a worry in the world. Then I started to wonder how Satorie felt about Palangis. When I asked Offisie about that he thought for awhile and then said, "You two better stay real close to me." We swam and fished all day and never saw one shark. Thanks Satorie!

Our 13-day stay at Niuatoputapu was well worth the stop... one of the friendliest places in the world. Just before we were getting ready to leave we were given a huge hand-woven rug. One of the locals had spent weeks (or months) making it. The rug was much too big for our boat, but we had to accept it or risk insulting our new friends. We held an open house on the boat to try and reciprocate and I think they enjoyed seeing a cruising boat. They all seemed to think it was funny for someone to live on a boat. They're probably right.

When we finally put to sea the weather wasn't all that great. It looked like we were going to have an uncomfortable trip. We were heading south about 120 miles to the Tongan island group called Vava'u.

My entry in the log book reads, "wind 25 knots on the nose, seas from all directions, reefed main and shortened jib." Definitely not one of our more comfortable trips. Shadowfax steered herself with our wind vane "Wayne" doing the steering. We just held on and, as usual, and hoped the weather didn't get worse.

The Tongan islands are either extinct or active volcanoes, which makes for exciting sailing. We had to keep a constant watch for any uncharted reefs or islands caused by recent volcanic activity. When nighttime fell and cloud cover limited our vision, we just hoped we would have some kind of sixth-sense that would warn us before we ended up on a reef.

The weather stayed the same for most of the trip and we finally sighted the island just two hours before dark on the second night. Ten miles out the wind dropped to almost nothing and we started the diesel so we could get in before dark. It would be too dangerous to try and enter the lagoon after dark. Our radar wasn't working, and the sat-nav wasn't working either, so we really appreciated the sunlight.

Vava'u consists of approximately 50 islands with a population of about 17,000. The highest point being 600 feet with almost all the islands within rock-throwing distance of each other. This protected the anchorages of Vava'u from almost all bad weather conditions.

Vava'u supposedly had been settled as long as 2,000 years ago, but the first European sailor (Spanish Captain Francisco Mourelle) didn't land until 1781. The famous explorer Captain James Cook visited the southern islands in

1777, but was told there was "neither harbor nor anchorage" by a Vava'u chief. This lie kept Cook from discovering the hundreds of protected lagoons and anchorages within the island group. Oh well, you win some and you lose some.

Vava'u was also a popular spot for tourists to fly in and charter a sailboat from the local Moorings Charter Company. We were able to get one of their excellent local knowledge charts of the area and all of the best anchorages were marked by number. What a hassle-free way to sail. We heard people on the radio all day long with the conversations something like this, "This morning we were at 42 but we're going to do some swimming at 13 before we have lunch at 26. How about meeting us at 12 for dinner before we go to the cookout at 32?" All 52 locations were within a couple of hour's sail of each other, and after visiting quite a few, we never found a bad anchorage.

We made it in before dark, and the cliffs on both sides of the entrance were impressive. No problem as far as the depth of the water. If the chart was correct we would hit the bow of the boat on an island before we would touch bottom. Most of the islands dropped straight into the sea to a depth of about 100 feet.

We headed into the maze of islands until we reached Mourelle Cove (#7) and anchored next to our friends Karen and David aboard the sloop Paragon from San Francisco. We had met them on our travels across the Pacific, and I think just about everyone knew of them because of their dog - a huge, shaggy, blind, sheep dog called Sir Buckingham. Still, "Bucky" seemed to like life on the 44-foot boat. Since Bucky was blind it made life a bit more challenging for David and Karen – as if sailing around the world wasn't challenging enough.

David and Karen had been sailing and diving the island of Vava'u for about a month before we arrived, so they were the best tour guides we could have hoped for. They knew which anchorages were the best to visit, and which spots were the most interesting to dive.

We had also talked to them on the ham radio when we were in Samoa, and they had asked us to bring them some supplies, including enough ingredients to make a pizza. Great friends, a perfect anchorage and a pizza were just about perfect after a rough passage.

When we arrived we found our reputation preceded us and a few boats wanted to order t-shirts and courtesy flags. By the time we left Vava'u we had more money then when we arrived. We even had a couple of orders to deliver down the line. What a strange job.

One of the things on the 'must do' list was to visit two caves we heard about. The first one, Swallows Cave, we were able to get to by dinghy. The entrance was so high we just might have been able to sail Shadowfax right into the opening. The interior was big enough to hold a few dinghies, as well as the thousands of birds we disturbed when we entered. There were so many panicked starlings flying around we were glad to be wearing hats. They must have had perches and nests up above, but we were afraid to look up - if you know what I mean. The water depth in the cave was almost 50 feet with the water being so clear we could count the stones lying on the bottom.

The next cave, Mariner's Cave, was a long, wet, 45-minute dinghy ride away and proved to be one of the most unusual caves we'd ever seen. Mariner's Cave was underwater. We had to dive 8 feet down to the entrance, and then swim 14 feet horizontally before popping up into the cave. Naturally, there was a local legend to go with it.

Many years ago there was a young, handsome, Tongan chief who fell deeply in love with a young girl from one of the outer islands. The only problem was that the girl was to be executed along with the rest of her family (apparently the reason for the pending execution was unknown). The chief couldn't let this happen to his beloved, so he swept her away and put her into Mariners Cave to keep her hidden. The chief brought her food and water for two weeks until he could arrange an expedition to Fiji and take her along.

When he left for Fiji he picked her up and married her along the way. When the chief returned from Fiji he was able to resolve the situation so she wouldn't be killed. And they lived... again you know the rest. Nice story, but I was never able to find out if the rest of her family got the ax or not.

The swim down and into the cave was wild. We just had to hold our breath and swim - hoping there really was a cave full of air at the end. When we finally surfaced we were in a giant dome-shaped cave with plenty of places to grab onto, or sit and enjoy the view. The water was so clear that plenty of light was allowed to enter. We spent most of the day swimming in and out of the cave and just enjoying the crystal clear water. Worth the dinghy ride for sure.

After sailing around the islands for a few days we thought we would head toward the capital island of Vava'u. The capital, Neiafu, consists of a small village with a safe (but crowded) anchorage and lots of small shops and markets. Most of the streets were paved, but the best transportation was by foot. We saw a few people with cars and old trucks, but with all the pigs and chickens blocking the road I think walking was definitely the quickest way to go. Since there really wasn't anywhere to go, it didn't matter that much anyway.

With the clock counting down toward another cyclone season we prepared to set sail and keep working our way south. Paragon joined us, and together we sailed 70 miles to the Ha'apai Islands, also part of Tonga. Again it was a wet and uncomfortable ride, but at least it was short. We left at two in the afternoon, and we were at anchor again the next morning by nine.

Ha'apai consists of a dozen or so islands and the area is cluttered with reefs and dangerous sailing conditions. The sailing guides said that sailing yachts usually steer clear of the area. Our planning put us there in daylight, so we didn't see any problem as long as we kept our eyes open for uncharted reefs.

Gretchen was on the bow pointing the way through one of the reefs when just off to our port side a huge whale broke the surface, flew out of the water and crashed back with a belly flop. He looked like an Orca (killer whale), but it happened so quickly we couldn't be sure. The next time he surfaced, he was too far off in the distance to get a good look. Never a camera handy when you need one.

We worked our way among the reefs until we came to a tiny opening into the lagoon and, along with David and Karen on Paragon, we dropped the hook. We could see small islands everywhere we looked, and they looked exactly like Florida – low elevation with fine sand beaches and covered with palm trees and Australian pines. It reminded us of home.

We anchored off the main town of Pangai, and again, we found friendly people everywhere. The old explorer Captain Cook was right when – in his ships log – he named the area "The friendly islands." The name didn't stick, but it sure seemed to be true.

A little farther south we stopped at an island called Uoleva and found one of the most perfect sand beaches we had ever seen. David on Paragon decided to take Bucky ashore for his first time in many islands so he could enjoy himself... at least until he was attacked by a large wild pig. Poor Bucky didn't like that very much. David managed to chase the pig away, and since Bucky was blind he probably had no idea what happened. Nothing was hurt except for his ego, so Bucky went back to the boat and to a much safer environment.

We again headed south and the hardest part about sailing 40 miles to the island of Nomuka was to find our way out of all the reefs and breaking waves. The sat-nav was still broken, so I was using the sextant to keep our position accurate on the chart. The reefs didn't seem to be where the chart showed them to be so the whole day was pretty stressful.

Once we thought we were in deep water we began to relax, and then the depth sounder dropped from 40 to 11 feet in a few seconds time. We swung Shadowfax to port and again we had to thread our way through another patch of uncharted reefs. This would be no place to sail at night. When we arrived at Nomuka we were whipped, so we decided not to go ashore. It's a good thing we didn't - we found out later that Nomuka was a Tongan prison island.

Five a.m. the next morning we raised the anchor and again headed south. This time we headed toward the capitol of all Tonga. Nuku'alofa on the island of Tongatapu 55 miles away.

Around noon, as we sailed along on another sloppy sail, we heard an unknown sound... like line being peeled off one of our fishing rods. We couldn't believe it. We dragged fishing lines constantly and we hadn't caught a fish in 11 months. When I went back to check it out I saw a huge mahi mahi dancing behind the boat on the end of the line. Gretchen took the rod and began to bring him in. Success! Fresh fish for dinner! The mahi was large enough to feed all our friends when we arrived in port.

We sailed into Nuku'alofa's main harbor, which was large enough for at least a hundred boats. The sailboats would drop an anchor and then tie their stern or bow to the harbor wall. Nuku'alofa is the hop-off point for yachts sailing to New Zealand, and the place was full of sailboats planning to head there for the upcoming cyclone season.

The 1,000 mile sail south to New Zealand was one of those passages that no one was looking forward to, so they tended to stop for a while and think about it. Everybody we spoke with had a horror story about someone who had made the trip before and had gotten "slammed" by a gale or rogue wave. When you sail that far out of the tropics the weather changes radically, and it's usually for the worse. We'd been staying in the southeast trade winds area, but by sailing toward New Zealand we were dropping down into the westerlies which blew (if you could believe all the stories) around gale force more often than not.

But screw the storm stories, what this many sailboats in one place meant to us was t-shirt orders. We were getting good at that. We bought more blank tees in town and spread the word. With the ham radio being the main contact with all cruising sailboats it seems we were becoming well known for great looking custom tees and flags!

While hanging out in Nuku'alofa and silk screening t-shirts, we were waiting for a "double high pressure" system to form over Australia (supposedly the best time to leave for NZ). We also had time to take a look around this small island. Lots of cars, people, shops, and even a professional rugby team. We managed to attend a game and Australia beat Tonga 58-14. Rugby isn't popular in the states and we didn't understand the game, but it was fun anyway. Like our football but without all the pads. With mud, spit and body parts flying, they kicked the crap out of each other.

Nuku'alofa isn't a big city. I guess you could call it a huge village, and we had a good time just walking around. We didn't get to do much walking on a passage – just lots of hanging on. On one of our walks we stopped at the New Zealand Consulate to tell them we were heading to their country. We also wanted to pick up our entry visas ahead of time if we could. Not as easy as we thought it would be - they made an appointment for us to come back the next day for an interview. We showed up on time and what a third degree interrogation they gave us. Very polite but intense. They wanted to keep the riff-raff out of their country, but somehow we slipped through and were given a six-month visa.

On the way back from the consulate we stopped to check out the King of Tonga's Palace (maybe invite him out for a beer), but when we arrived we found out that he was in Hawaii meeting with President Bush. We probably should have called first.

The locals loved their 400 pound King and they tell this story lovingly, so I guess it's okay if I tell it. One day while the King was visiting the United States he was walking along a path outside the White House. The President asked one of his aides who the little man walking next to the King was? His aide replied, "Lunch."

Just before we left the island we received a large package of mail. A good trick since no one back home knew we were going to Nuku'alofa. Apparently this package arrived in French Polynesia after we left, and someone just took a guess where we might be heading. They guessed pretty well. I wonder how many packages are still floating around out there looking for us.

We sailed out with a not-so-great weather forecast and we were looking forward to a little diversion on our way. We had a chart of a lobster-filled reef that we could anchor behind in the middle of the ocean just 300 miles away. Minerva Reef was said to be a little spot of paradise, and as we sailed alongside Paragon we hoped we could find it.

Almost as soon as we left Tonga we caught a yellow fin tuna! Our fishing was definitely improving. Maybe the fact that we had run out of lures had something to do with it. Without all those store-bought fancy lures we (by 'we' I mean Gretchen) started making our own out of colorful strips of plastic or string. Since this was the second fish we caught using our own lures, we decided to keep making them ourselves and not bother buying any - lots cheaper that way too.

The third day out we saw breakers on the horizon and altered our course to check it out. Just what we thought - Minerva Reef on the horizon. There are actually two Minerva Reefs, north and south, about 20 miles apart.

Minerva is a fantastically strange place to visit. There's really nothing there to look at... just a circular reef with a small lagoon in the middle and no land. At low tide only a small part of the reef is above water.

As far as we knew there wasn't a chart of either reef, so we were working off a mimeographed, hand-drawn chart someone had given us. We took our time trying to find the small entrance pass to the northern Minerva, and we found it exactly where our map said it should be. Once inside, Gretchen was at her usual place on the bow pointing out the coral heads as we motored around looking for the best place to anchor.

Paragon also entered the pass and we anchored next to each other in 20 feet of water for a comfortable stay of ten days. We were anchored in the middle of the Pacific Ocean - looking out at the water for hundreds of miles in any direction. You might wonder what there is to do at a place like that, but believe me it's a terrific place. We swam, ate lobster, walked the reef, ate lobster, did a few boat projects, ate more lobster, explored with the dinghy and filled our freezer with, yes, lobster. Dave on Paragon was the master at lobster hunting. He found at least six a day, but a few times he found as many as fourteen. It's a good thing we both had freezers onboard.

Thanksgiving rolled around while we were at anchor at Minerva and we managed to have a true Thanksgiving feast. You can guess what the main course was (lobster), but we also had hot apple pie, potatoes and a canned chicken that tasted okay but looked a little like road kill. What a fun place to celebrate an American holiday.

When ten days passed we dragged ourselves away to again sail south. We didn't go very far though. How could we be the "Minerva Reef Experts" if we didn't stop twenty miles away at the southern reef?

On the short sail we again caught a fish on one of our (Gretchen's) homemade lures. This time we caught my favorite, a twenty-pound mahi mahi. We hardly had any room left in our freezer, but we managed to fillet it and cram it in there somehow.

After we anchored at the southern reef we found it almost the same as on the northern reef - a tiny entrance, lots of coral heads and an anchorage in 35 feet of water. The reef was about a half mile from its charted location and the only real difference from the other Minerva was that the reef didn't offer quite as much protection. At high tide a swell came over the reef and made sleeping slightly uncomfortable.

We only stayed for three days, but it wasn't the swell that motivated us to leave. Cyclone Sena formed quickly 350 miles to the north of us and was heading in our direction. This was a little early in the year for a cyclone to form in this area, but not unheard of. We knew Mother Nature couldn't be trusted, and we really should have been on our way to New Zealand by then anyway.

You should have seen Shadowfax and Paragon go through the hectic fire drill of getting everything ready for going to sea. We heard of the cyclone through a ham radio weather report just as the sun set, which meant we couldn't leave until morning. No way could we leave Minerva Reef at night with all those coral heads in the way. We had no choice but to wait and let the cyclone get twelve hours closer before we could leave.

Fear is a great adrenaline booster, so as soon as the sun crept over the horizon we were threading our way out through the pass and pointing the bow south. We raised all the sails and kept the motor turning over to get every last ounce of speed we could. The 25 to 30 knot fringe winds from the cyclone were pushing us from behind and we made fast time surfing down the waves at over 10 knots. After two days we put a few miles between us and the cyclone (which was then heading slightly more east). I have to admit the best winds of the seven-day trip were from that cyclone breathing down our necks, but we were still happy to see it go away. It's no fun sharing an ocean with a cyclone. Scary stuff.

We caught two more mahi along the way with our homemade lures, but our freezer was still full of lobster so we let them go. We still counted them for bragging rights.

As we sailed closer we were reminded how far to the south New Zealand actually was as the weather began turning colder. Ah well, the southern hemisphere summer was coming, so the weather was bound to warm up... in a month or so anyway.

None of those "guaranteed" nasty westerly gales ever did hit us, and we approached New Zealand in good weather. It didn't look like we would be able to add to any of those weather horror stories we heard, except for that cyclone – cyclones make good horror stories. When we were 40 miles from NZ my log book states, "Heavy smell of earth, or moldy trees." Strange smells, but nice. Maybe it was their heavy population of sheep and cattle combined with their thick vegetation that produced the smell. Being at sea for extended periods seemed to heighten our sense of smell.

Chapter 18

Exactly at three in the morning we entered the Bay of Islands on the northern island of New Zealand. We were used to standing off and not entering any pass at night due to the lack of lit navigational markers, but New Zealand harbors are well marked and there were lit markers all the way to the town of Opua.

New Zealand consists of two main islands. The north island has approximately 44,000 square miles and the south island has about 58,000 square miles. Mountains run almost the entire 1,100 mile length of the two islands. The highest mountain is Mt. Cook, at just over 12,000 feet, on the south island. New Zealand also has a few active volcanoes along with hot thermal pools, geysers, and steaming mud pools.

It's possible that the first settlers were Polynesians who came from the islands to the north and east in 500 A.D. Around 1100 A.D. Polynesians from the islands of French Polynesia (possibly Raiatea) arrived and eliminated the first tribes. These Polynesians were to be called Maoris. These were the toughest of all the Polynesians - they would constantly wage war, and the losers would be eaten.

In 1642 the first European, Captain Abel Tasman, came to the islands under the Dutch flag. The first one to explore and chart both the islands was Captain James Cook. That guy really got around. I think he had explored and charted just about every place we had been (not to mention Alaska and Hawaii).

The New Zealand economy consisted mainly of farming. New Zealand has a population of just over 3 million people and 60 million sheep. Lots of cattle too. Not much problem getting a good steak.

As we sailed into the harbor the cold weather was getting to us. It was too early to clear in through customs and as we dropped the hook we could see our breath in the air. Definitely different than the humid tropics we were used to.

Early the next morning we motored to the customs check-in pier and found two officials waiting for us. Most boats clearing into New Zealand had been forewarned about what happens, and we were ready. The man from agriculture arrived with a four-foot-tall garbage bag and intended to fill it before he left. They were afraid of someone bringing in some kind of bug that would devastate their delicate farming economy.

The officials take all your honey, bacon, popcorn, hotdogs (actually all fresh meat, but not fresh fish). We were also not allowed to keep any eggs, either real or powdered. The bottoms of all our shoes were checked, along with our Tongan baskets and mats, for dirt or bugs. All our garbage was also put into his bag.

While the officials were looking around the boat to see if they had missed anything, one of them noticed we had a two-inch-tall bird hanging in one of the corners of the boat. This was your typical knick-knack type thing we had picked up somewhere. He noticed it had tail feathers of about a half-inch long. Well, he took out a pair of scissors and cut off the feathers. I guess he thought it might be of the diseased tail feather knick-knack variety. The bird looked funny, but I liked it better because it now had a cool story behind it.

While all this was going on we found the officials to be super friendly. They were sorry they had to do all this, so in return they gave us maps of the area, coupons for free drinks and even let Gretchen cut a few inches off the top of their bright red garbage bag to make more fishing lures (we were finding red to work best). We were told it would be safe to hitchhike anywhere in the country if we wanted to. We enjoyed meeting these officials and still remember them by name. A nice arrival.

David and Karen, aboard Paragon, had it a little tougher because they chose to bring a dog with them. They had known ahead of time what would happen, but it still wasn't easy. The dog was never allowed to get off the boat under penalty of death (the dog, not them). They also had to bring an inspector out to their boat three times a week to show the dog was still there. They could never tie to a dock and were also subject to surprise inspections. All this inspecting stuff cost them about $100.00 U.S. per month. What a pain.

After the check-in was complete we were able to get off the boat and look around. The first thing we noticed was the resemblance to New England in the States. Our first port, Opua, was set in rolling hills and lush green valleys. Evergreen trees shading Cape Cod-type homes could be seen overlooking the beautiful harbors. Every place we went we were greeted with, "Gaday, mate." We knew we were going to enjoy spending the six-month cyclone season in N.Z.

Our first excursion was to take a trip on an old steam locomotive to the town of Kawakawa. The historic train ride took us along the shoreline from Opua Harbor to the small town of Kawakawa where the train traveled right down the center of the street. Despite all the new forms of transportation, New Zealand has continued to use train travel as one of the most popular ways to get around.

The train we rode was built in 1864 as a result of coal being discovered in Kawakawa. The town grew along both sides of the track and has remained that way to this day.

On the ride into the town the conductor mistakenly told us the wrong time for the last trip back for the day (easier to blame the conductor than to admit we weren't paying attention). When we returned to the station the conductor offered to run the train just for us, and we ended up riding the train all by ourselves. It was easy to like these New Zealanders.

In every country we've tried to learn as much of the language as we could and even though they speak English in New Zealand, it was difficult to understand the accent. The following story shows what I mean.

A few days after we first arrived, Gretchen and I went into one of the local pubs for a beer. The pubs all seem to have a rustic look, and I think it's mandatory that they have posters on all the walls of rugby and cricket games. Anyway, I walked up to the bar and passed one of the locals on the way. I noticed he was carrying pitcher of beer. In my best Kiwi accent I asked, "Aye mate, what kind of beer is that?" He looked up and said, "Mate, this is Lein Ride and it's good." So I went up to the bar and asked for a pitcher of Lein Ride, and this seemed to confuse the bartender. He looked at a picture on the wall and then back at me. The only "pitchers" in New Zealand hung on the walls.

I pointed to one of the pitchers and he said, "Oh, you want a jug of Lien Ride" (instead of pitchers, glasses and cups they have jugs, buckets and handles). He took a jug and when he filled it I noticed my "Lein Ride" was really "Lion Red." I think learning Samoan was easier.

One day we decided to catch the ferry from Opua to the resort town of Russell on the other side of the bay. Russell is a quaint little village with enough history to fill two books. This was where many wars took place between the English and the local Maori tribes. The Maori culture was still very strong in New Zealand with their population being about 280,000.

We enjoyed walking around and checking out all the historic sites, but after the day was over we had to figure out how to get back. We decided to try our hand at hitchhiking to the ferry landing - it took us six hours... just in time for the last ferry. Taking so long wasn't because we didn't get a ride, but because the first ride we got was from an elderly lady who wanted to take us home for "tea." It wasn't long before we learned that "tea" meant dinner, a swim, and a fishing excursion with her 82-year-old husband. Apparently he was in charge of catching cat food for the entire neighborhood. I wish I had as much energy as these two.

Over the Christmas holidays we weighed anchor and set sail to explore a few of the 144 islands that make up the Bay of Islands area. The islands are hilly and heavily vegetated and most of them were considered parks, so there weren't very many homes cluttering up the area. We ran into plenty of friendly people in the different anchorages and even had a few invitations to come and visit them in other parts of New Zealand. We filed these away for future reference.

After our return to Opua we decided to look for a small motorcycle so we could get around easier. The people were so friendly that hitchhiking anywhere took all day. Buying a motorcycle was the best idea we had in a long time.

After a week of looking at bikes we went to a town about 30 miles away (hitchhiking) and we arrived in the pouring rain. Good incentive to buy transportation. We liked what we found and it was in our price range - a 125cc Yamaha electric-start street bike. Small, but it had to be small so we could fit it on the back deck of the boat. We rode it home in the downpour.

In between all our visiting and hanging out, we were selling t-shirts to the cruise ships and also at an outside market a few miles away. We asked the officials what we had to do in order to sell t-shirts since we didn't have work permits, and we were told, "It's only t-shirts mate. Just pay $15.00 to the Arts and Crafts Society and have at it." We came up with a few designs of local interest, nailed together a little stand, and away we went. We even figured out how to carry forty t-shirts, the stand, and the two of us on the motorcycle. What a business. We didn't get rich, but we made enough to get by... so far.

Our first long trip on the bike was 190 miles south to the big city of Auckland. We needed more blank t-shirts, and this was the best place to go. It's hard to find t-shirts without some sort of design already on them. Try it.

On the way we decided to visit someone we met while cruising the Bay of Islands. We stopped at the home of Rick and Barbara, which was more of a ranch than just a house. Rick built the house himself because he wanted an open design with a view to the backyard where he kept his 100 deer. He called himself a "hobby farmer," and told us that deer take very little work to raise. He told me that only once a year do they have to catch them all, tag them, and check them for T.B. In his next breath he said, "What are ya doing tomorrow mate?"

The next day I found myself standing in a corral with all these Bambies staring at me. I soon discovered this was no place for Topsider boat shoes. My job was to help ear-tag all the little guys while a vet checked the big ones for T.B. Hard work, but a great day. I still don't know much about deer, but it sure made raising deer look like a fun hobby.

The rest of the trip to Auckland was broken up by a stop at the Golden Arches. This was our first quarter-pounder since leaving Florida. It was exactly the same. Greasy, lukewarm and delicious.

Auckland is a typical city with lots of cars zipping around. I think you lose the knack for city driving if you don't do it enough, and together with having to drive on the wrong side of the road we were lost in no time. After a few hours of wrong turns we found the t-shirt joint and told them to ship our order to Opua. No way could we carry 400 shirts on the bike. Back at Opua we went to our favorite pub and had a cold "Lien Ride" to celebrate a successful trip.

We made it back in time for the "Opua Sailing Regatta" and managed to make a few dozen Regatta shirts to sell to the racers. We set up our little booth the day of the race and our second customer surprised us by asking us to house-sit for a couple of weeks. We had never met this person. She was given our names by a fellow yachtie and she said she needed someone to look after her home, dog, cat, cattle, horse and goat. Sure, why not... the deer tagging was fun so this sounded worth a try. Gretchen and I were thinking "hot shower" more than "goat feeding" when we said yes. We were always up for an adventure anyway. We stayed at her place the full two weeks and nothing died, so I guess we can consider that a terrific success. New Zealand sure was offering us lots of adventure.

Back on the boat we were trying to figure out what we could get into next. That was answered by a friend, Lou

Ann, from Florida, who decided to come for a visit. She had limited time and wanted to see the country. You can't blame her, right? New Zealand is definitely worth seeing and we were ready for the wham-bam trip of our lives - over 2,000 miles in seven days.

When Lou Ann showed up we rented a car and off we went. Let me think back and start at the beginning. We went through towns with names like Papatoetoe, Wainihinihi, Wharanui and someone told us not to miss Whikikamoocow, but damn if we could find it.

As I drove the rental car through the town of Whangarei I was trying to get a handle on driving on the left side of the road in a car with steering wheel on the right side. The car was a standard transmission and I found myself trying to shift with the window handle, and when I used the turn signal I ended up turning on the windshield wipers. During all this, the traffic was moving along at speeds of over 75 mph, which was more confusing as the speedometer wasn't in miles – it read 121 (kilometers per hour). We laughed most of the way and eventually had it figured out.

We wanted to stay near the town of Rotorua the first night and we arrived just after dark. We looked for a cheap place to stay as we had budget accommodations in mind. We pulled into a likely place and the manager was a friendly mate so we said, "Gaday, could you please show us your cheapest room." He gave us a big smile and did as we asked. It's hard to explain what the room was like, but Lou Ann summed it up best with the term "tool shed." We looked at each other and then talked about how we could see our breath in the mountain air. So, okay, we're wimps. We looked at the manager and said, "What have ya got with a TV and a heater?" He gave us another smile and said, "Good on ya!" (a favorite expression in NZ).

The city of Rotorua is located about two-thirds of the way down on the north island and is famous for its thermal activity. The curing powers of the thermal waters were known to the Maori tribes long before Europeans came to

New Zealand. Sixteen lakes surrounded by unbelievably green foliage added to the beauty.

Now let's talk about the smell. You can tell 25 miles away that you are getting near the thermal area. What a stink! The sulphurous odor is overpowering... like a hundred trucks full of rotten eggs sitting in the hot sun. It's strange, but after you're there for a while you can hardly notice any smell at all. Hard to believe you could get used to something like that.

With our super-speed tour we didn't have time to visit all of the thermal sights so we picked the most active, which was appropriately called "Hells Gate."

As we entered Hell's Gate the steam was shooting out of the ground everywhere we looked. We felt like we were in the middle of a giant cooking pot. In fact, the Maoris used these steaming pools to cook their meals. The water temperature in many places exceeded 212 degrees. Graphite in the water made it possible for the water to be hotter than boiling.

The second thing we saw was a sign that actually said, "Danger, we are not kidding. You risk your life if you wander from the path." No problem, with only seven days to see New Zealand we didn't have time for any deviating.

Right in the middle of all this boiling water there was what they called "mud volcanoes." Lots of mud bubbling, boiling and making a real mess. A sign here said if we threw any rocks into the mud they would make us go and get them. No time for that foolishness either... gotta go, time was wasting.

Back in the car we headed south. Past Lake Taupo, nice. Past the Kaimanawa Mountains, majestic. Through Ruahine range, like a desert. Even through a town called Bulls. Lots of beautiful real estate everywhere. More than a few times there were sheep just wandering around in the road without adult supervision. With the sheep outnumbering the people 20 to 1, we shouldn't have been surprised.

Our destination was the southern-most city on the northern island, Wellington. We arrived late and left early. We stayed at the Backpackers Lodge and went out to dinner. Been there, done that, Wellington.

The next morning we prepared to take the intra-island ferry to New Zealand's south island. Rental cars weren't allowed on the ferry so we dropped ours off, planning to get another one on that island.

The ferry was more like a small cruise ship than a ferry. It was 423 feet long and carried 850 passengers plus 60 cars. Two restaurants and two bars, along with a large TV room, made it a comfortable ride.

The three-and a-half-hour trip took us across the Cook Straits, which is famous for its incredibly rough waters. The wind would blow up to fifty knots against a four-knot current and the locals would say, "Good thing it's not rough today, aye mate?" These people are tough sailors.

The day we crossed the strait, the weather was nasty (or calm depending on who you ask) with the tops being blown off the waves. Shadowfax would have had a tough time trying to cope.

The first thing Gretchen did when we entered the ferry was to look for the casino. I think we were lucky. Two ferries make the passage - the casino was on the other one.

The South Island of New Zealand contains 58,200 sq. miles with a population of less than one million. You could be anywhere on the island and never be more than 68 miles from the water. A mountain chain known as the Southern Alps runs almost the full length of the island with 17 mountains having an elevation of more than 9,800 feet. Glaciers still cut a path through the southern mountains. The whole of New Zealand is less than five million years old (that's not really very old), so the mountains have a very jagged look as they haven't had time to erode.

Once the ferry started to cross we realized just how rough it was. The huge boat was tossed around and it wasn't until we entered the protected waters of Marlborough Sound on the other side that it calmed down. The ferry finally docked, and it was a mad race for the rental car. Gotta keep going.

While driving down the east side of the Southern Island we passed through tunnels blasted out of solid rock. We drove with a rocky volcanic black beach to one side and train tracks running parallel on the other side. At one point Gretchen said she thought she saw seals lounging around on the rocks on the beach... either seals or 400 pound wharf rats. We stopped to check it out. They were seals. There were dozens of them and we were able to get close enough for some terrific pictures.

We climbed back into the car and continued our drive south to the town of Kaikoura. We found a great place to spend the night called the "New Commercial Lodge." It was very old for a place with the word "New" in the title, but I knew this was the place to stay - rooms up top, bar down below and pool tables in the back.

Larry, the owner, showed us two rooms and told us the price. Gretchen noticed that one of the rooms had an extra bed and asked, "How much if all three of us stay in one room?" He gave me a big smile and a wink and said, "Good on ya," and then gave us a great rate.

That night in the bar everyone was smiling and waving at me. I probably could have been elected mayor. The next morning we thought it might be fun to make up Lou Ann's bed so it looked as though she hadn't used it. Great for the male ego.

The town of Kaikourais is said to have whales within a couple of miles of its beaches all year round, so the most popular tourist attraction was to climb aboard sightseeing boats to go whale watching. Unfortunately for Lou Ann, you had to book three days in advance. As for Gretchen and me, we saw quite a few at sea and usually pointed the boat away from them, so we couldn't imagine getting on a boat to go find them.

The next day we continued our travels south along the coastline to the famous town of Christchurch. The city's charm came from the tree-lined Avon River which wandered through the town. At least that's what the guidebook said. We flew by pretty quick.

From Christchurch we took a right and headed west into the mountain range. As the road cut through Arther's Pass in the mountain valley, we were treated to spectacular scenery on an unbelievable road. Many parts of the road were one lane which seemed to go either straight up or straight down. If we had met another car coming toward us, one of us would have had to back up for miles.

We saw a few strange looking parrots along the way called Kea Parrots. They are about the size of seagulls with bright green and red under their wings. Seemed like a strange place to find parrots since the weather was so cold, but there sure were a lot of them... awfully noisy too.

Once we were on the west coast of New Zealand we stopped in the town of Hokitika. Hokitika was New Zealand's answer to a California gold rush town. Huge amounts of gold had been found in the New Zealand mountains around 1864, with towns being built wherever the largest amounts were found. During the gold rush era, Hokitika had 102 hotels, with 84 of them being on one short street. Only three remained.

The town's special claim to fame was to have the only decent harbor on the west coast of the southern island. As many as 37,000 passengers arrived here, and more gold passed through this town than anywhere else. We were told that when ships were to enter the harbor the locals would go down to the pier and make bets on whether the ship would hit the rocks or the sandbar at the entrance. Looking out at the pass from shore I couldn't see how a ship could possibly get in. It looked like breaking waves all the way across. The prospect of a boatload of gold must have been enough to make captains try almost anything. Would I have tried it for a boatload of gold? Absolutely!

While walking around the town we were told that we should definitely check out The Hokitika Gorge. We decided to deviate from our chosen path and drive the 20 miles out of our way and have a look. We drove over a long, winding road to find a narrow wooden bridge crossing a deep gorge cut into the mountains with incredibly beautiful blue water at the bottom. Lou Ann described it best by calling it a perfect "tidy bowl blue."

With time running short we had to again head south along the narrow, steep, winding, bumpy, avalanche and earthquake-prone roads.

We made it as far south as the Franz Josef Glacier. New Zealand has many glaciers on the south island, but this one was easily accessible, which made it unique. The Franz Josef was over 7 miles long and fed by a snowfield 3,000 feet deep. The glacier flies along at the speed of 5 feet a day. As we walked the path to the glacier we were walking over the land where the glacier had been, and we could see the power behind it. Crushed boulders and eroded rock lined the entire valley. Worth the trip, but next time I'll wear a hat or maybe earmuffs. Glaciers equal cold – you'd think I would have known that.

Again, gotta go. If you ever make it to New Zealand don't miss the drive along the west coast of the southern island. The roads are narrow but in good shape, and the scenery incredible. "Pancake" rocks, formed by volcanic activity, line one side of the road at heights up to 100 feet. Lots of places to stop and sightsee along the way. We panned for gold at one stop (we got about $4.00 in gold each) and found a steam train to ride at another.

We continued north and came to a roadblock... a roadblock of solid cows. There were over 100 cows slowly walking along the street in the direction we were heading. With at least a half mile of cows to drive through, we took it slow and got some of the meanest looks a cow can give.

Not much further up the road we ran into a similar situation... except with sheep. There was a guy behind them on a motorcycle herding them along the road. This is hard to believe, but on the motorcycle he had two large dogs riding with him - one in front of him and the other in back. When one of the sheep strayed, he would push one off the bike and the dog would tear into the sheep with a vengeance. The sheep got back in line, and the dog (with a mouth full of wool) jumped back on the bike while it was still moving. When the next sheep got out of line, it was the other dogs turn. I was lucky if I ever got my dog to just come when I called.

After we made it through the sheep we made it full circle and arrived back at Picton and the ferry boat. With time ticking away we decided to make the crossing back to the north island by seaplane in order to save time.

We called a number from a brochure and the seaplane pilot arrived (looking as though he had a severe hangover) towing his plane behind his car – on what looked like a boat trailer. I asked him why he didn't just leave the plane in the water and we weren't very assured when he said, "It gets so windy in here that every time I leave it in the water she flips over." Next I told him I thought it was a good looking plane and asked if it was new and he said, "Naw, she's real old, but I had her painted up real good, aye mate?" All I could think to say was, "Good on ya," and got in the plane.

After we were all crammed into the plane he said he had to pick up some more people at a local resort. I thought maybe if they hung onto the wings we all might fit. As soon as we took off we landed again to pick up two more people and a screaming baby. The mother told us that the kid hated to fly and screamed all the way over. Wonderful.

We saw the pilot strap the kid onto the mother's lap and Gretchen commented that the big airlines should do that also. He replied by saying, "Well, I have to. If I don't, the kid would get splattered on the roof when we hit the bumps out there, and that makes quite a mess, aye mate?" "Good on ya," again.

For you airplane buffs, the plane was a Canadian left-hand De Havilland Beaver floatplane with a nine-cylinder radial engine. The pilot was just plain nuts.

Once over the Cook Straits we knew what he meant by the "bumps." What a wild ride, but we made it across and were glad to land safely just off the north island. As the pilot motored up to the dock, the wind caught the plane, and the wing slammed into a telephone pole which spun us away from the dock and put us aground. I felt sorry for the people waiting on the dock. They were Captain Marvel's next victims.

We picked up another rental car and made record time getting back to the Bay of Islands and Shadowfax. Our land adventure was over. We did just about everything except bungee jumping and touring the southern Fiordland - for that we would have needed another day.

After a sail around the Bay of Islands with blue penguins playing in our wake and a bit of relaxing on the islands, Lou Ann had to get back on one of those big birds and fly home. Our second year of the cruise was now over, and Lou Ann was about to cover the same distance in just a few hours. No doubt about it... our way of travel was slower, but definitely better.

Once Lou Ann left, Gretchen and I still had some time to kill before we were to sail out. We made and sold a few more t-shirts and spent most of our time in the town of Russell. We had moved the boat the few miles and anchored off the Russell fishing pier. We parked our motorcycle in the local church parking lot. Nothing to do but prepare to leave when our six-month visa (and cyclone season) ended.

One day when I walked in to get the motorcycle I was in for a little surprise. The poor thing was completely stripped. Headlights, mirrors, foot rests, battery, blinkers, kickstand and everything else that could be unscrewed was missing. It was laying on its side and looked beyond repair. Hard to believe but this story does have a happy ending.

I couldn't believe it... crime hits the little town of Russell. I walked the three blocks to the police station and read the sign in front, "Historic Russell Police Station. Policeman lives here. Please do not disturb." I have to admit that I did feel a little guilty walking past the sign to knock on the door.

After knocking on the door for more than a few minutes, I was glad to hear someone coming. When the door opened I met Russell's only police officer. Crocodile Dundee lives! He was about 6 feet 6 and weighed around 250 pounds (none of it fat), dressed in shorts, a ratty old t-shirt and no shoes.

He looked down at me and said, "Yea?" I told him what happened, and he said, "Go get it." I told him I really didn't want to touch it because it might have fingerprints on it that would help him find the thief. He said, "Good thinkin', when ya get it, put it here," and he pointed to his driveway.

Who am I to argue, so I got the bike and pushed it to his driveway. I was feeling pretty bad about the whole situation. "Dundee" came out to the driveway with his K-Mart fingerprint kit and went to work. At this point I didn't see much hope, so I went back to the boat to tell Gretchen what happened.

At 10pm the next night Gretchen and I heard someone outside knocking on the side of the boat. We were at anchor quite a way from shore and had no idea who it could be. We went outside to find 'Crocodile' in a tiny rowboat and smelling a bit like a brewery. He said, "Aye mate, got all ya stuff back. Tomorrow the puke who stole it will put it back together for ya, and then I'll have him wash it up real nice. From now on keep the bike in the jail behind my house where it'll be safe."

Sure enough, the next morning Gretchen and I went to his house (station) and found a kid of about 16 years old putting everything back together. Crocodile made the kid apologize, and then we went into his house and sat down to drink some of his home-brew beer. A happy ending and a great new friend to go with it (the cop, not the crook). He asked us if we wanted to press charges and we asked him what he thought. He said he knew the kid and thought he could scare him so he wouldn't do it again. I can only imagine how he intended to scare him, but we left it to his discretion.

A week before we sailed out a severe low pressure system blew through and caught us by surprise. Before I could get the dinghy secured, a great gust of wind came along and flipped it over with the Sea Gull motor on it. This was good news. I had visions of buying a new Mariner or Mercury outboard as I looked at the Sea Gull, which was now in the water with the propeller sticking up.

I flipped the dinghy back over, blew out the carburetor, cleaned the spark plug and crossed my fingers (hoping it would never run again), and pulled the starting cord. I couldn't believe it... it started up on the first pull. It never started with less than twenty pulls on a good day. Oh well, no excuse for new motor this time.

Our next port was suppose to be Australia, but we had heard so much about Fiji's 322 islands that we decided to sail to the north and check it out. After all, it was only 1,100 miles away.

May 16th rolled around, and we knew it had to be time to go. The southern winter was rolling in and we could again see our breath in the air. Time to bring the motorcycle aboard. We had thought about where to put it and how to get it there, so we put our plan into action. I brought the bike to a boat ramp while Gretchen met me there with the inflatable dinghy. Next, deflate the front chamber of the dinghy and roll the bike into the dinghy. Next, inflate the front of the dinghy while Gretchen held the bike, and then slowly motor back out to the boat (this attracted quite a bit of attention). Once back at the boat, we took the halyard from the mizzen mast and tied it to a bridle I had made. As Gretchen steadied the bike, I started to turn the winch on the mast, which raised the bike. So far so good. Once it was high enough, we swung it onto the deck and then lowered it.

It's true that the bike was only a 125cc Yamaha, but it looked as big as a Harley once it was on the back deck of the boat. Next, I had to tie it down. It sure looked out of place leaning against the rails on the port side. Gretchen made a cover for it out of a heavy plastic, and after spraying the bike with WD-40, I covered it and then proceeded to tie it down. I should have measure how much line was wrapped around that poor bike. I had it tied to every solid piece of the boat I could find. Hundreds of feet would be an accurate guess. The web of lines would have made any spider proud. The big question was whether or not this thing would still be on deck when we reached Fiji. No one had to remind me how rough it could get out there.

New Zealand was the same as all the other places when it came to saying goodbye. Too many new friends. Of course, we had to have one final party and make sure we had everyone's address so we could stay in touch. Leaving was always sad. We seemed to stay places a little too long for the term 'tourist' to fit, and not quite long enough to be called 'locals.' I guess we were somewhere in between.

The call for new adventure was so overpowering that we forced ourselves to weigh anchor and dip our flag in farewell and tribute to great new friends and a truly great country.

Chapter 19

As soon as we sailed out of the Bay of Islands, the brisk west wind filled our sails and off we went. We were clipping along at over seven knots with all our sails up when we caught the first of many fish on this passage. Within the next 30 minutes we caught a total of 5 fish - all in the 5 to 7 pound range. This almost equaled the entire number of fish caught during the previous year. We're sure it was because of the bright red lures made from the garbage bag we took from the New Zealand customs people. Gretchen had made a dozen or so lures from it, and it appeared that we were definitely on to something. Small strips of the red plastic were cut to resemble hula skirts and were tied onto the hooks using dental floss (a sailing necessity which is also used as sail thread in an emergency).

The first two days of the trip we were pushed along by a strong westerly breeze. The moon was almost full, the barometer was steady, and Shadowfax was in her element. When we hooked a 16-pound mahi mahi on our "garbage bag" lure I knew this was a change in our fishing luck. Dinner that night was Mahi fillets broiled in lemon and butter. My mouth waters just thinking about it.

Somewhere around the third day the wind backed to the south and continued to blow at a gusty 25 knots. The seas began to build, and the ride became uncomfortable. The seas were directly behind us and rolling under Shadowfax's keel - making us roll like an amusement park ride. I don't know who was the one to come up with the saying in most sailing books, "Fair winds and following seas," but all I can agree with is the fair winds part. That following seas stuff is terrible. It's like living inside a cement mixer. You get bruises on your bruises just trying to walk from one end of the boat to the other.

We tried lots of different sail combinations to stop the boat from rolling so wildly. We knew the spinnaker would be the answer, but the wind was a little too gusty to chance it. The spinnaker was our best sail and we really didn't want to shred it.

We tried the jib sail along with the mizzen staysail (which is a small spinnaker flown from the aft mast), but all that did was to block the wind from filling the jib. No choice but to drop the staysail - oops! The halyard got away from me and flew up to the top of the mast and through the pulley. The sail dropped to the deck with the halyard right behind it.

We were going to need that halyard again, so I asked Gretchen to hoist me up the mast so I could rethread the line through the pulley. Damn, what a nasty ride at the top of the mast! The view was great, and I wished I'd had a camera with me, but on the other hand, I wouldn't have been able to let go long enough to get a picture. On deck when the boat is rolling, the motion at the top of the mast is 10-fold.

After getting the halyard back through the pulley and me safely back on deck, we still wanted to come up with something to make the ride more comfortable. The answer was really quite easy. I know all of you long-distance sailors out there know what we did. We went down to the navigation station and looked at the chart for a different destination. If we changed course about 20 degrees and put the wind on the stern quarter, the boat would ride much better. Wow! What a great new destination... just a mere five days to the northeast was Minerva Reef. Perfect. We liked Minerva when we were there on the way to New Zealand, so we didn't mind going a little out of our way for a few more days of eating lobster at Minerva.

Once we changed course we pulled out the full jib and raised a reefed main, which smoothed out the ride perfectly so we could enjoy the trip.

Our fourth night out a huge tanker crept by about four miles to the west. The shipping traffic on the open ocean can be a threat to a small sailboat and that's why we kept night watches. This was the first ship we'd seen since leaving Tonga before coming to New Zealand, and it was the only one we had seen on the sail to Fiji. It would be easy to become inattentive during one of our late night watches, but one mistake could be deadly. When we saw a ship we would call them on the VHF radio to be sure they saw us and about half the time the reply was something like, "Wait a minute, I'll turn on the radar and see if you show up." Not very reassuring.

One of the more pleasant times during a passage is when you come off watch, crawl into your berth and get assaulted with a noise you can only smile at. Pods of porpoise come to play in the wake and actually 'talk' to you with their high pitched squeaking noise. The sound transmits perfectly right through the hull. Somehow it's a comforting noise, but after a while you want to get up and oil something.

Six miles off Minerva Reef we started to pick up the lobster on the radar (okay, that's a little exaggeration), and altered course for the entrance. The bad news was that we couldn't make it by dark... almost, but not quite. To try and enter at night or even at dusk would earn anyone who tried the "Idiot of the Year Award," so we just had to heave-to (stop the boat) and wait until morning.

The next morning we approached the reef and it looked funny... lots of little sticks sticking up in the air. It looked like a small marina. When we were in New Zealand we passed out a lot of our "secret maps" to enter Minerva, and told stories about having to beat the lobsters off your anchor chain, or having to keep your ports closed or else the lobsters would crawl in. I guess everyone believed us. Seven boats, besides ours, were anchored in the middle of the Pacific Ocean with nothing else in sight. Time to plug our t-shirt business and have a party.

We had 17 people aboard Shadowfax for a huge potluck dinner with everyone bringing a dish. We ended up with lobster cooked 17 different ways. We lost count of how much rum punch was consumed. We told everyone we planned on staying for a couple of nights, but we knew that wouldn't be the case. When had we ever stayed anywhere for only two nights? Two weeks was more like it.

It's hard to explain the feeling you get with a full moon reflecting on the water and the endless rows of breaking waves crashing onto the reef just a stone's throw away. A perfect truckstop for boats - and there was no way to spend any money no matter how hard you try... at least for us. We ruined that for other boats by selling them t-shirts.

We spent a quiet Memorial Day behind the reef, or maybe we had a big party Memorial Day. It depends on who you ask. We had to cross back over the 180 degree longitude line (dateline) to visit Minerva and depending on which side you set your calendar, it was either today or yesterday. Since we were going to Fiji, we kept our clocks on today while the boats going east used yesterday. When making the plans to visit one of the boats on a certain night, we first had to determine which team they were on so we wouldn't be late or early by a full day. Confusing.

Well, we couldn't stay forever so after two weeks we decided to up anchor and go. Our freezer was again filled with lobster, so we bid farewell to one of the most pleasant places on earth.

It must be about time for another rough weather story. We had good passages for the past few trips, and it was about time for Mother Nature to assert herself. The passage started better than it finished. We had a reefed main and a full jib and all looked well, but the night we left a small low pressure system developed over Australia and moved rapidly our way as it built in size. The wind stayed behind us (the good news) but as it increased to over 40 knots, the waves started to build and Shadowfax was soon surfing down the seas.

The steering vane was steering the boat, but we were a little worried about our approach to Fiji. Lots of reefs and our sat-nav wasn't very dependable. The sextant wasn't an option either because the cloud cover wouldn't let us see anything resembling a celestial body.

I was down below trying to rest and read when Gretchen came down from her watch and said, "Wow! Have you looked out there lately?" I went topside just in time to see a large green wave crash over the stern. Shadowfax was surfing down huge dark mountains of water with the hissing noise of breaking waves on both sides. Every few waves one would roll over the stern and slowly drain through the rails and back into the sea. One of the benefits of having a center cockpit like the one on Shadowfax was that we could manage to stay dry (mostly) and relatively safe.

The motorcycle tied to the back deck didn't look quite as safe. The lines seemed to be holding okay, but I was still worried about it. The waves would bury it often, and I wasn't sure the can of WD-40 I sprayed on it would be enough to keep the thing from rusting.

As we approached the Koro Sea around the Fijian Islands, we tried to hold an accurate course because of the many uncharted reefs in the area. We heard through the ham radio that Fiji was tough on boats. In the six months before we arrived, the reefs of Fiji had claimed six yachts. One was a Cal-46, like Shadowfax. We were told it was still mostly in one piece but high up on a reef somewhere to the south of Fiji. The captain - who was alone - was never heard from again.

This wasn't the case with most of the foundering yachts. It's true that most of the boats were a complete loss, but the owners only needed reef-walking shoes, not life rafts, to get safely to shore. Any examination of the local charts shows hundreds of tiny islands and reefs with charted wrecks on just about all of them. A scary place not to have an accurate position fix, which we didn't.

At three in the morning we were supposed to see the light marking the Astrolabe Reef, which sticks out 25 miles from the island of Kandavu. No such luck. I was fairly sure of our general position, so that meant that the light was probably not working. Nothing new there. We had been spoiled by

New Zealand where all the navigation markers were where they were supposed to be (and lit), but we remembered the rest of the South Pacific where markers of any kind were few and far between. Nothing to do but keep sailing, and watch and listen for any sign of breaking waves on a reef.

Daytime was never more welcome. Everything is always easier when the sun is up. After we were safely past Kandavu Island we only had a few more hours until our landfall at the city of Suva on the island of Viti Levu, the largest Fijian Island. The sun broke through and I was able to get a good position fix with the sextant, so it was time to check out our tourist information books to see what we were in for.

Chapter 20

The 322 islands of Fiji cover an incredible 274,000 square miles of the globe, but only have a land area of just over 7,000 square miles. 97 percent of the 274,000 square miles is ocean. Fiji is in the part of the Pacific called Melanesia where the customs differ slightly from the Polynesian Islands.

The islands are mostly mountainous with thick rain forests and over 3,000 species of plant life. Archaeological studies reveal that these islands probably had been inhabited as far back as 1500 B.C. The first European to see these islands was Dutch Captain Abel Tasman, who reported their existence but never landed. In 1779 the English explorer Captain James Cook was the first to land. He reported the natives to be fierce man-eaters and labeled the islands "The Cannibal Islands."

In 1874 Fiji became a British Colony and the islander's man-eating ways were stopped. The British brought in indentured labor from India in 1879 to work in the sugar industry, and today Indians make up fifty percent of the 750,000 population, which is more than the native Fijian's forty-five percent. In 1970 Fiji became independent and one of the major trade centers of the western Pacific.

The Indian majority was slowly being voted in as the political majority, and in 1987 the Fijian government was overthrown in a bloodless coup by Col. Sitiveni Rabuka. Rabuka, a Fijian, claimed he was "safeguarding the Fijian way of life." The free press was stopped, and the military dictatorship took complete control.

Later that same year, Rabuka thought his new government wasn't progressing the way he wished, so he staged a second coup. This time he claimed himself to be a General and also the new Head of State. Over 300 community leaders were arrested, and there were many reports of torture. The story doesn't end there. The day before we arrived in Fiji on June 10, 1991, Rabuka told his government officials that they were 'ineffective' and should all quit immediately. He also mobilized his military and reserve forces. We knew this would be an interesting stop.

As we approached the island of Viti Levu, we had no problem finding the tiny entrance pass. We had been told to look for a huge wrecked tanker on the reef at the east side of the entrance. An expensive marker, but easy to see. After traveling the 1,186 miles from New Zealand, to Minerva, to Fiji, we were ready to clear customs.

In each country it was a challenge clearing in and out, and it mostly wasn't a very enjoyable procedure. Since Fiji was in real political turmoil, we decided we should tell them about our guns. We wouldn't want to be arrested for gun-running in a country where people talk of torture.

We tied to the customs pier and the first official to board Shadowfax was the health inspector, and wow, was he angry. Gretchen had jumped from the boat to shore to tie up our bow and he yelled that absolutely no one could get off the boat for anything unless he said so. As he was yelling about this, the customs agent showed up and started calling the health official an idiot. The health inspector tried to throw the customs agent off the boat and was yelling that no one could board the boat, even a customs agent, without his say so.

We were in the middle trying to calm down both of these idiots. It was obvious that these men had hated each other for a long time, but they just happened to pick Shadowfax for their little war. Finally, a third guy came along and called the health official away, and we gave a big sigh of relief.

The customs agent stayed and asked us to fill out the usual stack of papers, while telling us what a jerk the health inspector was. When I came to the question about guns, I asked him what he wanted me to do with them, and he said, "You have no guns." I was sure that if we gave them to this man we wouldn't have gotten them back, so no problem. No guns here.

Once cleared in we motored the short distance to the most popular anchorage right off the Royal Suva Yacht Club. The Royal Suva Yacht Club had the word 'Royal' in it from the days of British rule. Nice of the Brits to leave the yacht club behind when they left.

Something else the Brits left behind in every country that had been under British rule was the English language, which made life a bit easier for us. Not everyone spoke English, but most seemed to know a little.

One of the first things we noticed about the anchorage was how crowded it was. Thirty sailboats from all over the globe were at anchor. Fiji is at a crossroad for yachts going in every direction. Word was out to sailors that this was a good, cheap place to provision, and an incredible place to get in a little snorkeling or diving. A few yachts had brought surfboards because Fiji is famous in the surfing world.

We made our way to the yacht club to introduce ourselves and to figure out where everything was. We were in for a pleasant surprise. We sat at the bar and found that a beer cost 40 cents and a T-bone steak was $2.00. While sampling one of their Fiji Bitter beers, we were told that the movie theater charged $1.10 for a double feature of the latest movies. Actually, we found out later that almost all the movies were as yet unreleased in the States. Somehow they were getting bootleg copies and showing them to the public. Definitely against the law in the U.S., but Fiji didn't really play by the rules.

No time to waste so we typed up a brochure saying, "Your Yacht on a T-shirt" and then listed different prices for different quantities. Then we added, "Makes a Great Christmas Gift" across the bottom and added pictures of sailboats to the design. We had 50 copies printed at the yacht club, and we were ready for step two.

Step two, get in our dinghy and go from boat to boat passing out our cool flyers. Up until now we had been letting word of mouth do our advertising, but it was time for a bold new plan.

Although the sailboats in the anchorage were anchored close together, it took us all day to visit just ten of them. The reason was that when we approached a boat, the conversation would go something like this, "Excuse me, we're from that boat over there and we print custom t-shirts with an exact picture of your yacht on it. Here is our brochure." The reply was always something like, "I'm sorry but my English isn't so good. Why don't you come aboard and have a rum drink and well talk about it." We've had rougher jobs.

At the end of the day we returned to Shadowfax with five separate orders for a total of 110 t-shirts. We told everyone we needed 50 percent down as a deposit (we needed money to buy the blank shirts). We returned to Shadowfax a little drunk, but definitely happy. Luckily Gretchen had written all the different orders down, which was a really smart idea because the next morning our brains felt a little fuzzy.

The hard work was about to start. Most of the boats were planning to leave in four or five days, so we had to get moving. Gretchen was in charge of t-shirt acquisition, and I was in charge of tracing the boats from a blown up picture and then cutting a screen that would allow us to apply the silkscreen ink to the shirts by squeegee.

The main streets of Suva were lined with shop after shop, which were all run by Indians. When you walked past one of the shops they would try to grab you and pull you inside sell you something. This made Gretchen's job of finding t-shirts extremely tough, but after she got the hang of their way of doing business, I think the storekeepers got the worst of it. She knew what she wanted, and when she found it there was no way in hell they could get her to pay more than she intended.

The place she found to buy the t-shirts was a huge warehouse with shirts piled to the roof. Very few were in boxes, so she had to sort through mountains of shirts... picking out the good ones from the bad ones and sorting them into sizes. She ended up paying only $1.50 per t-shirt. Good quality too.

What a business. We were selling the shirts finished for $8.00 each for an order of less than 2 dozen. Our first week in Fiji we made over $800.00. As yachts left Fiji, just as many new ones sailed in to replace them.

When the Fiji Yacht Club held a cookout for all the boats in the anchorage, we talked our happy little customers into wearing the shirts we made for them. This gave us the best advertising we could get. All night we were talking to people about prices, sizes, colors, designs and, of course, how fast we could finish an order. We also had a stack of courtesy flags all finished and ready to add to their t-shirt order.

One boat with an older couple onboard approached us saying, "You're the t-shirt people. We've been looking for you." They explained to us what they wanted and supplied us with a line drawing of the boat (which saved me a couple of hours work). By the time they had added up all the shirts they needed to send relatives, friends and anyone else they could think of, the total was over 200 tees. Our fame was spreading. Even the ham radio was helping to pass the word. By the time yachts arrived they knew just what they wanted. Lots of work for us, but we needed the bucks.

In between all these orders we managed to see a bit of Viti Levu Island. For the first time since New Zealand we unloaded the motorcycle and took it to shore. We just reversed the order in which we put it on board... the only difference was the size of the crowd watching as we did it. I think the large crowd was watching and secretly hoping to see it get dumped in the water. Everyone loves a bit of drama.

Once we had the bike on shore we wanted to be legal, so we went to the local police station to see if we could register it. After visiting the police, customs and the local registry and getting no good answer, we did what the police captain told us to do. He said, "Ride it. Who cares? If anyone stops you, just give them my name." We rode the thing all over

155

the island with our New Zealand license plates and never had a problem. A little less complex than the U.S. vehicle registration office.

One of our more memorable rides was when we were investigating back roads and inadvertently rode into a military prison. Not our fault, they shouldn't have left the gate open. As we were riding along the edge of the rain forest and taking pictures, it became apparent that we were on the wrong road when we saw the prisoners working in the fields and a dozen or so guards converging on our location. The first thing I thought of was to say to Gretchen, "Maybe it would be a good idea to hide that camera."

We played the role of dumb tourist and talked our way out of it. The guards couldn't understand who we were, why we were there, where we were trying to go, or our explanation that we were just lost. After ten minutes, and lots of cheers and waves from the prisoners, the guards finally let us pass. The New Zealand registered motorcycle was never mentioned.

Our stay in Suva was worth it. We stayed for two months making t-shirts, checking out the scenery and trying out all the different restaurants. What a great little city. No highrise buildings but lots and lots of little shops - more than half seemed to be selling only watches.

After leaving the city we wanted to check out some other areas of Fiji, and to stop at traditional villages we needed to load up on kava. Kava (or Yanggona) is the dried root of a plant in the pepper family, which when ground by a mortar and pestle can then be wrapped in a large cloth (like a tea bag) and dipped into a bowl with a couple gallons of water. The drink that is created is a tranquilizing, non-alcoholic brew that looks a little like used dishwater. The reason we had to load up on kava was because we wouldn't be allowed to visit any of the villages without performing a ceremony called a Sevusevu, which requires this kava stuff.

When it came time to sail out, we actually had to tell everyone "no more" as far as the t-shirts went, but we did take some orders for people who were sailing in the same direction... promising to meet them at a small island called Malolol Lailai in a couple of weeks.

We stocked Shadowfax with lots of provisions (including 500 t-shirts) while we were in Suva. We knew how this money thing went - sometimes we had it, most of the time we didn't - so we stocked up while we could. Another bright point in our stay was when the Sea Gull outboard finally self-destructed.

When it quit running I didn't get excited. After all, the thing always quit for no apparent reason. But this time when I took it apart I saw that the head on the motor had split in two. Finally! No amount of Super Glue would save it this time!

One of our t-shirt customers told us about a Japanese yacht that had just sailed in with a Yamaha 2hp they wanted to get rid of. They had bought it a couple of months before and had dropped it in the water before they ever used it. They had it cleaned and it ran, but they decided they didn't want a motor that had been 'dunked'. These people must have been new yachties. If they asked around the anchorage they would have found that just about everyone's motor had been underwater at least once.

We told the Japanese couple all this because they seemed like nice people, but it didn't matter. They had already bought another motor and just wanted to get rid of this one. No problem. A hundred bucks later we owned a new 2hp motor. What a deal!

After our goodbyes, and getting the motorcycle secured on deck, we raised anchor and sailed out the pass with ten knots of wind and clear skies. We weren't planning to go very far. The island of Mbengga was only a day's sail away, and that was where we decided to head.

Mbengga was the Fijian island where the legendary 'fire-walkers' came from. The island is about three miles long, four miles wide, and mountainous. The island also offered a few protected anchorages, or so it appeared on the chart.

Each anchorage had a small village on shore and we picked the best looking cove on the chart and sailed on in.

We anchored in a picturesque setting off a tiny village with steep mountains on all sides and colorful reefs dotting the anchorage. With Shadowfax securely at anchor we grabbed some kava and went ashore to present our Sevusevu. The Sevusevu is a very ancient ritual where a visitor presents his gift of kava to the village chief and asks for permission to visit his people, fish in his water, or walk on his land. The short ceremony is mandatory for every village we visited, even if the villages were right next to each other.

As we pulled the dinghy up on the shore we were immediately met by one of the natives and led to the chief's hut. Most of the huts were made of tiki thatch, but a few were made of old pieces of wood that looked more like driftwood than lumber. The chief's home was one of the wooden type. When we entered the chief's house we found him sitting on the floor waiting for us. Actually the floor was all there was to sit on... not a stick of furniture anywhere.

We had read about how to present the Sevusevu, so we knew what to expect. I approached the chief and sat next to him, I placed the Kava on the floor in front of him (never hand it to him) and then just waited. His daughter stood by the door and interpreted what the chief said to us since the chief could only speak Fijian. He performed a couple for short chants, with some hand clapping and other rituals, and his daughter told us he was welcoming us to his village and to enjoy our stay.

Once the Kava was accepted, we were free to roam around and check the place out. This small village was the kind of place that comes to mind when you think of the Fijian Islands. Friendly natives with lots of small children running around narrow dirt paths in between tiki thatch huts. Just about all the food they needed they were able to grow in the hills behind the village. The rest came from fishing in the lagoon. The huts and paths were incredibly clean, and you could see the pride these people had in their surroundings. It's true they didn't have any money, buy they were far from poor.

Behind one of the huts we found a dozen or so kids playing a game. We watched for a while, and it looked like full-contact baseball. One of the kids would pitch the ball (small coconut) to another kid who would hit it with his bat (large stick), and then everyone else would chase and tackle the kid who caught it (bare handed). They really seemed to be having fun, and it wasn't until I started to pass out a few balloons that the game broke up. Balloons were always a hit. I could twist up a balloon-dog in seconds!

That night while comfortably at anchor a strange phenomenon took place. The wind picked up to 20 knots from the east, and the hills and valleys of Mbengga took this wind and funneled it into our protected anchorage in gusts as strong as 60 knots. No way could we get any sleep, so we took turns with watches in case the anchor started to drag. We also couldn't move the boat until daylight because of all the reefs and coral heads in the lagoon. What a nasty night. The wind threw Shadowfax around on her anchor from one side to the other whenever one of these wind bullets slammed into us.

At first light we dinghied ashore to apologize for having to leave their beautiful village so soon, but they did understand the problem. In fact, we were told that this intense wind was a common problem for their village.

As soon as we left the bay the wind calmed down and we started to look for another village to visit. In no time we found a bigger village to check out. This village turned out to be the fire-walking village of Rukua.

Once Shadowfax was again safely anchored, we dinghied ashore to present the Sevusevu. We were met by one of the locals and he led us to the chief's hut. This chief's hut was small like the other chief's hut in the first village, but it was made of concrete instead of wood and tiki thatch. We were told that the Peace Corps had donated enough concrete for most of the homes in this village of 200 people.

We laid the yanggona root (kava) on the floor in front of the chief and again noticed the fact that there wasn't any furniture anywhere in the house. The chief of Rukua was a bit younger than the first chief. He didn't look a day over ninety. Fire-walking must be a healthy thing to do.

After being accepted to the village, we thanked the chief and left to look around. Immediately we met a few of the men who just returned from farming their crops on the mountainside. As with the other village, they were able to grow all the fresh vegetables they needed for their village, and even have some to sell or trade with other villages. They explained they always have enough to eat - except when cyclones rolled through.

When I asked how often cyclones hit the area we were told, "We have at least one cyclone every year that will damage the crops and destroy a few homes, but about every five years we get one that makes us rebuild our entire lives." This fact seemed to upset us a lot more than it did the locals. After a few thousand years of this, they must have been accustomed to cyclones making a mess.

We were taken on a tour of the village and were again impressed at how spotless everything was. Even if a building was falling apart, it was still clean. At the end of our tour we were invited to a kava drinking party that night. We had no idea what to expect, but we knew it would be one of those experiences we would never forget.

They told us to watch from the boat for a blinking flashlight on shore and that would be the signal for us to come in for the party. Very double-oh-seven-ish.

At eight that evening we sighted the light and went ashore. Our host, Simonie, led us into his concrete hut and had us sit on the mat covering the floor. With the exception of a small bench in the corner, I again noticed the lack of furniture. When I asked why nobody seemed to have any furniture, he said all he needed was the bench. He said he would sometimes take it outside and sit on it to watch the sunset. I don't think it ever occurred to him to sit on it inside the hut. After all, he had a perfectly good mat.

The kava bowl was carved from one piece of vesi (hardwood) and could easily hold three gallons of kava. I was told that I was to be the guest of honor and would have to lead the drinking. I was sure I could handle a job like that.

Simonie made a production of preparing the drink with chants, hand-clapping, and quite a few mystical movements. Once the kava was prepared and the five people present were seated around the kava bowl, I was told to say the word "talo," which means serve. Simonie filled half a coconut shell with the drink and instructed me to say "bula," which is a greeting, and then to clap once and drink the entire contents.

I can't say that my first drink of kava was pleasant, but it wasn't exactly terrible either. It tasted like wood mixed with water, which is exactly what it is. Once I finished the drink I clapped three times and said "matha," which meant empty. The coconut was again refilled and passed to Gretchen. The ritual was repeated until everyone in the room had finished a drink.

The first effect we noticed was that our lips and tongue went numb. I couldn't help wondering what we had gotten ourselves into this time. More people started wandering into the hut, and each time it was again up to me to say talo and start the process all over again. Before we knew it there were 7 people sitting around the bowl, and Simonie had refilled it three more times. After the first couple of gallons we didn't mind the taste and, in fact, started to enjoy it.

Throughout the night I questioned everyone about this fire-walking routine. When I asked them who in the village did the walking and how they practiced, I was surprised at what I was told. They said that fire-walking is in their blood; therefore, everyone was a fire-walker - women included. As for practicing, they knew from birth that they could do it, so what was there to practice. The men said they must avoid women and not eat coconuts for two weeks before they fire-walk. The women were smart enough to let the men do all the fire-walking, but they didn't doubt for a second that they could do it. A few of these Mbengga fire-walkers have travelled the world and performed in front of kings and presidents.

At one point during the kava ceremony we ran out of ground up root and had to step outside to grind up more. The root was ground in a large mortar with four of us taking turns doing the pounding. The next step was to put the kava in a cloth sack and soak it in water in the kava bowl. This step was once done by having the village virgins chew and spit out the root and water into the kava bowl. I don't know if they stopped this because of health reasons, or from the lack of willing virgins, but we were glad they used the cloth sack.

The kava party lasted well into the night, and we had a terrific time talking to everyone and saying "talo" whenever it looked like someone was ready for a drink. I didn't want to keep anybody waiting or show that we 'Yanks' couldn't keep up. The next day we were told that my timing was good... just a little faster than they were used to.

As we walked from the party back to the dinghy, I noticed the full effect of a night's worth of kava drinking. I couldn't really walk straight, and my vision wasn't exactly up to par. Once back on the boat and down below, Gretchen walked right into the main mast. Maybe this stuff had something to do with their abilities to fire-walk. I'm glad I never got the urge to try fire-walking, but I was sure this wouldn't be my last kava party.

After a pleasant three days at the village of Rukua, we sailed away with a crowd of new friends waving from shore. We decided to sail 100 miles to the western side of Viti Levu Island. We left at dusk for the overnight sail in not-so-nice weather. The wind was strong but behind us, so we didn't see any problem other than just another rough ride.

As the night came over us, squally weather rolled in and the winds increased to just over thirty knots. Our course would keep us between reefs for the whole trip, so we had to stay extra alert for current changes or wind shifts. If we went a couple degrees off course for as little as a half hour, we could end up on a reef. As the seas built, the trip became exciting. Actually, thirty knots in the daytime could be considered exciting. Thirty knots on a dark night with reefs all around is nerve-wracking.

The next day we sailed up to Navula pass for a somber entrance. This was where a fellow sailor we knew had lost his boat on the entrance reef just a few months earlier. Fortunately no one was killed, but the boat was a total loss. Maybe knowing how many yachts had been lost in these waters helped to keep us a little more alert.

Our reason for sailing to this part of the island was to find Fiji's main airport near the town of Nadi. Friends from Florida were going to fly in and visit us for a couple days on their way to Australia. We were sure we could give them one of our wham-bam tours in the short time they would be there.

We managed to get Shadowfax anchored, and ourselves to the airport the next day to meet their 5am flight. It's hard to imagine that they could travel in one day the distance it took us over two years to travel. On the other hand, look what they missed.

After lots of hugs, we managed to get their luggage into a taxi and made our way back to the boat. We were anchored off the sandy beaches of the Regent Motel. The motel management kindly let us leave our dinghy on their beach. They even arranged for our 5am taxi and happily answered all our 'tourist type' questions. The Regent bar had a huge kava bowl – always full – and free.

After Jim and Dede's long flight, we thought a leisurely sail to the island of Maloilo Lailai 15 miles away would help them unwind. Their adventure had to start somewhere, but we didn't think it would get exciting quite so fast.

We were sailing with a great wind and all the sails pulling us along at six knots when we first noticed a large sailboat a half-mile behind us. The boat appeared to be one of those million-dollar racing yachts, which I was sure would pass us in no time. As the yacht approached, Dede said what a pretty boat it was and went on to ask if maybe they were getting a little too close?

If you pay attention to sailing rules (we do) an overtaken vessel (us) is to maintain course and speed while and overtaking vessel (him) is supposed to keep clear. I wasn't all that concerned. I thought the owner probably wanted to pass close to get a look at Shadowfax and wave, just as I would have done if I were passing him.

We later found out, however, there were two people on board, and they both thought that the other one was on watch as their autopilot kept them on course. The rules that say to maintain course and speed also say, "If maintaining course and speed doesn't work, run away." Well, not quite in those words, but that's what they mean.

When this huge boat was close enough for us to read the labels on the winches, I spun the wheel to head Shadowfax into the wind as Gretchen said, "Excuse me, sir. Would you mind turning your wheel to starboard a little?" Again, those weren't her exact words, but the people scrambled to take control.

The collision was avoided by inches and once we were at anchor we saw the big yacht anchored nearby. The boat's very red-faced owner dinghied over to apologize. Amazingly he asked if we were the Shadowfax he heard about that silk-screened t-shirts. Of course we accepted his apology. We took new customers any way we could.

At Malolo Lailai we anchored off a small resort called Musket Cove. An enclosed lagoon with tiki thatch huts along the shore made the place really picturesque. Since Jim and Dede could stay only a couple of days, we couldn't rest very long. They were tired after their long flight, but sleep gets in the way of a good time, so off we went to explore.

On the back side of Malolo Lailai we found the village of Solevu. Solevu was a mix of concrete, tiki thatch and wooden huts. The chief's home was by far the largest, and it was entirely made of tiki thatch and bamboo poles. The place must have taken hundreds of hours to build. When the four of us entered to present our Sevusevu, I wasn't the least bit surprised to find a mat covering the floor and not a stick of furniture anywhere.

This time the Sevusevu ceremony took a bit more time, with lots of hand clapping and chanting. At the end of the ceremony, our yanggona root was accepted and we were welcomed to the village.

While we were presenting the kava to the chief, a few of the village women placed mats outside their homes and displayed triton shells and other items they made in the hopes that we would buy something. With a resort nearby, these people had learned the tourist game. It was a little sad to see the old ways of a gift for a gift give way to money, but at least inflation hadn't set in. They were selling $200 triton shells for ten bucks.

We spent a couple of relaxing days at Malolo Lailai Island and managed not to get into any trouble, although we did try. The return sail to the Regent to get Jim and Dede to their flight was uneventful, but I found myself looking over my shoulder for approaching boats a little more than usual.

We took their luggage ashore that afternoon so we wouldn't have to deal with it at four in the morning, which was their departure time. I don't know which one of us finally looked at the calendar and figured it out, (Gretchen, I'm sure), but we were a full day off schedule. Their flight out was the next day. Not a problem, Shadowfax was more fun than the country of Australia anyway. I'm just glad someone noticed before we all showed up at the airport at five in the (wrong) morning. Being near the International Dateline was like a perpetual Twilight Zone.

So now what? A free day with nothing to do. We thought the best thing to do would be to rent a car and check out a few back roads (keeping alert for prisons).

On the other side of Viti Levu Island, the city of Suva is in a rain forest and it would rain almost every day, but this side of the island was very dry. The mountains had more of a desert look, and the little bit of existing vegetation seemed to be screaming for more rain. This side also has more resorts as the climate is more enjoyable for tourists.

Our Fiji drive started out harmless enough. We rode past miles and miles of sugarcane fields and watched as the cane was loaded onto small railway cars that would take it to be processed in the sugar mills of Lautoka, one of the larger towns.

After a little sightseeing we found a dirt road to check out. After we were on the road for about a half-hour we spotted a tiny hand-drawn sign that said, "Pottery Village." Under the sign were a dozen children who were waving and pointing for us to turn toward the village. We're easy... no problem. The kids started running alongside the car as we headed down a narrow, winding road. When we came to a corner I noticed that the road ended right at a river. I looked around for the kids and saw that they were all gone. I started to wonder if this was some kind of Fijian ambush run by ten-year-olds.

When I looked at the other side of the river, I saw all the kids waving for us to cross. Jim was in the back seat, and I heard him say "No!" just as I punched the gas and dumped the clutch. Rental cars are used to this stuff. The car shot across the river without being pushed too far downstream, and we popped out at a small village with ten small huts and a large pottery hut.

We were led into the pottery hut and saw hundreds of items for sale – mostly tiny knick-knack-type- things. The average price for something was $.50, so how could we refuse?

The Fijian lady who was in charge insisted on being called "Lady Di." We had such fun laughing and talking with all the people of the village. It's hard to imagine that we bought $40 worth of $.50 items. The entertainment was worth it, and the village needed the money, so we didn't mind.

After we left our new friends at the village we looked at the map and it showed a dotted line along the dirt road we were on. It showed that if we followed the dotted line far enough we could get back to Nadi and civilization. These back roads are always good for an adventure, so we took off along the narrow, bumpy, dusty trail. There were so many people walking along this trail we had to continually wave. I felt like I was running for political office. Vote for me! Vote for me!

We stayed on this incredibly rough road for a couple of hours before we decided to stop and ask, "Can we get there from here?" We saw three women walking along the road and when we told them where we were going, the expression on their faces was priceless.

The tallest one looked at us and said, "Nadi!?!' She then looked up the road in the direction we were going and said, "There are lots of rocks up there." As she said this, she held her hand up at waist high to show how big they were. Then she said, "You won't be able to get past the trees either." No hand signals were needed as we all knew how big trees are. Then she continued, "You people better go back." Our rental could cross rivers, but I didn't think it could cross the great divide. Oh well, it was fun while it lasted.

A couple of hours of retracing our steps (again waving the entire way), we cheered when we hit the paved road. It was almost dark, so we headed back to the Regent Motel and their kava bowl.

The next morning we put Jim and Dede on their plane and then headed back to Malolo Lailai Island to get back to our t-shirt orders. A regatta for cruising sailboats was leaving from Malolo Lailai and sailing west to the country of Vanuatu (formally called New Hebrides), and we knew we could get some t-shirt orders. We arrived a week early to pass out our brochures. We also decided to join the race.

This Regatta was called the 12th Annual Musket Cove Regatta, and just over 40 yachts showed up for the 511 mile sail. What a party! The regatta was a huge celebration with pig roasts, fun races, more pig roasts and rum flowing like water. Most of the 40 yachts were from New Zealand or Australia, and the rivalry between these two countries made for quite a bit of fun. America was so far away that we didn't really count.

The first thing I noticed about these Kiwis (New Zealanders) and Aussies (Australians) was their seamanship. These guys are great sailors. A few fun races were organized to race around the island, and these people really sailed hard. About half of the yachts were serious racers and they treated every race like it was the America's Cup Race. After a few "my boat can beat your boat" chants at the bar, we were to see some million-dollar yachts with crews of ten go through the paces.

Another interesting thing I noticed was the preparation of 40 yachts going for a 500 mile passage. Very intense! Everyone was running around trying to get things fixed, mailed, bought, secured and organized. Even though we had made many of these 'jumps' before, we found ourselves running around like everyone else. I guess organization is contagious.

The rules of this regatta were a little unusual. Fishing was mandatory. The first boat in was disqualified and had to buy the last boat a case of beer. Blatant cheating is allowed, and there were special handicaps for yachts with ironing boards, hand-drawn charts, a washing machine or children. We were the only boat with a motorcycle on deck, and we were sure that would count for something.

Even though the rules made for a fun race, at least half of the boats were intent on winning, and we convinced them they needed custom t-shirts to wear at the victory dinner. When one boat ordered a couple dozen shirts, it snowballed as their rivals saw what they were wearing. Kind of a "keep up with the Joneses" sort of thing. We discovered that when we went up to a boat from Australia, all we had to say was, "That Kiwi boat over there got a couple dozen and we thought you might want a few." We went through the shirts we bought in Suva in no time and had to sail back to the mainland twice to buy more.

All in all, we had a great time at Musket Cove even though we had to work so hard. Plenty of parties and new friends. Lots of these long-distance cruisers were slowly heading to Australia, which gave us lots of new people to hang around with. We figured if we hung around with these Australians long enough, we might learn and understand Australian. Definitely a hard accent to master.

The regatta started on time with all the boats showing up. The serious racers slipped past the starting line with all of the cruisers trying not to get in their way. Shadowfax crossed the line somewhere in the middle of the pack.

The sail to Vanuatu was a relatively easy sail with the seas not all that huge. As soon as we left Fiji in our wake, it was almost a straight downwind sail with strong trade winds pushing us along. To top it off, this was to be another one of those fantastic full moon passages. One of the most impressive times sailing on any ocean was when a huge full moon lit the way. Midnight watches in the tropics, with steady trade winds, your favorite music, and a full moon, makes life about as good as it can get.

Immediately we put out our fishing lines to try out a fancy new lure Gretchen had bought in Fiji. It looked like a fish with eyes and even had the right colors. It would dive, jump and skip across the water enough to make us think we had a fish on the line all the time. We put that lure on one line, and one of Gretchen's homemade lures on the other line. We didn't use fishing rods very often; we just tied the lines to a cleat and hoped the fish could do six knots with us as soon as we hooked him. Not very sporting, but we were in it for the food.

Within a couple of hours we caught a three-foot mahi mahi and barely had it filleted before we hooked another one. It's easy to guess which lure we caught them both on. The fancy, store-bought lure skipped along behind us as Gretchen's homemade lure did all the work of actually catching fish.

That first night at sea we could see lots of lights all around us from the other racers. It was important to keep a good watch when sailing in a crowd like that. It would have been very embarrassing to ram into a fellow sailor. We were kind of "sailing for America," so we had to behave ourselves. We had already proved to them that everything they heard about Americans being true "capitalists" was true. We sold almost all of them something.

You would think with 40 boats leaving at the same time, and sailing on the same course, we would always be in sight of at least one other boat. Not true. After that first night we never saw another boat. That shows just how big those oceans really are. After the second day we couldn't even reach anyone on the ship's short range VHF radio. We started to wonder if we were going to the right island.

The forecast was for perfect weather with a strong high pressure system moving off the coast of Australia. With such great weather we thought it might be a good idea to put up the spinnaker. After all, we were in a race. We might as well try to go fast.

Our spinnaker was something to see. Most spinnakers have fancy designs and colors. Ours had what looked like a giant lion throwing up into a giant boot. Back in Fiji one Kiwi was heard to say, "Those Yanks look pretty good out there, mate, but they gotta get some help for that poor lion." I'm sure whoever designed the spinnaker didn't have that design in mind, but that's the way it came out. The sail came with the boat and was our best sail - almost new and not that difficult to put up.

Even though our spinnaker wasn't hard to handle, we usually took it down at night. A squall rolling through after dark would create havoc, making it necessary to 'tackle the lion.' But since this passage had such a great weather forecast we decided to leave it up. Besides, we really didn't want to come in last. If I said we had a hassle free run that night, I would be lying.

The weather stayed great, but Murphy's Law followed us in another way. At 11:30pm the spinnaker sheet broke (the line from the boat to the sail). I was just getting to sleep below, with Gretchen on watch, when I woke to a sound like a rifle shot. I flew up on deck to find Gretchen trying to sort everything out. We managed to drop the sail and get a new line on it, but our troubles weren't over yet. When we raised the sail, another line tried to tie itself around our forestay, so we had to drop the spinnaker again.

We could have left it down for the night, but by our third try it was becoming a quest. If we had been crew on one of those multi-million dollar race boats we would have been fired. By the fifth try we managed to get everything in order, and I went back down to sleep. I'm sure after all that exercise I slept better anyway.

As the sail was giving us all this trouble, the rest of the boat was going through its usual breakage of boat stuff... as with any passage. I suppose I could fill a few pages with all the things that go wrong on an ocean passage. Things either break, snap, bend, or as the case with our outside stereo speaker, jump ship. One minute it was there and the next, poof, gone. King Neptune must have been building a stereo. Even though we had to be prepared, it was better not to think about everything that could go wrong with a sailboat: Lines running everywhere with most of them having tons of pressure between ends, and mechanical and electrical equipment that Columbus never had to deal with just waiting to start on fire. All we could do was to deal with it without making a bigger mess in the process. No matter how bad I make it sound, we would never get any sympathy. After all, we were sailing around the world. It's not supposed to be easy.

It's actually just as easy to come up with a list of nice things about a passage. Clear trade wind-filled days, visits by friendly porpoises, the sound of the waves hissing as Shadowfax surfed down the hills. Of course there was always the promise of future exotic ports and the memory of all the friends we had made and places we had seen. In the battle between the good and the bad of long distance voyaging, there's no doubt that the good is a hands-down winner.

Chapter 21

To get back to the race, and since we we're heading to the country of Vanuatu, I should tell you a little bit about the place. In 1774, Captain James Cook sailed to these islands and named them New Hebrides. They remained the New Hebrides until just recently. In 1980 the group of islands won their independence and changed the name to Vanuatu. This made them the youngest country in the Pacific. Vanuatu consists of 13 large and 70 small islands with a total population of approximately 120,000. The area has five active volcanoes, which made earthquakes common throughout the area. In the year 1914, there was a ridiculous compromise between the British and the French when they agreed to rule the islands together. A joint interest, or "condominium" as it was called, created two sets of laws, two police forces, and even two sets of currencies. For such a tiny country this plan never had a chance of working, although the natives put up with it until 1980.

I've skipped over an incredible amount of history about these fascinating islands. Many books have been written about Vanuatu and its past. The first dozen or so missionaries who were sent there were eaten. There were pirates everywhere, and there was forced slavery... not to mention what happened during World War Two. Read up on it. It's good stuff.

Something else that should be mentioned is the local language. It's called Bislama, and I'm sure you've heard it called Pidgin English. If someone looks at you and asks, "Plane bam it falls down wanem time?" they are asking, "What time is the plane due?" There are entire political speeches written in the local newspaper in this amazing language.

Well anyway, you are probably wondering who won the regatta. It wasn't Shadowfax. We started somewhere in the middle and finished the same way... right in the middle. The boat that came in first (by a huge margin of a day and a half) was a 72-foot catamaran, which looked like a giant Hobie Cat. Didn't Dennis Conner pull that trick once in the America's Cup Challenge Race?

This huge boat even got out of the race rule of buying the last boat a case of beer because one of the boats, to this day, hasn't finished. A 42-foot sloop lost interest about halfway and headed south to another destination.

Vanuatu was probably one of the most primitive countries we visited. The country even had villages we weren't allowed to visit. Secret cults and native ceremonies were common. But the port we landed at, Port Vila, didn't fit that description. Port Vila is a small town which seemed to have only one street, with dense jungle on all sides. Shops, markets and even a casino were scattered along the road, making it look like a very modern, but tiny, city.

Vanuatu was one of the easiest countries to clear customs. Actually, it was being in the race that made it so easy. Vanuatu wanted the race to come back each year, so they did their best to make it easy on us.

We sailed in, anchored, and were met by a small boat full of officials who didn't even get out of their boat. We were asked our names, and then they gave us "gifts from the community." The gifts were a couple of six-packs of beer and soda, t-shirts, and coupons for free stuff in town. That's it. We were cleared into Vanuatu.

Once we went ashore to check out this out-of-place town in the middle of the jungle, we were able to figure out the reason this town existed. Lots of New Zealanders were vacationing there, so we asked one of them how this little town got there. He said, "This is a tax-free country, mate. No income tax, no corporation tax, and no capital gains tax." Later we found out that about the only tax was a ten percent hotel tax, which was paid on the honor system. It had to be, because there was no auditor or even a tax collector. We were also told that over 1,000 foreign companies were registered to do business there, and more than 75 banks were operating from post office boxes.

Even though the race was over, the celebrations were just starting. More pig feasts and with prizes for everybody. We won the award for the boat with the "best radio schedule." We never made contact with anybody during the race, but I can't say we really tried.

With all these yachties partying and drinking, the t-shirt and flag business went nuts again. We were getting more orders than we could handle. After a week of drinking and printing t-shirts we needed a break, so we took a little time off to sail around the back side of Efate Island. The thirty miles we sailed took us back at least 200 years and showed us the true Vanuatu.

We found a great anchorage in a small cove at the mouth of a freshwater river. The jungle was close on all sides with parrots flying overhead by daytime and bats flying overhead by night. Mountains were poking up everywhere, and to top it off, we had a volcano off in the distance.

Small villages were scattered throughout the jungle with a commune-type vegetable gardens up the river where the locals were growing their crops. Whole families would paddle by in their dugout canoes on their way up the river to work, or back to their homes on a small island about a mile away. Everyone seemed shy until we managed to get one of the canoes to come close enough to be able to give the kids some balloons. From then on, getting to know the people was easy.

Every day at least a dozen small dugouts full of families would stop by to give us vegetables and fruits and to just visit. We in turn took our dinghy up the river to visit them in their gardens. Whenever we tried to have a conversation with someone, we were never sure if they understood us. We, on the other hand, were positive we didn't understand them. The language of Bislama was hard enough to understand, but it got quite a bit worse when it was spoken at a hundred miles an hour.

Anyway, it didn't matter. By this point in the trip we had learned that you don't have to speak another person's language in order to get along with them. We had a great time inviting a few of them aboard and showing them around. An interesting thing we discovered was that no one liked the taste of any kind of soda. The only drink we had that they could stand was our water, and they didn't like that very much either. They were used to the water from their river, not our water which had come from wells in Fiji.

As we met more and more people we decided to dig deeper into our lockers and find as much clothing as we could to pass on to the families and their children. It was obvious that they needed clothes and also obvious that they were proud. The only way we could get them to take our clothes would be in trade situation.

We started to tell them we needed fruits and vegetables, and when they brought bananas and papaya we would trade for a few shirts or pants. We gave away lots of clothes, but Shadowfax was starting to look like a floating vegetable market.

During our fourth day at this great location one of the village chiefs paddled out from the island a mile away and wanted to invite us to his village church the following day. We accepted his offer and settled down for the night, wondering what kind of adventure this would turn into.

Bright and early the next morning we started the dinghy (so far the new outboard started every time) and slowly made our way over to the village. The village was small with mostly tiki thatch huts. The population was just about 300 people, and half appeared to be children. Their lives were simple, but they were by no means easy. Every day the men would paddle their canoes (in any weather) the mile across the bay to work the fields. The women would take all their children, while the father was at work, and paddle themselves the mile across the bay to collect fresh water to bring back to the village.

We pulled the dinghy up on the shore and were escorted down the narrow dirt path by an assortment of children, dogs and a few farm animals. Most of the people we passed on the way were dressed in their Sunday best (Lots of clothes we had given away). We expected a very simple church service, and as usual, everything wasn't always as it appeared.

The church was a large barn-type, wooden building with windows and holes for flow-through ventilation. The seats on the left were for the women, and the ones on the right were for the men. Gretchen and I were allowed to sit together on the men's side, as over 100 villagers filed into the building. A few more people stayed outside to watch through windows.

Once everyone was inside the tempo changed. Out came four guitars and a Casio rock and roll electric keyboard. A small generator was started behind the church to power the keyboard, and all of a sudden we were in a church revival with everyone singing, clapping and cheering. Very upbeat! Various groups, and a few by themselves, walked to the front of the church and sang their hearts out. It reminded me of a talent show. After each performance everyone applauded and cheered.

We couldn't believe it. This village must have spent two year's income on the instruments and the generator. It couldn't have looked more out of place anywhere in the world. From what we could get out of trying to follow the service, it appeared they'd made up their own religion. Years ago, when the missionaries landed on these islands they probably had less luck converting the locals here than anywhere else they were sent. Most of them were eaten, and in fact, you can shake hands with one of the men who claims to have enjoyed one of the last missionary feasts. It wasn't that long ago.

All in all, we had a great time trying to follow along in the songbook we were given. All the songs were in Bislama and one of the more catchy tunes went something like, "Praise um God, Praise um God, Man no Good, Praise um God," sung to what sounded like a Beatles tune.

After the church service we said our goodbyes and made our way back to Shadowfax to get ready for the short sail back to Port Vila. We needed to get back and finish up a couple of t-shirt orders and prepare for the 300-mile passage to the country of New Caledonia.

On the sail to Vila we had to round a headland called Devil's Point with the wind and a very strong current against us. At one point we were sailing along at just over five knots through the water with the current against us at six knots. We were sailing through the water at a good clip but the current was pushing us backwards. As we were crashing through the seas and going backwards, I glanced over the stern and saw the largest fish we had ever caught hanging on one of our fishing lines (Gretchen's homemade lure, of course).

We pulled aboard a five-foot wahoo! Boy, were we happy. Gretchen dragged it into the cockpit, and I spent the next couple hours cutting it up into fillets. We froze 20 servings aboard Shadowfax and passed out 20 more, which pleased all our friends back in Port Vila tremendously.

We spent one more week in Vila trying to finish up our t-shirt and flag orders when the word came down to us from the local customs agent that they would like it if we quit buying all their country's blank t-shirts. It seems the one and only silk-screen business in Port Vila tried to buy some t-shirts for their business and couldn't find any. Apparently they heard stories about a crazy American woman who was running around buying up all the supplies. It was time to leave anyway so we said our goodbyes and sailed away.

Chapter 22

The passage to French controlled New Caledonia was like spending time in a cement mixer. The wind was again behind us, but the seas were huge and from every direction. Shadowfax tried her best to cope, but the seas were just too much. In the deep trough of the waves the sails wouldn't get any wind so they would just flap, and then when we rode to the top of the wave the sails would fill and snap with a noise like a whip. Not very easy on any of Shadowfax's parts.

The first group of islands we sailed past were the Loyalty Chain Islands of New Caledonia. We'd been told that the natives on these islands weren't very friendly and that it wouldn't be a very good idea to stop. We always found it interesting when we heard something like this. There was obviously only one thing to do. Sail in and check it out.

The largest three islands in this group are called Ouvea, Lifou and Mare Islands. We decided to stop at Mare. We sailed up to a small, beautifully green, mountainous island and tucked Shadowfax under a sheer cliff and dropped the anchor in the shallowest water we could find – 65 feet. Norfolk pines covered the island, and a pine scent filled the air. The water was so clear we could see the anchor lying on the ground as a huge grouper swam up to investigate this new object in his territory.

A few locals were fishing from shore, and we could see them pointing and talking. I stood on the stern of the boat under our largest American flag and waved. One of the locals rowed out and we found out what all the rumors were about.

The locals had nothing against us, as it seems they like Americans just fine. Their problem was with the French government. The natives wanted their independence from the French and apparently they were willing to fight for it. Shots had been fired, and yachts and shipping were being warned away so the locals wouldn't get any support.

We didn't stay very long, but it was a welcome rest from those crazy seas, and we did get to put another false rumor to rest. As long as you don't mind an occasional bullet flying over your head, the Loyalty Islands are a perfect place to visit.

Just 100 miles to the south was the main New Caledonia Island of Grande Terre. We left Mare Island just before dark so we could make landfall early the next day, which gave us enough time to check the books and see what we should expect.

The islands of New Caledonia had a population of approximately 145,000 with the main island being the fourth largest in the South Pacific. The islands are mountainous with the highest peak of 5,400 feet being on the main island. The main island is completely surrounded by a 500-mile coral reef - a scuba diver's heaven!

The French explorer Captain Bougainville discovered these islands, but it was the British explorer Captain James Cook who named them. In 1768 he named them Caledonia, which is the Latin name for Scotland. These islands became part of the French colonies in 1853 and were used as a penal colony.

During World War Two the islands were a prime target for the Japanese because for their strategic location. The U.S., French and New Zealanders maintained large bases on the islands and fierce battles were fought with the Japanese over their control and the surrounding shipping lanes.

Shadowfax coasted into the entrance pass on the northern side of the island with Gretchen on the bow "reef spotting" and me at the helm weaving past the shallows. Thunderstorms followed us in, along with a few patches of heavy rain. We had to motor around to the south side of the island to the capital city, Noumea, to go through all the clearing procedures.

Checking in was a relief, as we only had about a dozen papers to fill out. In fact, we were given a free night at the dock and a loaf of great French bread (I'm of the opinion that all French bread is great). We didn't mention the guns.

Noumea is a modern city with lots of shops, restaurants, and tourists. The population was around 60,000, and the roads were jammed with cars. Pretty hectic, but we figured if you can't beat 'em, join 'em, so we put the motorcycle ashore and entered the flow of traffic.

As usual we tried to find the legalities of using our New Zealand registered motorcycle, and none of the officials had an answer. So we got on and went for a ride.

We drove around Grande Terre Island, and the more we saw, the more we liked it. As soon as we exited the city we found incredible hills, valleys and waterfalls. Not very many people live outside the city, so we found mile after mile of vacant beachfront property looking out over calm lagoon waters. It seems that with French Polynesia and New Caledonia, the French control some of the prettiest real estate in the Pacific.

On one of our longer drives we decided to make a trip to the northern coast. We'd been told the island was pretty desolate on that side, and that made it sound worth checking out. We followed a well-paved road that turned from time to time into clay – all the time never seeing another car or motorcycle. We were starting to think it was true and that nothing was ahead on the northern coast. I was starting to hope for at least one lonely gas station.

Gretchen spotted someone just sitting on the side of the road so we stopped and asked if there was a gas station in our future. Our French was almost non-existent, but we managed to get the message across, and he got the message back to us that pretty much said, "Dream on." We should have asked him what he was waiting for, but since he didn't seem to need any help, we turned around to head slowly back toward Noumea.

Only a couple of minutes went by before two French Police caught up to us and yelled for us to pull over. I was sure we were busted for riding the New Zealand registered bike, but once we pulled over the police zipped on past. We waited a few minutes for them to come back and they never did.

I started the bike to continue on as Gretchen pointed out a couple of cars speeding along toward Noumea. They were two jeeps full of camera equipment and a film crew. Just behind them about two dozen police on motorcycles went past, then a helicopter and a few pickup trucks painted in bright colors with various advertising plastered all over them. This was getting strange. Minutes earlier this road was completely deserted, and now it resembled a parade without an audience.

The next group to pass answered our question. Bicycles... dozens of them going as fast as they could. This was an international bike race hosted by the New Caledonian Government. More police flew past, and a few cars started to pull over to watch. We walked over and found someone who spoke perfect English, actually perfect British, who was with the English team. He told us the race would go on all day, and the only way to get back to Noumea would be to join the flow and try not to get in their way.

We did just that and found it to be a blast. We passed dozens of police along the way, and they must have thought we were part of the race since we had a foreign motorcycle. As we closed in on Noumea, the crowds became thicker until standing room only lined both sides of the streets. We started waving and smiling as we putted along down the road. At least if we ran out of gas it would have been no problem getting a fill. Our audience would surely have helped part of the race crew.

What an experience. When we finally made it back into the city we went to the first ice cream shop we found and had a couple of sundaes to calm us down. After paying $17.50 for two ice creams (we had forgotten how the prices were on these French Islands) we felt a little calmer.

The longer we stayed the more we appreciated the city of Noumea. Officials told us it would be okay if we wanted to stay through the next cyclone season. We were even told we would able to work legally if we decided to stay. This was a tempting offer and we talked it over for a while, but decided it was too risky to stay right in the middle of the cyclone belt without any insurance on the boat. We were both looking forward to spending cyclone season in Australia anyway. Good on ya mate!

After two weeks in the city we again loaded the motorcycle onto Shadowfax and strapped it down for the 900-mile trip to Australia. We sailed out of Noumea with plans to check out the Isle De Pines (also part of New Caledonia) just 30 miles away before we made the big jump toward Oz. We were told the island had beautiful caves on shore and lots of lobster living in the reefs.

To get there we had to stay inside the circular reef that surrounds New Caledonia and sail east. Actually, we had to sail over reefs for almost the whole way. As long as the weather stayed clear we could see the shallows, but in bad weather the route would become treacherous. Many of the reefs and coral heads reached the surface, with no indication on the chart that a reef was even there.

Isle Du Pines is a small resort island where everyone from Noumea would go for vacation, but the place was quiet and un-crowded and the roads mostly unpaved. I could see why they liked to vacation there. What a difference from the city.

We anchored in different locations and explored parts of the island. After asking some locals about finding the caves we'd heard about, we finally found one. No signs, no tourists, and in fact, no road.

Deep, dark and full of stalactites and stalagmites. Bats flew around our heads as we went deeper into the cave and disturbed their sleep. What an eerie place. The cave angled down until we reached a lake at the bottom. Incredible! We were later told if you used scuba equipment it would be possible to swim and dive for miles farther into the cave. It was obvious that to try it without being an experienced cave diver would be crazy... but tempting anyway.

For our lobster dinner - nothing. Not one lobster living near any of our anchorages. It was still worth the trip though. Isle Du Pines was another reason why New Caledonia would be a great place to stay for a while. But we hadn't changed our minds about staying, so we prepared for the jump to Australia.

We considered a passage of less than 500 miles to be no big deal (It's amazing that you get used to something like that), but when they stretched up around 1,000 miles, we took extra time preparing. Over that length of ocean anything could happen. I guess a trip of just a couple of hundred miles could be just as dangerous, but we had started to consider those just short jumps. Since the passage to Australia was about 800 miles, we stocked at least one month's supply of food and as much water as we could carry, which was about 200 gallons.

When everything was packed, stowed and tied down, we were just about ready. Gretchen turned on the ham radio and tuned it in to the Pacific Ocean Weather Net so we could get one last weather report before heading out.

The weather reports we were able to get for the Pacific, when the ham radio could pick them up, came from Rarotonga in the Cook Islands. A dedicated guy named Arnold, who worked at the airport, would take time out every day to relay weather and navigational information to yachts in the Pacific Ocean.

As we worked on the boat the weather report came in loud and clear, and we couldn't believe what we heard. The first thing I said was, "Aww, come on. It's way too early."

Cyclone Tia had formed and was almost in full swing to the north of New Caledonia. Tia was predicted to move right through our location and continue south. Maximum winds were up to 80 knots, and the forward speed was ten. Man, we hated those things.

I put Tia's position on the chart and plotted its forecast position for the next four days. Then I put our future positions on the chart if we decided we wanted to leave and run ahead of it. I didn't really think that would be a very good idea, and when the future positions showed the cyclone catching us on day three, we started to make plans to stay until it passed.

Next, we reviewed the charts to see where the best 'hurricane hole' was. The chart showed a good-size bay on the southern side of Grande Terre Island that looked like the perfect place. If I had to sit down and draw the perfect hurricane hole, this would be it. Far back in the bay a small river branched off and took two ninety- degree bends, finally ending in a small circular harbor surrounded by mangrove trees. The chart showed the water to be shallow with a sand and mud bottom. Perfect.

We sailed Shadowfax the 30 miles back to the main island and up into the bay named "Bay Du Prony." That chart was correct and we were able to get the boat all the way into this narrow river. We entered the small harbor at the end of the river and secured the boat with three anchors and a few lines tied to mangrove trees. What a nice place to spend a cyclone. We were surrounded on all sides by mangrove trees and steep hills just like the chart showed. We were also surrounded on all sides by sharks.

Shark fins were cutting through the water everywhere we looked. None of them appeared all that big, but with this many sharks in one place it was awesome to watch. Maybe they knew that bad weather was on its way and they swam to the safest place they knew. The water was murky, and we were sure we didn't want to go swimming to see if they were friendly. We didn't really want to use the inflatable dinghy either, but we did.

Once we had Shadowfax secure there was nothing to do but wait, so we took the dinghy ashore to investigate. We still had a day and a half to see what this cyclone would do. As Tia got closer we would know more about its wind direction, which would then help to decide which way to tie our bow to keep Shadowfax pointed into the wind.

Once ashore, we walked along the river for about a half mile until Gretchen found a small waterfall that she could dam up at the bottom to make a bathtub. New Caledonia had lots of places like this, and again we found ourselves talking about staying through the season. Nah! Australia was calling!

Back on the boat we tried to imagine what would happen if this cyclone made a direct hit. Lines could break, trees could fall and the water could rise. We planned out different strategies, while the cyclone was deciding to leave us alone.

Tia just grazed Grande Terre Island as it passed. We sat securely in the anchorage as winds of only 30 or 40 knots funneled through the mountains. Not bad, Shadowfax could deal with that. No problem.

We moved Shadowfax out toward the bay entrance so we could take off as soon as the weather looked okay and we gave the seas a couple of days to calm down before we took off for the passage.

When the seas calmed enough and the weather report was good, Gretchen went up on the bow to raise the anchor. It wasn't until the anchor was stowed and we were on our way that I noticed it was Friday. I don't know how many of you have ever heard of the superstition about starting a passage on Friday, but it is definitely a no-no. As we were thinking about what we should do, I remembered a conversation I had in New Zealand about boating superstitions.

There were a couple dozen yachtie-type people hanging around the Opua Cruising Club and I asked what they all thought of the hundreds of sailing superstitions. This really got everyone's attention. It seems that the boating world has its own superstitions that make all the land-based superstitions (like throwing salt over your shoulder or walking under a ladder) seem tame.

When I asked what superstitions they believed, everyone started talking at once. Here are some of them: Never set sail on Friday. Don't ever whistle on a boat. Don't own a green boat. Don't set sail on Friday. Never talk about or name your boat after a horse. (So much for the name Shadowfax). Whistle forward of the mast if you want more wind. Put a naked woman on deck if you want less wind. Never, never start a passage on Friday. Don't sail on the first Monday in April or the second Monday in August. Never eat chicken on a boat. The list goes on and on, but the "never leave on a Friday" was mentioned the most.

I tried to find out if anyone knew where any of these crazy ideas came from, and not one person had any idea what it was all about. Crazy stuff, but it was obvious that the most prevalent superstition that was repeated over and over again was never to start a passage on Friday. Gretchen and I thought this would be as good a time as any to test this crazy superstition. Maybe sailing on a boat named after a horse along with eating chicken on the passage would cancel each other out.

We sailed through the entrance channel and immediately the wind picked up to a perfect 25 knots off our stern quarter. We sailed at a steady six knots toward Australia.

What a perfect trip. Hundreds of porpoise kept us company most of the way, with a few turtles coming to the surface to check us out. For a few hours we had at least fifty pilot whales surfing down the waves with Shadowfax. A pilot whale looks somewhat like a huge porpoise with the blunt nose of a whale. More cute than scary.

As we approached Australia the shipping activity picked up, and at one time we had five huge ships in sight all going different directions. We called the ships on the VHF radio and found the crews monitoring the radios to be very talkative. I suppose those people didn't have a whole lot to do. Talking to us probably kept hem awake. We were trying to get one of them to throw us some ice cream, but no way. It would have been easier to talk them out of all their charts.

Chapter 23

Australia is geologically the oldest continent in the world, and is also the smallest. The continental U.S. (excluding Alaska) is just about the same size as Australia, and the entire population was only just over 17 million (about the same as New York). Archaeological studies show hat the first people arrived there as many as 30,000 years ago... probably from Asia.

Captain James Cook charted the east coast of Australia in 1770 and claimed it for England. After losing the U.S. Colonies, the British thought this would be a good substitute, and also thought Australia would be a good place to set up a penal colony. By the time the British stopped using the country as a prison in 1868, there were over 150,000 convicts on the continent. Many people we met while we were in the country could tell us what crime it was that their ancestors were said to have committed. Many times with a bit of pride in their voice.

For the land, diverse is a good word for it. A mountain range stretches along the east coast reaching a height of over 7,000 feet. Beyond the mountains to the west, there is everything from beautiful rivers and pastures to hundreds of miles of desert, which has claimed the life of many travelers who have gone on a 'walkabout' never to be heard from again.

Probably one of the most famous places to visit in Australia is the Great Barrier Reef off the northeast coast - 1,250 miles of reef to be exact. At some point we were going to have to weave our way through it before we sailed out of the country. The animal life in Australia is truly extraordinary. The rain forest contains such things as kangaroos, which can jump as far as 27 feet. Also koalas, wombats, wallabies, dingos, bandicoots and platypus can be found in different parts of the country. I also should mention the 1,500 species of spiders, 140 species of snakes (the rattlesnake of the U.S. barely rates in their top 20 for toxicity) and the shark-infested waters. To top it all off are the saltwater crocodiles which grow to a length of over 20 feet. On the bright side, we heard chance were low of ever running into the vicious Tasmanian Devil.

The bird life is noisy and colorful. Pigeon-size parrots were everywhere with cockatoos and kookaburras filling all the trees. Australia also has a huge, flightless bird called an emu that looks a lot like an ostrich.

We were definitely excited about getting to Australia... one of the biggest milestones of the trip. The plan was to stop somewhere for the upcoming cyclone season and set up shop selling our t-shirts. We weren't sure where we wanted to stay, but we decided to head for a small port called Bundaberg to clear in.

As far as the passage went, I think the log book sums it up best, "Fast, perfect sail, comfortable, no fish." Even the list of "things that broke" was held to less than a dozen items. I'm glad we were able to put that "Don't sail on a Friday" thing to rest. If we were wrong... well, better not to think about it.

We tied to the customs wharf at the mouth of the Burnett River on Thanksgiving Day after a total of five and a half days at sea. Australia was known to be the toughest place in the Pacific to clear customs, and our experience proved it to be true. We didn't mind being searched, inspected, folded, stapled and mutilated, but we did mind when the officials were arrogant. At least the customs officials were the only rude Australians we met during our nine-month stay.

After we were cleared into the country, we were free to roam around and find a secure place to anchor. We motored farther up the Burnett River, which led to the small town of Bundaberg.

Once we were anchored and had made our way to town, Gretchen summed it up best then she said she was "shell shocked." Big Macs, Pizza Huts, Sizzlers and grocery stores chock full of everything you could want. The small islands of the Pacific didn't offer much in consumer goods, and we had forgotten what a shopping mall was (which on our budget was probably good). Even though Bundaberg had all these things, it was still a pleasant small town and we enjoyed walking from end to end. An enjoyable place, but not the one in which we wanted to spend cyclone season.

After a week of hanging around Bundaberg and getting reacquainted with civilization, we raised anchor to sail 30 miles south along a protected, shallow waterway until we came to a pass called Wide Bay Bar - locally known as Wipe-Out Bar. We arrived near the pass at dusk and decided to stop and sleep for the night before we headed out the pass to continue south.

The next morning we explored a few of the back channels and then tied to an old rickety pier. A few locals were fishing from the pier, so we struck up a conversation which eventually led to a discussion about the pass called Wide Bay Bar. We were told, "Wide Bay's closed, mate, too rough. Breakers. Currents. It's a mess." We were also told that within a couple of days it should calm down and be reopened. The weather didn't appear to be very stormy, and the wind was down to ten knots, which made all this rough water talk a little hard to believe. We decided to stay put until the 'locals' gave us the okay. If you sailed around the world without heeding the advice of locals in their waters, I don't think you would make it very far.

Our stay turned out to be enjoyable. None of the local boats wanted to tie to our rickety pier, so we were free to stay as long as we wanted. We just had to watch the tidal range, which was 9 feet, which would hang Shadowfax by her dock lines if we didn't keep adjusting them.

Across the narrow strip of land between the bay and ocean, we got to stretch our legs on the ten-mile-long deserted beach. One of the fishermen offered to take us in his four-wheel-drive truck to a nearby town, and what a cool ride! The truck drove right down the beach, which was also their main road... at least at low tide. We had just arrived and we were starting to like Australia a lot.

After a few days of adjusting dock line we were told that "Wipe Out Bar" had calmed down enough for us to make it out... possibly. We left at the break of dawn and followed all the shrimp boats that had also been waiting for the pass to calm. Once out into the pass, we could tell why this place had acquired such a reputation. Five miles out, the depth of the waster was still the same as it had been at the entrance – ten feet.

The sea seemed extremely rough for such calm weather, with every third wave crashing over the bow. Gretchen said this was one of those times that it was better not to look. No problem for Shadowfax though. She crashed through the waves and strong incoming current and broke into calm waters at just about lunchtime.

From 'Wipe-Out,' we made a fast 70-mile passage south to the Mooloolaba River - fast because of the 40-knot northerly wind that smashed into our stern shortly after leaving the bay. The local weather report called for "a chance of squalls," and since it blew like crazy and rained for the next six days, I guess they were right.

The Mooloolaba River entrance was a little on the small side, but without any sandbars or major obstructions, we didn't have any problems getting in. Once we were in, we did two things that were totally different.

The first was to find a marina to dock Shadowfax. And the second was to prepare the boat so we could leave it for a couple of weeks. We always lived at anchor, so we found it unusual to stick the boat in with a hundred other boats that all seemed to just sit without ever going anywhere. We found a pretty little marina at the end of a short canal, but I don't think Shadowfax liked it very much. I think she's much more comfortable swinging on her anchor line.

For the reason we were leaving the boat, I have to back up a couple thousand miles to the Fijian Islands and the Regent Motel. When we returned after dropping our friends Jim and Dede off at the airport, our dinghy was on the beach at the Regent tied to a tree. As we untied the dinghy we met Murray and Pam Rowley who were in Fiji on a working vacation from Australia. We became friends and spent a couple of days with them in Fiji. When they left to fly home, they told us to be sure and look them up when we got to Australia. Whenever somebody said something like that to us, they had better keep the coffee hot and the beer cold.

We called Murray and Pam when we arrived, and with true Australian hospitality they offered to come pick us up and take us to their home. It felt strange leaving Shadowfax behind, but we packed a few things, checked the dock lines and took off to spend Christmas and New Year's Day with a real family at a real home with a real tree. Christmas trees on the boat tended to be a little short.

The Rowley family accepted us immediately. The fact that Murray's house had a pool, spa, tennis court, four horses and two dogs didn't make it very tough on us. Gretchen and I didn't mind mucking out the stables, playing with the horses and getting our hands dirty instead of salty, although I'm pretty sure that stuff wasn't dirt.

After a terrific two weeks at their house we decided to go back to the boat and sail it up the Brisbane River, which would be closer to Murray and his family. They were moving from their beautiful house on the river to a house even more beautiful, and they asked us if we would help them move.

Again we were down to our last few dollars, but this time it was a little different. We were told by the customs agent when we entered the country that we wouldn't be allowed to work "in any way, shape, or form." He told us if we did, and were caught, we would be told to leave within 24 hours. Being thrown out in the middle of cyclone season didn't sound like a whole lot of fun, so we decided to keep a low profile as far as working was concerned. We really didn't have a choice though. We had to work a little, or not eat for the entire cyclone season. Five cyclones at the same time were rolling around different areas of the Pacific and we didn't want to end up rolling around with them.

Even with working in 'low profile' mode, Australia sure was a great place to kill time and we stayed at the small marina in Mooloolaba for about a month before sailing for the Brisbane River. The Australians at the marina were incredibly hospitable and kept insisting that we "stay for one more party, mate." Not to mention silk screening a few shirts for them – they promised not to tell.

When we finally broke away from the marina, after saying the usual 1,000 goodbyes, we exited the Mooloolaba River to find 30 knots of wind and a six-foot swell waiting for us. After being tied to a marina for so long, everything was out of its secure place.

Stowing things on a boat is an art. Imagine taking your china – yes, we did have some china – and then trying to secure it inside your washing machine so nothing would break when you turned it on. During long passages we would stuff towels in between noisy glasses or anything else that was banging around. Anyway, after the first few minutes we were able to get almost everything stowed, and the sails set for a leisurely 42-mile sail to the Brisbane River entrance.

We entered Moreton Bay a few miles before reaching the Brisbane River entrance and it was such a nice bay we decided to anchor for the night - maybe two. We anchored between Moreton Island and six huge, rusty old ships that were sunk in a group as a fish haven.

Moreton Island is about 20 miles long and is 90% National Park. Miles and miles of beach with hardly a person in sight. Moreton Island was advertised as having the world's highest sand dune - a strange claim to fame - but the place sure was beautiful. Even the six ugly wrecks that were sunk in a few feet of water were fascinating to look at. Millions of tiny, multicolored fish were using the wrecks to hide from their larger predators. It looked like a gigantic aquarium.

Our one or two night stay turned into four nights, but we finally raised anchor and headed toward the entrance to the Brisbane River. In order to catch the incoming current to help us get up the river, we stopped and anchored until we thought the current should be with us. We were told by locals that it would be almost impossible to get up the river against the current, and by using the local tide and current charts, I tried to figure exactly when the current would change. I also called the Brisbane River Control on the V.H.F. radio to get their opinion. When I was sure we had it right, we raised the anchor and headed toward the entrance.

We entered the river against a four-knot current, and I kept telling Gretchen, "Don't worry, it'll change any minute." We crawled up the river hour after hour, memorizing every tree we passed. At one point I though we should just anchor off to the side and wait, but then I'd tell myself, "any minute now," and kept going.

Just after dark we rounded a corner and the city of Brisbane came into sight. What a beautiful sight too! Glass towers lit up, huge paddlewheel tour boats, and people everywhere. Gretchen and I weren't very hot on cities, but this one was impressive. After places like Tonga and Fiji, this was an awesome sight.

For transient yachts like ours, Brisbane had installed pilings along the edge of the river for boats to tie to. Very thoughtful of them. We tied the bow to one pile, the stern to another, and joined the thirty or so boats that were already there. For a backyard we had the Brisbane Botanic Garden. The Botanic Garden Park is huge, with acres of foliage, narrow walking trails, and free rock concerts on the weekends. We had to pay the city of Brisbane a small fee for the use of the pilings, but it was definitely worth it. Believe it or not, the city of Brisbane even included free washing machines right at the dinghy dock for us to use.

As a side note, the current finally turned in the right direction at just about the time we tied to the pilings. So much for local tide tables and current diagrams.

We were happy about the whole piling situation. Shadowfax was secure and away from nasty cyclones, and we were also just twenty minutes from Murray's house by motorcycle. Our first project was to make the motorcycle legal in Australia.

When we cleared in we were told by the nasty customs man that no way would we be able to legally use the bike, and to never put it ashore. Of course, we didn't believe him. There is always a way. We found our way to the registry of motor vehicles in Brisbane and told them what we needed. Their answer was something like this, "No problem, mate. Bring the bike in and let us have a look. If it looks okay, well give you a letter giving you written permission to use it for six months. If you find yourself still here in six months, come on back and well give you another letter. No worries."

Gretchen and I went back to the boat and lowered the motorcycle into the dinghy to bring it ashore. This time we had a bigger crowd watching from shore then we ever had before. We were getting pretty good at lowering it into the inflatable, and we managed to dinghy to a boat ramp without dropping it into the river. Whenever people watch us do this tricky maneuver, I'm sure they just pretend to root for us... really hoping to see us drop the thing into the drink. Maybe because that's what I'd be thinking if I were them. I guess we all have a dark side.

We rode the bike to the registry (remembering to drive on the left) where our new friend sent someone out to inspect it. Ten minutes later we had a very official-looking letter saying just what we were told it would say - six month's use. The hardest part to believe is we got through all this without paying anything. No one seemed interested in money... they just seemed to want to help us out.

There were lots of things for us to take care of while we were in Brisbane. We had to provision the boat for another long haul, and we had to get all the nautical charts we would need. In the States we bought charts to get us to Australia, but no further. Of course, before we restocked the charts, we had to figure out where we wanted to go.

Our original plan was to go from Australia south through the Indian Ocean to South Africa, but friends from other boats we had met were trying to talk us into sailing with them toward the Red Sea and the Mediterranean. After talking it over and looking at a map of the world, we decided to head for the Red Sea. Instead of possible gale force winds around South Africa, we would have to deal with the crazy political situation of the Red Sea countries. Clearing customs in those places would be interesting.

We also had to get a few t-shirt orders to pay for all the supplies and charts we needed along with enough money to apply for a cruising permit for Indonesia. The cost for the permit was $175.00 U.S. with a three-month waiting period after submitting it.

We rowed around telling people on boats tied to the pilings about our custom t-shirts and flags and since most of the boats were also deciding where they planned to go next, the courtesy flag business was a hit! Since every boat sailing into a new country needs to fly that country's flag as a courtesy, every boat needed flags – lots of them. Boats sailing toward Africa (either south or north), or east into the Pacific, needed flags for at least ten countries. At $10.00 to $15.00 a flag, we could make $100 or more from each boat. Gretchen had two sewing machines aboard and could get all the material locally. We were in business.

With our persistent (and sometimes annoying) salesmanship, we were able to make enough money to apply for the Indonesian cruising permit and to start ordering our charts. We had learned a lot since leaving the States as far as charts went. We were just about the only people who had real charts aboard.

Copies... that's the way to go. Sailors who needed charts got together and swapped what they had - all copies - with what they needed, and then someone would gather up all the charts and take them to make copies. For $.50 we could have a full-size chart copied. The charts came out great, but even if they didn't, we found most reefs and islands not to be exactly where they were charted anyway.

While all this was going on, we were also helping Murray and his family move. Lots of heavy work, but we still managed to have a blast doing it. Once we had them moved into their gorgeous new home, we moved in too - at least most of the time. For the three months we were in Brisbane, two of them were spent with Murray and his family.

His new house had a pool and tennis court, so we had no trouble keeping ourselves busy whenever we stayed. To be made part of a family like the Rowleys was definitely an honor. Greater friends can't be found. Staying with them also helped us as we tried to master the Australian language – one of the toughest in the world, mate. The statement, "Fair dinkum mate see yaat the uni after breckie for a barbie thisavo," actually means something.

As cyclone season tapered off we started to prepare for the next leg of the trip. To leave Australia we were going to have to sail 1,500 miles up the coast and behind the Great Barrier Reef until we sailed "over the top." The charts for the trip showed miles and miles of reefs with nothing but the word "un-surveyed" written on the chart. On the bright side, we could spot dozens of anchorages that looked to be shallow and protected.

Before we left Brisbane we made a deal with a cat. Actually, we made the deal with the cat's owner. The people who owned this cat owned a beautiful black sailboat named Fram. Ralph and Phyllis had sailed out of California and had to fly back take care of some business. They had no idea what to do with their 15-year-old, mean and unstable, Siamese cat with a name we couldn't spell.

We offered to take the cat for five or six months until they returned from the States. The catch was we had to sail 750 miles north to the city of Townsville to get the cat, and we wouldn't meet up with Fram to give the cat back until Bali in Indonesia. Or maybe Singapore. It looked like this feline was going to be our boat guest for awhile.

Brisbane was one of the hardest places we ever had to leave. A huge park for a backyard, tons of new friends on the other boats around us, and the motorcycle conveniently parked nearby. But most of all, Pam and Murray, along with the rest of their family. They had adopted us as much as we had adopted them. Good friends for life no matter how many miles we put between us.

After our goodbyes were said, we loaded the motorcycle onboard and untied from the pilings to motor out the river – this time with the current pushing us along. Our first stop was the same place we anchored months earlier - off Moreton Island where all the fish-haven wrecks were sunk.

The plan was to stop for one day so I could jump in the water to clean all the river scum from the bottom of Shadowfax. Since Australia had so many dangerous animals, I got into the habit of listening to the radio before I ever went into the water. Australia would broadcast shark alerts on the radio and TV, and just before Gretchen and I jumped in the water we heard an alert on the radio about Moreton Bay, "Large schools of sharks have been spotted feeding in the area. Swimmers should take caution until further notice." Scratch one bottom cleaning job. The water was a little murky, and we didn't want a shark to confuse us with a tasty trout.

We left Brisbane in the company of the sailboat Princess Del Mar with Jim and Gwen from California aboard. They said they would keep us motivated and moving so we could get to the cat before the owners had to fly out. We figured we had to sail 50 miles each day for the next two weeks to make it on time, and since Jim and Gwen were early risers we might have a fair chance of making it.

We wanted to get some miles behind us so we sailed for two days and nights in rough conditions against a fairly strong current. We rolled around uncomfortably, taking watches and trying to sleep. It's impossible to get into a routine when sailing in rough weather for only a couple of nights. When morning finally comes, you feel about as rested as a fighter after the tenth round. When the wind goes against a strong current, the waves seem to stand straight up, as was the case for us. When the sun rose we realized we were better off when it was dark and we weren't able to see the size of the seas.

The best thing about a trip like that is stopping, and Lady Musgrove Island was a welcome sight. The island reminded us of the coral atolls of French Polynesia. We motored through the entrance pass, followed by Princess Del Mar, and weaved around the coral heads – called 'boomies' in Australia – and up to the small island. There was a slight swell entering the anchorage, but we figured it had to be from all the rough weather we'd just been through.

Although Musgrave looked like an atoll, it was actually called a "fringing reef" and was the most southern part of Australia's Great Barrier Reef. Whatever they wanted to call it, it was still a great place to dive and clean the boat bottom. We were anchored in 15 feet of water and we could see the bottom perfectly. More importantly - no sharks in sight. We did see a 6-foot sea snake swim by, but no place is perfect - well, almost no place.

Since we'd been at sea for two days we figured we were ahead of our 50-mile-a-day schedule, so we stayed put for two days. We worked better under pressure.

If we thought the sail to Musgrave was bad, we weren't ready for the next passage. Rain, high winds, squalls and just about zero visibility followed us for the next 100 miles. At least by this point we were in the lee of the barrier reef, which helped to keep the seas at a respectable height.

One of the stronger squalls that flew through that evening caused us to drop our sails and start the motor so we could continue to make way. This was when I spotted the slight leak on our motor's water pump. Not good. I loosened the cap on the water reservoir so the motor would run without excess water pressure. No parts stores within a few hundred miles, and of all the spares we had, we didn't have a spare water pump.

As we arrived at Great Keppel Island, we marked another 95 miles off our trip and anchored in seven feet of water. Two hours after being safely anchored, and a breakfast of pancakes and bacon, we were just able to move Shadowfax before being grounded on a very low tide. In a few places along the Australian coast the tides could be as much as 17 feet and we promised ourselves, "No more anchoring shallow." We hadn't been aground since leaving Florida, and we didn't want to break our record.

The anchorage off Keppel Island had a larger sea swell than the Musgrave Island anchorage, which didn't make life aboard very easy or comfortable. We checked out one of the local cruising guides and it claimed that Keppel was a "lively" anchorage. It also claimed that was to be the case with most of the anchorages all the way up the coast. From this point north we knew it was much too dangerous to sail between the reefs at night, so we had to grin and bear it while rolling around uncomfortably in the anchorages.

The weather was still squally, but bright and early the next morning we were off again, heading north, with Princess Del Mar sailing right beside us. A few porpoise kept us company during the day with a couple pilot whales off in the distance. No matter how bad the weather became, visiting porpoise always seemed to pick up our spirits. Sleek and playful, they would ride with our bow wake and swim on their sides so they could look back at us. Nice pets - at least for as long as they stayed with us.

Our next stop was a truly beautiful place called Pearl Bay. Again there was a swell, but it was calm enough for us to remove our sails to fix a few small rips, a never-ending job with 20-year-old sails. Soon we'd have more thread and tape than sail.

Pearl Bay was a deserted cove with a huge sandy beach and Norfolk Pines covering all the hills. We enjoyed walking the shore and swimming near the beach, but Pearl Bay had one problem. It was a bombing range. On the up side, this meant there probably weren't any saltwater crocodiles left to eat us. We liked the bombing range so much we stayed for an extra day. At five the second morning, Jim and Gwen on Princess Del Mar were yelling over to us, "Hey guys! Anchors up. Gotta go."

Even though we didn't want to leave, we were glad we did. We woke to a clear day with perfect wind. Gretchen pulled out the spinnaker, and we flew along all day. It's funny how anyone could consider 10 mph flying, but there you go...

Besides the weather and enjoying a great sail, the day had a low point. When I looked in the engine room while we had the generator on to run the freezer and charge the batteries, I discovered all the oil had decided to leave the generator and spill on to the floor. It's not easy to clean up four quarts of oil on a moving boat. No matter how many rags and paper towels you have aboard, you're sure to use them all.

Like the leak I discovered in the water pump on the main motor, the seal on the water pump on the generator was the problem. As water passed through the seal, it over-filled the generator oil pan and all the oil leaked out onto the floor. At least we could still run the fridge with an alternate pulley from the compressor to the main motor. I'd have to be at anchor in order to clean all the saltwater from the generator to be able to use it again.

The weather was so clear, and we were moving along so nicely, that we decided to do another overnight sail. The way looked clear of reefs so we decided to go for it.

The next morning we arrived at another "lively anchorage" at Brampton Island. Brampton was the first island in the famous chain of islands called the Whitsundays.

The Whitsundays are a chain of over 70 islands which were discovered by Captain James Cook on the Whit Sunday of 1770 (Man, that guy went everywhere). All the islands are mountainous with lots of rock formations along the shoreline. The area reminded us of The Bay of Islands in New Zealand, except it was much warmer and, of course, more "lively."

Up again at five the next morning for another great sail with Princess Del Mar prodding us along. This time we used all the working sails and flew along in the protected waters behind the Great Barrier Reef. By evening we had made it to the largest island, Whitsunday Island, and anchored in the protected cove named Cid Harbor. Protected but "lively."

Getting up early was becoming a little old, but again at five in the morning Princess Del Mar was raising anchor and calling for us to do the same. We motored from the harbor in a complete calm and had motored about two miles before the water pump on the main diesel motor let go for good. All the water drained from the motor, and that was that.

We raised the spinnaker to try and catch every puff of wind, but there weren't all that many puffs to catch. Jim and Gwen on Princess Del Mar offered to tow us, but we figured if we waited long enough the wind would come up. After all, what would Captain Cook have done if his water pump quit?

After three hours we noticed the current had carried us four miles backwards, but we still weren't ready to quit. Princess Del Mar was quietly waiting in the wings for us to give up and accept a tow. We were persistent and kept saying, "Give us just another hour. I'm sure the wind will come up." After four hours the spinnaker was still hanging limp and almost dragging in the water. We pulled it down and accepted the tow.

Princess Del Mar towed us to a place called Arlie Beach 10 miles away. As soon as we put the anchor down in the small cove, we started to talk over what to do next. We called Phyllis and Ralph (from the "cat" boat) on the ham radio and told them what part we needed. Townsville is a small city and we thought they might have a chance of finding a water pump. We definitely wouldn't find one in Arlie Beach.

We were in luck! Phyllis managed to find a pump and get it on a bus. With only 24 hours left to pick up the cat before Phyllis and Ralph had to fly out, we had our work cut out.

The bus with the pump arrived at 8pm and with almost dead batteries, I managed to get the pump changed. Candles, flashlights and a few band-aids were the key, and by five in the morning we were back together and ready to leave.

Ironically, when we were ready to leave we had plenty of wind and off we went, not needing to use the motor. The spinnaker went up, and we made great time. We sailed all day and all night with the spinnaker and coasted into Townsville with minutes to spare.

Townsville is a city with a population of about 100,000 people. I think most of them knew we were coming for the cat. The people most interested in this cat exchanged were the customs and agriculture agents. It seems we couldn't just take this cat from their boat to ours. We had to fill out a couple of tons of paperwork and then have an escort from the agriculture office come with us and take pictures (for their files) during the exchange. The agriculture agents went over a pile of rules about things we could and couldn't do with a cat aboard. We had to sign that we read and agreed with the rules. It seems New Zealand and Australia were both ultra-concerned about bringing animals into their countries.

One of the more interesting "cat" rules was that we would never be able to tie to a dock while we were in the country. If we needed fuel, we would have to arrange for someone from agriculture to meet us at the dock so they could watch to be sure the cat didn't get off the boat. We were told that if this cat happened to die, we would have to keep him aboard until we could show him to someone to prove he didn't run away. The fines for screwing up were in the thousands of dollars. We had no idea that owning a pet could be so intense. I think the transport of uranium nuclear rods would be easier.

To top it off, Phyllis told us the night before we arrived that the cat had attacked her while she was sleeping. She said the little sucker tried to tear her eyes out. Damn.

Once we had the cat aboard we were able to slow down a little and quit waking up at five in the morning. We still had a long way to go, and from Townsville north the reefs of Australia had a reputation of eating boats. The chart showed lots of anchorages along the way, but we weren't very impressed with what we had found so far. It's hard to sleep with the boat moving like the inside of a cement mixer.

After a couple days in Townsville – and completing a t-shirt order for 5 dozen shirts – we were off again and on our way toward the top of the country. Almost as soon as we left Townsville things got interesting. We had to sail by a live bombing range.

We were told through the V.H.F radio that we had to give the Australian Air Force's target at least a five-mile berth while they were bombing. We wanted to have a front row seat as we sailed by, so we stayed about five miles and a couple of inches away and slowed down. What a show. The Australian Air Force attacked a big pile of rocks with fighter jets with the kangaroo emblem on the side. They came in low and fast and totally obliterated this poor pile of rocks. I thought maybe I should get the white-out and take those rocks off our chart. Stupid rocks got the shit kicked out of them.

After a few more nights of uncomfortable anchorages we found one that we just couldn't talk ourselves into leaving. Hinchinbrook Channel weaves its way along a mangrove-lined shore that started to close in on us the farther we went up the channel. There was absolutely no way any sea swell could get to us. In fact, Hinchinbrook would have made a great cyclone hole if we had needed one.

Princess Del Mar was still with us and we had also joined up with another American boat, Perigrina, with Ed and Sandy aboard. Each morning we would get up and call each other on the radio to see if anyone wanted to leave yet. After finally finding a calm spot to hang out for a while, all we wanted to do was relax and maybe look for crocodiles.

We hadn't seen any of these famous Australian saltwater crocodiles anywhere, and Hinchinbrook looked like the perfect place to find one. Gretchen and I climbed into our inflatable dinghy and took off to investigate the area with Ed and Sandy following us in their dinghy. I had a good idea that an inflatable dinghy wouldn't be a whole lot of protection against a pissed-off crocodile, but we kept looking anyway.

It was probably lucky we didn't find any crocks lurking around, but at one point we were all tensed up and looking over at a log that could have been a croc when Sandy was attacked... not by a crocodile, but by a two-foot-long fish that jumped and hit her square in the face. With everyone thinking about man-eating crocodiles, this got our hearts pumping overtime. We quit looking - the fish escaped.

After a week we finally talked ourselves into leaving Hinchinbrook, so with not much wind we slowly made our way north, and after another rough anchorage at a place called Dunk Island, we moved on toward the town of Cairns. We planned on making one more stop before getting there, but when we dropped anchor at Fitzroy Island, it was as if we anchored in the middle of the Pacific Ocean. We lasted 20 minutes and then raised anchor to head toward Cairns and a much calmer harbor.

Cairns is a wonderful place, and we stayed two weeks. We put the motorcycle ashore and enjoyed all the local color; Pizza Hut, Sizzlers, Mac's and other exotic-type places. Cairns is a tourist town. They mostly made their living off the Great Barrier Reef - Diving trips, snorkeling, fishing and boat rides. This was also our last civilized place to re-provision and fix all our busted stuff before Shadowfax sailed to Indonesia.

We were able to find just about everything we needed and we had a generator water pump flown in from the States.

Cairns would have been a nice place to stay for a full season. It's true that they get their share of cyclones every year, but we found a couple of anchorages on the chart that might have made good cyclone holes. Next time around maybe...

Just before we sailed from Cairns, a couple of sailing buddies on another boat sailed in with a broken motor. I thought I would do my good deed for the month and see if I could help. Their problem wasn't all that severe, and they even had the correct spare part on board. Once they were back together and running, they happily waved as they sailed off into the sunset - and right up onto a reef.

They crashed into the reef at a place called Hope Island just a few hours to the north of Cairns. Another testament to the dangers of Australia's Great Barrier Reef. They bent their rudder and needed to be towed back to Cairns where they could haul the boat for repairs. We promised ourselves that from this point on we would do no more night sailing until we made it past the dangerous reefs.

We hated to leave such a nice place, but we sadly sailed from Cairns and headed north past Hope Island and right into the calmest weather we had seen. Not a breath of wind and absolutely no sea swell. Pretty eerie after so much wind and motion for so long. All we could do was drop the sails, start the motor, set the electric autopilot and enjoy the scenery. Lots and lots of nothing.

Actually, by nothing I mean no homes, people or roads. All we could see was mile after mile of rain forest and mountains. Beautiful country.

We motored along until we tucked in behind Cape Bedford, a cozy little harbor where we found a small industry. They were selling beach sand by the boatload to resorts overseas – U.S. included. It was pure white sand that looked like snow. It was so bright you needed sunglasses to look at it. I started to wonder how much that sand would cost. A funny thing to sell.

We continued north in a dead calm heading toward Lizard Island, or as the advertising said, "The best diving on the reef." Lizard Island is a small island that includes a research station and a small resort. Someone told us that the resort charged over $500 per night per person, but we never went up to the desk to ask. I guess that's how rumors get started, huh?

The water at Lizard Island was crystal clear. We anchored Shadowfax in the only sandy spot we could find. Reefs surround the island, which makes it a great place to dive and snorkel. The visibility in the water in Australia seemed to be terrible most of the time, but when the trade winds stopped blowing, the water cleared up immensely.

Underwater we saw beautiful live coral and thousands of colorful fish. Even giant clams that looked big enough to swallow a human. A huge cod moved in under Shadowfax, and he was definitely big enough to eat a human.

After a couple of days of swimming and playing, the wind finally came back up and we sailed away from Lizard. In fact, it was almost blowing a gale. With the wind screaming behind us, we were sailing as fast a Shadowfax could go.

I couldn't help wondering what Captain Cook did when the wind was blowing like this. He didn't have any charts and he had to get his ship through all the reefs. Actually, he did crash into one reef while sailing along this area, but he was able to get the boat off and refloated without too much damage. He had to offload everything from his ship to do it... even a few bulkheads.

With the wind blowing so hard, every anchorage we found was again "lively," and it was in one rough cove in the middle of nowhere that Gretchen got "crook with the wog." Sounds tough, doesn't it? Actually, that's Australian for "sick with the flu." For the next few days I got to play single-hander.

We sailed to a calm anchorage on the west side of Flinders Island for a few days so Gretchen could recover. Flinders has quite a few large caves with Aboriginal paintings dating back 2,500 years, and even though Gretchen was still "crook," she managed to make the five-mile dinghy ride and three-mile walk to see them. The caves are huge and it was easy to imagine what a rough life these people must have had. Over the years lots of cyclones rolled over this tiny island.

Once we made the five-mile dinghy ride back to Shadowfax we decided to visit a fuel barge anchored nearby. Two people lived aboard this small barge, and their job was to sell diesel and water to the many shrimp boats in the area. There wasn't another fuel stop within 500 miles and it sure sounded like a lonely job, but the people aboard didn't seem to mind. They also had never heard of anything called a "shrimp boat." In Australia they are called "prawn trawlers."

Gretchen was starting to feel a little better, so once again we raised anchor and sailed north on a strong easterly wind. We had only been sailing for a couple of hours when we saw something off in the distance that looked like a sailboat high and dry on a reef. Sure enough, as we approached we saw a 40-foot sloop stranded on a reef. It sat there so perfectly that it looked like a car on a showroom floor. We sailed as close as we could to see if we could help, and we managed to get the owner on the radio. He said, "I think I miscalculated." Ya think?

He hit the reef at two in the morning with a strong wind pushing him farther up. We offered what help we could, but he said that he'd been on the reef for two days and a tow boat would be there in a couple of hours. We later heard he did get towed off the reef with only rudder damage and a number of huge dents in his steel hull. I guess if you're going to hit a reef, it pays to have a steel boat.

The next few stops were all about the same. One of the cruising guides to the area summed it up by saying, "Apart from a superb beach and ideal anchorage, the islands have little appeal." I don't know who wrote that, but it sure sounded like a good review to us. A nice beach and a secure anchorage was usually just what we wanted.

One anchorage was the small harbor at Portland Roads. Only a couple of buildings lined the shore, and once we dinghied ashore we asked one of the residents how many people lived in the town. She stopped and put her hand to her chin in deep thought and said, "Ten, I think." She then said that a few years earlier her husband was hired to take a census for the area. She said he traveled 1,200 kilometers and had come up with only 40 people.

Sailing north from Portland Roads the scenery changed radically from lush rain forest to arid and bleak. Australia sure seemed to offer a little bit of everything as far as scenery was concerned. With the speed of a sailboat, you don't miss any of it.

We'd been doing pretty well with the fishing along the Australian Coast, but it was at a place called Margaret Bay where the tuna almost jumped right into the boat. We caught 11 mackerel and 4 tuna on the sail north, but at Margaret Bay the water was literally boiling with fish. As soon as we sailed toward the anchorage we hooked two tuna, both in the 40-pound range. We also had three hooks bent straight from what must have been huge fish. Great fun to fish like that.

From Margaret Bay the only place we could make it in a day sail was a place called Hannibal Island, and none of the cruising guides had anything good to say about it. One of the books summed it up by saying, "At best, poor to miserable." Since we still didn't think it was a good idea to sail the reefs after dark, we made way for Hannibal thinking it couldn't be all that much worse than the incredibly rough anchorages we'd been to already.

We sailed in and dropped the anchor in 50 feet of water just as the sun was setting, and we could tell right away that we weren't going to have a very good night. It was so rough that a booby bird that was trying to land on our radar couldn't stay on. After a miserable night trying to get what sleep we could, we raised anchor at first light to continue the sail north to the last anchorage before sailing "over the top."

Besides being the last anchorage, Escape River was also known for its vast number of saltwater crocodiles. We thought we might have a good chance of seeing one along the shore, but first we had to get past breaking seas at the sandbar at the entrance. All the guide books had good things to say about the Escape River anchorage, so we were determined to find a way in.

As we approached the entrance to the river we sailed back and forth trying to find the deepest water. Once we were sure we found the safest route, we just sort of rode the waves in. Our depth sounder showed a low of seven feet, but we managed to get in and anchored without hitting bottom.

Right away we noticed something different: no swell, nothing, flat calm. What a great anchorage compared to the last few. Even though we never saw any crocodiles, it was still one of the best anchorages along the entire east coast of Australia. We were sure that once we rounded Cape York at the top of Australia and 'took a left' we would find more calm anchorages like this one.

From Escape River we sailed at an average of 6.9 knots with a 30-knot wind and finally made it over the top. What a great feeling! The sailboats Princess Del Mar and Perigrina also rounded the top with us, and a party was definitely in order. It was also the Fourth of July.

Cape York was an unusual place for a fourth party. Nobody their but us Yanks - and the crocodiles who had been successfully hiding from us during our time in Australia.

This ended our 1,500 miles of day sails, and we were past the worst of the dangerous reefs. Our next passage was to sail west across the Gulf of Carpentaria toward the small town of Gove on the northern coast of Australia.

The 350-mile sail across the gulf was slow with strong winds against us. Our average speed was only four knots, and the size of the seas kept us from getting much sleep. When we finally got used to it, we were just about at Gove. We couldn't even fish along the way because of all the seaweed in the water. After we caught a few pounds of weeds, we just pulled in the lines and quit trying.

Gove was definitely one of the more interesting places we had seen in Australia. The town of 5,000 people was created as a mining community. Bauxite was the product, and just about everyone was involved with the mine in one way or another. To keep people happy and to make it easier to live in such a bleak area, the company offered free transportation, free movies, and free cookouts on the weekends. A giant company swimming pool was built next to the large company supermarket. This unexpected place to provision before we sailed off to Indonesia was a welcome sight.

We enjoyed the stay and we were even allowed to use the transportation and to see as many movies as we wanted. The residents seemed to be happy with their little town, even though everything was always covered in the red dust from the mine. Years later we could still see shades of the red in our sail covers.

What we couldn't do was go out at night. The locals told us the crocodiles controlled the beach where we would leave the dinghy. They told us that at night the beach was infested with the crocs, and if we were late getting back to our dinghy we would have to stay on shore somewhere and wait until light. It's true that we wanted to see a croc before we left the country, but this wasn't exactly the way we wanted to do it. We made it back to the boat every night before sunset.

Time to go to Indonesia. We were excited - and a little nervous. All the stories of pirates and political problems kept us on our toes and alert during the passage. We had no idea what to expect when we arrived.

Chapter 24

There are over 13,600 islands in Indonesia making up a chain stretching for 3,200 miles. The population is well over 170 million. Indonesia is also known as the "Ring of Fire" because of its 400 volcanoes. An average day could have 70 active volcanoes rumbling, along with three earthquakes. The country is home to the volcanoes Krakatoa and Tambora, which erupted and became the world's greatest volcanic cataclysm.

The Indonesian economy is mainly from oil drilling. I know when you think of the major oil producing countries Indonesia doesn't come to mind, but it should. Indonesia is a member of OPEC with over a million barrels of oil per day being produced. We knew we would definitely fill Shadowfax's fuel tanks with cheap fuel.

Before sailing north from Australia we said goodbye to our friends on Princess Del Mar and Perigrina because they weren't sailing in our direction. We wanted to find someone to sail through Indonesia with us, but it appeared as though we would be on our own for a while. With all the warnings we had of pirate attacks, sailing along with another yacht would have been a good idea.

The 400-mile sail north was one of our better passages. We had fair winds and averaged seven knots most of the way. No real problems except for our getting there too early and having to heave-to until daylight.

Our first port of entry was the village of Saumlaki on the island of Tanimbar. As we sailed into the harbor and dropped the anchor, we were astounded at the difference a few hundred miles can make. Instead of the bleak, uninhabited, desert look of northern Australia, we were looking at lots of green foliage and an active village.

The village had dozens of wooden buildings all leaning to one side or another. People were fishing from the main dilapidated dock - which was also leaning radically - and in general, everyone in the village was staring at us. We guessed that checking in through customs was going to be a memorable occasion.

We inflated our dinghy and made our way toward shore, armed with all our ship's papers as well as a small list of words of the local language. When we tied to the dock and climbed ashore we had to shake hands with everyone in sight as we headed toward the local police station to announce our arrival.

A young Indonesian boy, who spoke fair English, decided he wanted to be our guide, so we followed him up the steep hill to the police station. We had to keep stopping as he introduced us to everyone along the way. We entered the station and found a place to sit until somebody showed up. We could tell this was going to be a big production that could take most of the day. Tourism was something new to Saumlaki.

A smiling policeman showed up, and we followed him into his office. A 10-foot python snake was in an aquarium in the corner of the small room. We filled out a few papers and forms, but all this official really wanted to do was smile, be friendly and get his picture taken with us in front of the station. No problem. Friendly people are always easy to get along with.

Next step was to go to the harbormaster. He was almost as friendly, but he wouldn't "officially" welcome us until we gave him 14,000 rupiahs ($7.00 U.S.). And that was that. It didn't take us as long as we thought to clear in, but then we were told we should stop at the mayor's office and let him welcome us too. We spent an hour or so trying to find his office (our guide had to go to school) before we gave up the search and started to investigate the village.

Walking around town we saw for the first time the typical construction of Indonesia. Lots of buildings close together and built partially over the water. Wooden frames covered with grass thatch. The homes along the shore were also the same type of construction, but with dirt floors. The building code must have been something like, "If it can stand on its own, it passes." The boats in the harbor seemed to be built to the same code, except constant bailing was mandatory.

As we walked around the village, word travelled and it seemed like every villager came looking for us to invite us to their homes for dinner. By sign language we politely refused everyone - except for one person who owned the local hotel. It was a tiny hotel and we figured this would be a good chance to learn about the local culture.

The dinner was great, with lobster, rice and lots of local vegetables. The most common meat in Indonesia was dog, and I think we had ours medium rare. I hope Rover had a good life. All in all, we enjoyed the dinner and we tried to learn as much as we could about Indonesian culture. The Indonesian language was just about the easiest to learn of any place we'd been so far. A few of the younger people spoke a little bit of English too.

After a pleasant four-day visit we again raised anchor and pointed Shadowfax west. Before leaving we were given wood carvings and woven mats for gifts. We knew that the next person to sail to Saumlaki would wonder what was up with all the Shadowfax t-shirts people were wearing.

Even though we were sailing along the chain of Indonesian islands, the next one we were to stop at was a long 500 miles away. The cruising guides stated this area usually didn't have much wind, but we were having a great sail with a 15 to 20 knot southeasterly breeze. So far we were liking Indonesia just fine. Friendly people, cheap prices, and plenty of wind. Not a bad combination.

After a relatively uneventful four-day sail - except for putting another rip in the jib sail - we sailed into the lee of Wetar Island and dropped anchor in 20 feet of water at the mouth of a small river. My entry in the log reads, "Rough crossing bar at mouth of river, almost broached." Actually it's not as bad as it sounds. I was referring to the dinghy ride into the river after we were safely at anchor.

Wetar was a beautiful mountainous island with no villages in sight. Parrots flew overhead, and small Indonesian boats sailed past in the distance. We couldn't help but launch the dinghy to investigate this fast-flowing river that wasn't shown on any of our charts.

Once we made it over the shallow bar at the river's entrance, we continued to alternate between motoring when the river was deep enough, and pushing along with the oars when it wasn't. About a half-mile up the river we came to an old deserted village and beached the dinghy to check the place out. It was fun trying to figure out who lived there and why they left such a nice location. We also kept our eyes open for the clouded leopards, wild wart hogs, and sun bears that might not appreciate our traipsing around their area. Our guide books listed many wild animals to watch for, including Komodo Dragons.

About a mile further up the river we came to some rapids flowing down from the mountainside. We walked along the side and carried the dinghy up a little way so we could ride the rapids back down. Not a very wise thing to do with the family car (our dinghy), but it sure was lots of fun. We carried the dinghy back up and did it again... three times. When we made it back to the boat a few hours later, we had three holes and a few rips in the dinghy to repair. A little super glue and patch material and we were good to go.

With another Indonesian port behind us, we headed west toward Alor Island. A great tourist destination it wasn't. When we went ashore at the village of Kokar and asked a local when the last time westerners visited the village we were told "tidak pute," which meant never. Again, everyone was friendly enough, but it was the first time we were introduced to one of their stranger customs.

It seems that all Indonesians have a room in their home that is for anyone in the village to enter without permission, or even without knocking, for the purpose of resting or just to visit. The outside of our boat fit that category. At almost every anchorage in Indonesia, the locals would just climb aboard without asking and take a seat in the cockpit until we noticed. Sometimes we would wake up in the morning to find a couple of people in the cockpit quietly talking.

This practice was unnerving, and we did learn the word "no" quickly, but there was no way for us to educate a whole country to the peculiar ways of Americans about our privacy. All we could do was to look for an anchorage without a village nearby if we wanted time to ourselves. It was hopeless whenever we anchored off a small village.

Before we left Kokar we were able to get a stalk of bananas for a few pennies and nothing looks better than a stalk of bananas hanging in the rigging. We were also offered four big lobsters, but we had a little trouble figuring out what it was they wanted us to trade. They kept saying "gooching" and rubbing their stomachs.

Gretchen looked in our little Indonesian dictionary, and she found it- they wanted our cat. They didn't get very many fat "goochings," and ours was looking good. We were becoming attached to the little guy (not to mention that he wasn't ours) so we politely refused and offered t-shirts and balloons instead. They weren't as happy as they would have been with the cat, but the trade was made. I guess they thought we were saving our gooching for a special occasion.

78 miles later we found ourselves at Kawula Island anchored off the village of Leba Leba. Talk about picturesque. We anchored Shadowfax in the middle of three smoking volcanoes. All the place needed was a few dinosaurs. But we would have to wait for Komodo Island to see the dinosaurs.

As soon as the anchor was down we were attacked by the locals. A half dozen small boats packed full of people rowed out to welcome us. Once they arrived they started climbing aboard. A slightly scary experience, but they were just friendly people with no more on their minds than just to meet us. After a couple of hours of this madness, our cockpit was still full. We tried to get the point across that we wanted to rest after our passage. No way did we want to be rude to these people, but just as we were about to get a little more strict, they seemed to get bored and finally left.

The next day as we walked around the village we ran into a German couple along with an Australian couple who were in search of old weavings for a museum. They invited us to join their quest, and we jumped at the chance. I bet we still would have joined even if we had known it involved walking to the top of the volcano.

Our new friends had hired an old van with bald tires to take us to the volcano along non-existent roads. We had steep cliffs on both sides with large rocks for a road. Whenever we passed through a village it was like a one-car parade. People would come out of their homes and wave as we went by. At one point we stopped to take a few pictures of the volcano, and the local school let the kids out so they could come to see us. I'd brought about 100 balloons, which made me the most popular person in our little group - at least until my supply ran out.

Once we made it to the base of Lewotolo Volcano we started to walk up the path toward the top (we were happy to see a path). We walked for hours in what seemed like a straight up climb. We had to stop and rest plenty of times on the way, and this gave the village women a chance to get past us on the narrow path. The women who were walking to the top of the mountain were carrying supplies on their heads, and the women walking down the volcano had jugs holding gallons of water on theirs. We were holding everyone up by walking so slowly. They flew up and down the mountain as we huffed and puffed. We thought we were in good shape, but these women were amazing.

We finally made it to the top and the little bamboo village that was our destination. We found few people, but lots of artifacts. This village was where the natives paid for their wives. The "bride price" was expensive. Men would pay the father of the bride for the rest of their lives so they could get a good wife. Elephant tusks, moko drums (hand-made bronze drums equal in bride price to 40 cattle) were just a few of the things that a husband would have to give. In return for all this, they would get a wife that could carry water on her head – while carrying two babies and building another – and run up and down a volcano for the rest of her life. It's and interesting concept, but I was sure Gretchen wouldn't go for it.

After taking lots of pictures we started the long walk down the mountain along with a group of children who were running ahead pretending to be our guides. They ran up and down the mountain as sure-footed as goats until one of them made a mistake and fell. He cracked his head against a sharp rock - blood was everywhere.

I took off my shirt to use as a bandage, and Gretchen used her belt to hold it in place. There were no hospitals or clinics for hundreds of miles, so all we could do was get him back down the mountain. He was conscious, but in pain, as we tried to hurry our way back down. He walked on his own, trying to act tough, but when we finally saw his house and mother in the distance, he started crying and running for home. We went to his house to see what we could do, but his mother seemed to have everything under control. We left after someone was sent to try and find a doctor from another village. Poor kid.

Once back on Shadowfax we sailed from our scenic volcano anchorage with plans to stop 25 miles away at a small village on Solar Island, but they scared us away. As we were circling the anchorage right off the village, it looked like half the village had run down to the shore to wave. The other half ran for their small dugout boats. We were about to be invaded by (and I'm not kidding) over 1,000 overly friendly people. Ten or twenty we could handle, but this looked terrifying. It looked like an aggressive crowd at an English soccer match. We waved and smiled as we sailed away.

From that fiasco we sailed into Flores Straits and past a pod of playful whales that were the size of houses. Beautiful creatures to watch. Most were easily as big as Shadowfax, but some were much larger. They didn't seem to care about us, and we continued on to a place called Konga Bay - quiet, calm, and deserted. What a difference from the village on Solar Island. We were in need of a quiet night, so we anchored, kicked back, and enjoyed the solitude.

We only stayed one night, and then we were off and sailing along the south side of Flores Island for a two-night trip to the tiny island of Nusa Kodi. Komodo Island was only a few miles away, and we were excited about seeing the Komodo Dragons that we had heard so much about. For those of you who have never seen any of the National Geographics specials about the dragons, Ill fill you in with a short recap.

The Komodo Dragons are actually monitor lizards. They are typically about 10 or 12 feet long and weigh up to 300 pounds. They are the sole survivor of the carnivorous dinosaurs that lived in tropical Asia 130 million years ago. They were discovered on Komodo Island at the turn of the century. The last count put the total number of lizards at 7,000. They control their own population by eating their young, along with most of the goats that wondered around the island.

Since Nusa Kodi Island was close to Komodo Island we were hoping we would see a few dragons. We didn't think they could be all that dangerous. After all, they're just lizards. But no luck. We found plenty of monkeys, and even a couple of wild deer, but no dragons. Well, the island of Rindja was a stone's throw away, so we raised anchor and headed there to continue our search.

We anchored in a protected bay with beach on all sides and started to explore. Monkeys were running all over the beaches, and even a rat (which looked to be half the size of the dinghy) ran along the shore. It seems they grew things big in this area. While motoring the dinghy just off the beach Gretchen pointed out a huge log and wondered if it could be a dragon. When the log got up and walked into the woods, we were fairly sure it was.

It took a couple of more beaches before we spotted one that we could sneak up on. I think we were lucky. The thing was only about four feet long and took off when it saw us. We were starting to think about how dangerous those things might be. These dragons looked muscular, and the fact that they killed and ate large animals finally started to sink in. We wandered back to the dinghy.

After seeing this small dragon, we wanted to see more so we raised anchor and headed for Komodo Island. Komodo doesn't have a protected anchorage so we tucked the boat in as best as we could. If the weather turned nasty, we would have to leave in a hurry.

When we went ashore we met tourists from all over the world who were there to see the dragons. Komodo has about 50 huts people can rent for the night, but the guests are told that they must stay in their huts after dark and never to go out for any reason. Apparently these lizards would, and had, eaten tourists. This was one park where the dinosaurs ran free, and the people were locked up. You could tell they weren't kidding – these monster lizards were everywhere we looked. At night it would be easy to trip over one as they blended in with the landscape. Logs with teeth.

Near the shore there was a small building where drinks and food were sold, and we could see this was a popular spot with the lizards. A particularly large dragon sat a few feet away from the building and a small crowd had gathered to take pictures of it. One Japanese guy looked away after snapping a bunch of pictures, and the thing ran for him at warp speed. We all screamed at him to run, and the lizard was at the spot where he was standing in less than two seconds. Man, these things are fast. It worked out okay though. This guy looked back to see what was happening, and his adrenalin took over. In less than a tenth of a second he jumped straight up and over the rail that went around the restaurant. When the dragon got to the spot where the man was, the lizard stopped and became as still as a statue. Okay, now we were officially scared of these things.

We happened to arrive on the day that they fed the lizards to show tourist just how carnivorous they could be. What they did was to take a live goat, kill it, and throw it into a 20-foot deep valley. I've never seen anything like it. Gruesome but impressive. I've heard they don't do this anymore, but the way it started was with a long walk as you follow four guides as they lead the goat down a long path. The guides all have long sticks in case they have to beat away attacking lizards. As the small gathering of tourists follow along everyone was trying to not make friends with this doomed goat. It was hard to get your head around this whole affair. The locals had been doing this for so long that the dragons knew where to wait and what to expect. We arrived at the edge of a small cliff and one of the guides slit the throat of the goat and tossed it off the cliff. Dozens of lizards of all sizes attacked and ripped apart this poor goat. It looked like a bad monster movie and I can see why they would stop this weekly goat feeding routine. We all realized the lizards eat goats in the wild, but an organized goat sacrifice seems a bit much.

When we arrived back on the boat, the weather stayed calm and we were able to spend the night anchored off Komodo. Early the next morning we were off and sailing along the north side of Bumbawa Island. Up until this point the shoreline was mostly scrub grass with thin vegetation and almost no palm trees. Instantly, as soon as we sailed from Komodo, we had lush rain-forest-type stuff so thick you wouldn't have been able to chase a lizard ten feet.

We were able to stop every night along the way and found one beautiful place after another. Lots of friendly faces and no place to spend money. That's really good sailing. Actually, most of it was motoring, but so what, we were in an OPEC country and cheap diesel was easily had. The only breakage was our electric autopilot which decided to stop working. I tried taking it apart but with no luck. If I couldn't get it fixed we would have to wait until we arrived in Singapore. Singapore is known for its electronics and western-type shopping malls so we were hopeful we would find whatever we needed.

It must have been the week for electronics. The next day when I was walking past the nav-station in the boat, I noticed smoke coming out of the sat-nav. It appeared to be stuck and just blinking like a stoplight. Prognosis - dead forever. When I took it apart to see if I could see any obvious problem, like a loose something or other, it looked like every circuit had been fried. Oh well, we could use the sextant until we managed to get a replacement.

In Singapore we were planning on getting a GPS navigation system. These things were new at that time and just becoming available under the $1,000 price tag. A GPS for the boat would triangulate our position (using satellites) and update itself every second. These were still new to sailors, and when we would ask someone who owned one what they thought of it, they would just smile and go into a 20 minute speech about how unbelievably, incredibly, fantastically stupendous the thing was. As for me, I couldn't imagine knowing absolutely within a few feet where I was all the time. It sounded too good to be true. No matter how fantastic having a G.P.S. would be, it would take a pile of money to get one.

Once we rounded the island of Lombok we stopped for the night at a little island called Gilli Air, which translates to "Island in the water." Very original name. Gilli Air was nothing but a small resort and bar, but we really enjoyed it. We could practice our English and drink way too much with a few Australians who were hanging around the bar. It surprised us to be out in the middle of nowhere and find something like this. Indonesia has some great beer... I think. I have a photo of that bar with me sitting with a few people and a table full of empty bottles. Other than the photo I don't remember any of it – hence the view that Indonesia has great beer!

From the anchorage to get to that bar we managed to cut the bottom of the dinghy up getting it over the reef surrounding the shore, but a little more Superglue and that was that. Superglue and duct tape will get you pretty far in the sailing world.

Our next stop was famous Bali Island. We arrived in Bali on Independence Day - theirs, not ours. Indonesia declared its Independence from Holland in 1945 after the Japanese occupation ended, but the country didn't officially win its independence until 1949. Parades and celebrations were the order of the day, and every boat in the harbor was flying every flag that they could get their hands on. We were just in time for all the parties. Nobody could fault our timing.

Let's see, how can I describe Bali? It was not like anything we had seen in Indonesia. Bali had almost one million tourists a year, with about five million of the locals trying to sell everyone a watch. It was like one big bazaar. There were also lots of beaches - topless - and motels. The price of an item would vary from one foot to the next. One of the best deals was the local Pizza Hut – all you could eat for $2.50. You can see where our priorities were.

Gretchen and I went to visit a famous local temple and the taxi driver charged us $10.00. We then ran into a couple who paid $40.00 each for the same taxi ride. We found that it was expected to cut the prices of everything by at lest half before even beginning the bargaining. We bought a hand-carved three-foot-long blowgun that was in the shape of a dragon for $7.00. The price started at $50.00. Shopping like this was fun, but you had to keep your wallet in your front pocket and stay alert. We were told that Bali had a famous school where they taught pickpockets their trade. A fun place, but what a jungle.

Our third day in Bali we were told of a huge cremation celebration about to take place. It was going to be the largest one in 50 years. CNN was there, along with the BBC and a few of the other major TV news networks. They were going to cremate the dead of one of the local royal families. The guy had been dead for 30 years, and they had been planning for this cremation since that time. Since his death a few more members of his family had passed away, so they were going to cremate them too.

The preparations were elaborate to say the least. Huge multi-colored towers were carried down the main road by dozens of people. Hundreds of thousands more gathered to watch the procession. Priests walked along holding burning incense and ringing bells. Wooden gongs were throbbing in the distance, and everyone was chanting. Their religion was primarily Hindu, and it looked to us to be a very colorful religion.

There were so many things going on at once that it was hard to follow. First the family washed the corpse and then wrapped it in cloth. A raw egg was rolled across the body to fall and smash on the floor... removing all impurities. All this time the fancy procession was marching down the street to "the place of burning" where everybody was piling up offerings to be burned along with the bodies. We saw a bloody ox head go by - freshly cut - along with many chickens, and bolts of beautiful inlaid gold cloth. Once everything was set to burn, they used a torch to light the fire. Well, they had quite a bonfire. They torched all this stuff along with all the family pets - still alive.

When this was over there was still a lot left to do. The family searched the ashes for the bones of the dead, and then arranged them to look like the body. When this was done, they carried them to the sea. We were told there was still a week's worth of things to do before the bodies were laid to rest, but we lost interest and headed back to the boat.

Meanwhile back at the anchorage, it was crowded with other sailboats. For us, crowded was good. We passed out brochures, and before we knew it we were about as busy as we could stand. Gretchen found a place to buy the blank t-shirts and the material to make flags, so we went to work. Nice to be busy (especially since we were broke). A few of the yachts had heard of our shirts through their ham radios, and since we had our eyes on an expensive GPS we worked as hard and as fast as we could.

We stayed in Bali for just two days shy of a month. I guess we must have liked it. Lots to do and cheap food to keep us happy. Ashore, at just about any local restaurant, you could get a huge dinner of cashew chicken and a beer for about a buck. Delicious.

If you wanted to spend more, you could go to one of the many resorts that lined Nusa Dua Beach. They were some of the most beautiful resorts we'd ever seen. Hand-carved stone walls with intricate wooden carvings everywhere you looked. The resorts along the beach were so large it took us 20 minutes to walk from the beach to the lobby. To this day we haven't seen a resort anything like these. Incredible places.

Meanwhile, back at the t-shirt business we got an interesting order. Gretchen and I tried not to be intimidated when we saw a huge yacht, so we put on our best smiles and dinghied over to the Sheik from Saudi Arabia and his mega yacht. One problem about a huge boat like this is trying to find a place to knock on the hull to get someone's attention. There should be a rule where any boat over 60 feet has to have a doorbell.

Anyway, we managed to get someone's attention and we were invited aboard. To us the yacht was huge, but we were told they were using it only until their new boat was finished being built. They told us the new yacht was being built in New Zealand and it would be the biggest sailing yacht ever constructed by that country. They also said that since they wouldn't have this boat much longer, they didn't need many t-shirts. They explained that 85 shirts with five print locations and two colors should do it.

What an order! When the shirts were finished, they looked more like football uniforms than t-shirts. They liked them so much we were told if sailed to South Africa to meet them there, they would give us and order for at least 500 shirts for their new boat. We appreciated the offer, but just took the money and started looking through the boat catalogs to decide which GPS we wanted to buy when we got to Singapore.

Before leaving Bali we became owners of a cat. Through a ham radio net word trickled down to us from California that the owners of the cat we were cat-sitting for needed to talk to us. They said to call them in the U.S. when we arrived in Singapore. They also passed word along that they wouldn't be coming back to their boat - which was still back in Australia - for at least a year. Oh well, we had become attached to the mean little ball of fur anyway so we didn't mind all that much.

Once we finished all our orders and quit screening shirts, we provisioned the boat, polished up the sextant, and off we went with great memories of Bali. Another destination that was definitely worth the visit.

We were able to day sail for the first couple of days, but the anchorages we found were some of the worst we'd ever seen - exposed, large see swell, and dangerous. If we thought some anchorages in Australia were bad, these were even worse. Gretchen and I had both caught some kind of flu, so we didn't want to sail overnight. Since the electric autopilot was broken, and there hadn't been any wind for us to use the steering vane, we would have had to hand steer all night. Anchoring in uncomfortable anchorages was the lesser of evils.

After we felt a little better we decided to put some miles behind us and do a couple of overnight sails. The wind never came up very much and we had to steer in a flat calm for two days. We shortened our night watches to two hours each and suffered through it without being able to get much sleep. It's amazing how tired you get trying to stay focused and keep on course for only two hours. Then you get to rest for only two hours before you have to get up and do it again. You start to look and act like a zombie. The fact that most of the time the cloud cover was so thick the sextant was just an expensive paperweight made it all the more important that we hand-steered a perfect course.

One of those dark nights sailing through Indonesia is still one of the most memorable nights of the whole trip. The sky was socked in with thick clouds with not a star in sight, and the water had a phosphorescent glow that was as bright as a full moon. Talk about being disoriented. It seemed like we were sailing upside-down. I could plainly see the time on my wristwatch from the glow of the water. It felt supernatural. Sometimes a school of fish would swim by, and it looked like a Disney World light show. Eerie and fascinating at the same time.

After sailing west for a couple of days, it was time to take a right and head north toward the South China Sea and Singapore. The small island of Karimun Jawa was sort of in the way, so we figured we would stop for a night's rest before taking off for the 620-mile passage to Singapore. At the end of two weeks at Karimun Jawa, we still didn't want to leave.

When we motored into the tiny harbor we dropped the anchor not intending to go ashore. We just wanted to get some sleep and get on our way, but after being anchored for only a few minutes, Nurul, one of the locals, swam out to welcome us and invite us ashore for a party. We could hardly refuse an offer like that, so we launched the dinghy and made our way to shore.

We found a typical Indonesian village with small wooden huts lining dirt roads. Decorations had been strung along the roads, and we could see a large crowd of people in what appeared to be the town center. It looked as though the whole village was taking part in a party of some kind. We later discovered they were gearing up for a week's worth of celebration for a wedding and a circumcision. Every one has been to weddings, but a celebration for a circumcision was something new to us.

When the crowd of people saw us walking toward them, quite a few ran up to greet us. In the town center we saw a

40-foot pole standing straight up in the middle of the road. At the top of the pole was a circle of prizes and gifts that were free to anyone who could climb up there and get them. It may sound easy, but the pole was entirely covered in thick black grease that made climbing it almost impossible. All the young men of the village kept trying, and each one would seem to get a little higher as the grease was wiped off. We clapped and cheered until a young man finally made it to the top and started tossing down all the different prizes. What a fun way to start a party.

After a full day of celebration we made it back to Shadowfax with no intention of leaving the next day. We had been invited to a local wedding, and we were told we would be the first foreigners to attend one of their weddings. That sounded like a good reason to stay. Weddings are always fun.

We arrived early and saw that the wedding was a mix of Indonesian and western dress. I think "colorful" would sum it up. I don't think there is such a thing as a bad wedding, and this one was just as much fun as most. Food, singing, dancing and gallons of tea made for a great time. Even though everyone at the wedding appeared to have a good time, I should mention two people who seemed not to have such a great time. I don't think the bride and groom liked each other very much. It was an arranged wedding, and they had only met each other a couple of times. After the wedding they shook hands and went in different directions. The groom sat by himself in a corner for the rest of the evening. We wished them both luck... it looked like they were going to need it.

After a day's rest aboard Shadowfax, we were invited to be special guests at the island circumcision. Nurul had come out to invite us, and with our limited Indonesian and his limited English we often got things mixed up, so Gretchen and I looked at each other and then back to Nurul and said, "An Island what!?" To which he said, "Cut, cut," as he made his fingers work like scissors. He also told us to be sure and bring our camera so we could be their official photographer. When Nurul left we still weren't sure we knew what was going on, but we knew it would be one of those times we wouldn't forget.

The day started out with a huge feast of rice, fish and green stuff, and moved right into a full-scale parade around the village. Dragon costumes and masks were worn with drums and bells keeping the beat. The parade didn't really pass by anybody on the street, as everyone was in it. As it passed houses, the people would come out and join the procession. The 12-year-old and 10-year-old boys who were to be circumcised were pulled around in a hand-made float that was built out of wood and cardboard in the shape of a jeep. I was given the honor of wearing the dragon costume for a while, which was a blast. The costume was incredibly elaborate and colorful with working jaws and someone else in the back working the tail. Biting was allowed, and I tried not to miss anybody.

After the parade came the singing and dancing. The local emcee played records and announced the singers on equipment they brought over from Jakarta, the capitol of Indonesia, on Java Island. After a couple of hours of the singing and dancing it was time for the circumcision, so the emcee had to take a break. After all, he was the closest thing to a doctor they had.

We grabbed our camera and followed the crowd. We entered, along with half the village, a three-sided hut with a dirt floor. The 12-year-old sat on his father's lap while the villagers stood in a half-moon circle around the boy. We were up front and had the camera ready. The 12-year-old's job was to sit and smile as this guy came at him with a double-edge razor blade that had been sterilized with alcohol and fire. This was one brave lad. The faces of the people watching were just as interesting to watch as the boy. Boys and girls of all ages, along with the adults, watched with a bored expression. They seemed much more interested in watching us Americans. After all, we were something new, and circumcisions were old hat. One 6-year-old girl sat on the floor and played marbles through the whole affair. Gretchen, on the other hand, wasn't looking so good. She wasn't all that keen to see a doctor with a needle, never mind dirt-floor surgery with a razor blade. She went outside to try and keep from passing out.

I can't blame her as it was really something to see. After a roll of film had been shot and they had cleaned up all the blood, they gathered up the alcohol and razor blade and went to the hut with the 10-year-old to start the procedure all over again. He tried to be brave, but passed out about halfway through the procedure. I was sure whoever developed our film in Singapore was going to be in for a bit of a shock.

The party continued late into the night with the emcee back on stage playing loud, distorted music through concert speakers. A good time was had by all – except for a couple of brave young guys – and we managed to get back to the boat by midnight... still a little bit in shock over the day's events.

Before we knew it two weeks had flown past and we only had eight days left on our Indonesian cruising permit. Since we had a seven-day sail to leave the country we decided we had better get motivated and head north. Goodbyes were said to all with our new friends trying to talk us into staying. The village chief even said he would write a letter giving permission for us to be late checking out of the country. We declined the offer, raised anchor, and sadly sailed away.

What horrible weather we smacked into. Big seas and tons of wind coming from the direction we wanted to go. So much for the sextant. The cloud cover was so thick, with lightning crashing everywhere, there was no way to get a position fix with either the stars or sun.

Just before dark that first night out, Gretchen was sleeping, and I looked behind us to see two perfectly formed waterspouts heading our way. It looked like both of these waterspouts were heading right into the wind just like we were. I altered course and crossed my fingers as they crossed our stern less than a quarter mile away. They passed so close I could see the water explode where the funnel hit. I was a nice guy and didn't tell Gretchen about the waterspouts until three days later when the weather had cleared.

So that was that – almost four days of nasty weather without an accurate position fix. All we could do was to hold the best course we could and hope we didn't smash into a reef or an island. At least with that much wind the steering vane was happily steering us along.

Along the way we could hear lots of ships on the radio, and by talking to them we discovered the weather wasn't the only thing we had to worry about. Each time we spoke with a ship - or just heard them talking to each other - it seemed all they talked about were pirates. We were told that the closer we got to Singapore, the better the chance that we could be attacked. It seems these professional pirates would approach a ship - usually a large tanker - with their boat and throw grappling hooks up and over the side of the ship. They would then climb up over the side and take control. The ships usually had at least one week's payroll aboard (about $10,000 U.S.) and they would always give it up without a fight. It was better to let the insurance companies cover the loss instead of getting killed. We were also told that these pirates were heavily armed and used extremely fast speed boats. A few of the larger ships would keep their high-power saltwater fire hoses constantly trained on their own ships at positions where they thought the pirates would board. This was happening at a rate of about 200 attacks a year and increasing rapidly.

The good news for us was that there was no reason for a boatload of professional pirates to board a 46-foot sailboat. What could they possibly get from us? A few hundred bucks (our G.P.S money) and a selection of broken electronics would be about it. If they had to split up everything they got between five or ten people, I'm sure they would be a bunch of pissed off pirates. Besides, I'm sure they had an idea they might have to fight for even that. I don't think we would go quietly like a large insured tanker would.

Anyway, every morning we would turn on the ham radio to listen to the ships talk about the "pirate alerts" for the day. We kept the guns ready and loaded just in case. Sailing in this area sure was stressful. No accurate position, nasty weather, pirates, and a cat that bites.

We sailed north up the Karimata Straits until we came to Pulau Karimata Island and anchored for the night in the middle of nowhere. The third morning of that passage the sun came out long enough for us to get a position fix with the sextant, and since the island was in our way, we sailed into a small lagoon and dropped the hook. We didn't want to stop, but the weather had been so bad and we were so tired, it seemed like a good idea.

We probably would have stayed longer if the anchorage was better, but after one rolly night on the hook we turned to the west and headed for Bintan Island, our last stop in Indonesia. The weather was still bad, with solid cloud cover, but the sun broke through often enough to figure out where we were. At six in the evening - the night before reaching Bintan - we sailed across the equator and back into the northern hemisphere for the first time in over three years. Now summer was again summer, and hurricanes would spin counterclockwise. We felt closer to home, but we would miss the tropical southern Pacific Ocean.

To clear out of Indonesia we stopped at Tanjong Pinang on Bintan Island, and when we met the customs official we discovered they wouldn't have cared if we stayed longer than our cruising permit allowed. They probably wouldn't have minded if we never left. Indonesia is so large, and has so many islands, the northern end acts like it's a completely different country than the southern end. Oh well, another great country in the ol' passport, and we were on our way to the busy country of Singapore.

Singapore boasts that they have the busiest port in the world for shipping, and we spotted over fifty tankers and ships during the short 45-mile sail from Bintan. Actually, Singapore has a few interesting things worth mentioning.

Chapter 25

The island country of Singapore is only 244 square miles in size (about the same size as Chicago) with a population of 2.7 million people;   76% Chinese, 15% Malay, 6.5% Indian and 2.4% other. In 1965, Singapore became independent from the Malaysian Federation and is now a democracy with majority vote rule. The official language is English (nice for a change) and the city was probably the cleanest in the world. The streets were spotless due to the strict laws and enforced penalties. Littering was a $1,000 fine - heavily enforced. People who smoked anywhere except outside, or at home, were fined $500 - again heavily enforced. Chewing gum was prohibited to have for personal consumption or to import - the hardest litter to clean up. Failure to flush a public toilet carried a minimum fine of $150. I don't know who checked up on that one.

As for a drug problem, there wasn't much of one. The penalty for having a small amount of marijuana - death - tended to keep people honest. Crimes which carried a jail sentence, like theft or possession of a Playboy magazine, also included a specified number of lashes with a cane. Singapore was a safe city, as long as you were very careful to obey all the rules - and always remembered to flush.

We anchored on the northeast side of Singapore off the Changi Sail Club. The Sail Club wasn't very convenient because we had to dinghy almost a mile against a very strong current to get to the dinghy dock. Once we made it to the dinghy dock, we had to pay $20.00 a week for the use of the dock. Since Singapore usually dealt only with tankers, there really wasn't anyplace else for a sailboat to go.

In the city we discovered one electronics store after another. Shopping was definitely what Singapore had to offer and we couldn't believe how it was possible for that many shops to survive. From what we could tell, the prices weren't that great. A video camera worth $1,000 in the States would cost you the same $1,000 in Singapore.

We were ready to give Singapore our money for a GPS, and since we were in the land of electronics we didn't have any trouble finding many to choose from. The problem was they were $600 cheaper in the States. Hard to believe we were in the center of an electronics universe and we had to have West Marine out of California ship us a GPS. We bought a hand-held Garmin GPS for $800, and what a great new toy! I figured that knowing where we were all the time would be a good substitute for the boat insurance that we didn't have. Much less chance of crashing into a reef with this plastic marvel.

Getting the autopilot fixed was another story. This vast knowledge of electronics in Singapore wasn't helping us at all. We couldn't find anyone familiar with the kind of autopilot we had, but we did find one guy who told us he would take a look at it if we brought it in. It took three hours to disconnect it from the boat, but we brought it in at nine in the morning. As I placed the unit on the counter we became a little nervous when we saw the repair guy already drinking a cold beer. We left the autopilot anyway, and for $120 we got it back in what he claimed was working condition. Not a bad price - but the only way to tell would be to install it and test it out.

In between our running around trying to get things fixed, we did take time off to check out a little bit of Singapore. We made our way to the Singapore Zoo and thought it was one of the most professional zoos we'd ever visited. Acres and acres of beautifully landscaped vegetation surrounded islands of animals. That's right, islands. None of the animals were in cages. They were on very large islands surrounded by water. It looked like they had plenty of room to roam instead of being stuffed inside small cages.

Other than going to the zoo, we didn't find a whole lot that we could do without spending piles of money - which we didn't have. Singapore was definitely geared towards shopping and not much else. A loaded credit card would have made it a lot more fun.

When we finally had everything fixed and ready to leave, two weeks had passed. We stocked the boat with food, a few more charts, and figured we better get out of such an expensive place - we were down to our last $12.00. All the other sailors who were in Singapore also had huge lists of things to buy or fix, which meant selling t-shirts was impossible. Nothing for us to do but get out of the country and head for Malaysia.

We sailed from Singapore with fair weather and a foul current against us, but it was great to be on the move again. There were so many tankers anchored all the way around the island of Singapore that we had to weave our way around them, while also keeping our eyes open for the other ships that were underway. A messy place for navigation, but what the hell, our GPS let us know where we were - our speed, direction and time of arrival in any weather. Cool.

We were going to head north to the Malacca straits, which meant we would have to dodge ships for hundreds of miles. Over 200 huge ships and tankers motor up and down this narrow waterway every day. In some areas the straits were as narrow as 25 miles. Outside of the shipping channel the local fisherman would string miles and miles of nets. What a busy place.

Two memorable things happened on the way out of Singapore. One was that we were hit by a dreaded "Sumatra." Sounds bad, huh? Exciting anyway. A Sumatra is the name for a whole pile of wind that came out of the west in gusts of over fifty knots... at least that's what they called it in this part of the world. We discovered many places like to name their winds - I just think of it as a big pile of wind.

The second problem was a lot worse. The electronic autopilot had the same problem it had before we arrived in Singapore. Bummer. With the usual light winds of the Malacca Straits, we were back to our least favorite pastime... hand steering.

Chapter 26

Malaysia has a land area of 128,303 square miles and a population of about 18 million. Sumatra Island, Indonesia, is to the west of the Malacca Straits, and Thailand borders Malaysia to the north. The South China Sea is to the east, which makes this part of Malaysia a huge peninsula.

We wanted to day-sail up the straits as much as we could because of all the tanker activity, so our first stop was the island of Pisang, only 20 miles away from Singapore. A 200-year-old lighthouse on Pisang Island helps ships and tankers find their way and I have to say that Malaysia wins the "Great Lighthouses" award. All the way up the coast we saw one after another - old, kept like new, and all operating. Usually there was a huge mansion at the foot of the lighthouse where the lighthouse attendant lived. Sounds like a comfortable job to me.

Once at anchor I noticed the water in the Malacca Straits was the color of mud with a little oil mixed in. With all those tankers using the waterway every day, it could have been worse.

I'm not sure why I picked this first anchorage to get in the water and clean the bottom of the boat, but I did. The water was warm but so dirty that I could only see a couple of feet in front of me. We hadn't hauled the boat to paint the bottom since New Zealand, so I had to jump in and clean it every month or so. Really no big deal, it would only take an hour or so and it was usually an enjoyable job. Except this time.

The Malacca Straits has more sea snakes than anywhere we'd been, and with such terrible visibility there was no way to see them coming. I wasn't all that worried about it until a three-foot-long snake drifted by my facemask only a couple inches away as I cleaned the prop. I didn't appreciate that very much, but since I could see it, I stayed in the water and continued to work on the boat. It was about five minutes later that a plastic garbage bag floated by and wrapped itself around my legs. I couldn't see what it was, and my mind was thinking "snake," and it scared the crap out of me. I flew into the dinghy and didn't get back in the water until Thailand.

We sailed our way up the coast – along with quite a bit of motoring – trying to find someplace acceptable to anchor each night. A couple of nights we just had to drop the hook near shore in an unprotected area. Safer than dodging supertankers at night though.

One scenic little harbor we found was at Water Island, which was only a few miles from the historic town of Malacca. Malacca is about 500 years old, and a few of the original buildings are still standing. At least that's what the tourist books said. We could have taken the ferry over to take a look, but with only $12.00 to our name, paying for a ferry ride wasn't on our list of things to do.

Our prospects of increasing our sailing funds looked promising as long as we could make it to a place called Port Kelang, about half way up the Malaysian coast. It also promised to be a great party. We plotted a course for Port Kelang.

Port Kelang was the starting point for the Raja Muda Sailing Regatta. This one sounded great - 55 boats, 300 people, with Heineken Beer as one of the sponsors. We put the pedal to the metal, and we made it to Port Kelang with two weeks to spare. Plenty of time to talk the racers and cruisers into buying some t-shirts. We also had to make enough money so we could join in the fun. The cost of joining the regatta was $225.00. We were only $213.00 short.

We motored up to the Kelang Yacht Club and found a protected area tucked in behind a small peninsula. The current ran strong with the tides, and it was so crowded with boats coming for the regatta that the only way for anyone to stay was to pick up one of the yacht club moorings. Anchoring was out of the question, and there was an $8.00 per day charge for a mooring. Luckily, they trusted us when we said we couldn't pay until we made some money. It looked like this regatta was going to cost us a fortune.

Fortunately, the people joining this regatta were as interested in t-shirts as the people in the Musket Cove Regatta were back in Fiji. Once we went through all the shirts we had on board, Gretchen found a new supplier in the nearby capital city of Malaysia, Kuala Lumpur (locally known as K.L.) and we were in business.

Lots of hard work, salesmanship and rum drinks later, we had enough money to pay the dockage, restock lots of t-shirts, and join the regatta. Just two days before the official start of the regatta we walked up to the race office with our $225.00, and it looked like the 'Saint of Sailboats' was taking good care of us. Our conversation with the race officials went something like this.

Us: "Hello, we would like to join the regatta."

Them: "Sorry, we're full, no more boats."

Us: "Aw!"

Them: "How about if you give us $25.00 each, and you can be a Ghost Boat. You can eat, drink and go to all the parties, but if you win we can't give you the trophy."

Us: "Gee, I guess that would be okay."

Sometimes life can be kind. A few of these race boats had been shipped down from Hong Kong and had crew of up to 20 people. The only way we could have possibly won was if one of those huge tankers ran over all the other boats. As for the parties, that's all we wanted!

The regatta consisted of three legs of about 100 miles each, with dinners and parties before and after each part of the race. It was tough, but somebody had to do it. The sponsor Heineken held up their end well by yelling "free beer!" so often it was disgusting. Lots of fun and new friends made the whole thing definitely worthwhile.

Some of the race boats that had been shipped in for the regatta were fun to watch. These people were intense in their preparations. They were spending small fortunes to win this race. The money they spent just on their sails would have floated Shadowfax for years. Crews had flown in from all over the world to take part in this regatta, with most of them planning to continue on and join the next regatta, The Kings Cup, in Thailand.

Once the regatta started we could see a problem right away. Each leg of the race started at sundown and ended the next day when the boats made it into the next port. Since we were being lazy and didn't want to sail overnight, we decided to leave in the morning so we could be in at the next anchorage wide awake for all the parties. The fastest boats in the race would always see us safely at anchor when they arrived at the finish line, and they started to wonder how "that boat with the motorcycle strapped to the deck" could be so fast.

The ports along the coast of Malaysia where we stopped were wonderful. It would have been nice to have had more time to look around. One of the ports, Georgetown on Penang, was one of the stops along the way where we got to spend a full day.

Penang was the first trading post for the British in the Far East in 1786. What a mix of cultures. The city is a large one (population almost 300,000) offering just about everything anyone could need, from huge western-type supermarkets to tiny local shops. Gretchen and I traveled around the city by something called a 'trishaw' that cost only a dollar per ride. A trishaw is a bicycle that pushes two seats along in front of it. In New York City-type traffic, the guy pedaling us around would head the wrong way down one-way streets to save himself a little pedaling. Sailing around the world and dodging supertankers was definitely safer than travelling by trishaw. But we did load the trishaw up with lots of groceries from all our new t-shirt profits. Sailing with money was never as comforting as sailing with full food lockers.

After another dinner and party in Penang, at the oldest hotel in Malaysia, we were off again on our way north. This time we had plenty of wind and a great sail. It takes a bunch of wind to get Shadowfax really cranking, and we were sailing with the rails in the water and all sails full. Again, we were sailing during the daytime instead of at night with the rest of the racers, but since we were the only boat in the "Ghost Division," we could bend the rules any way we wanted. The finish line was on the island of Langkawi, and we were at anchor before any of the racers even started.

Langkawi is a group of 104 islands all clustered around each other - custom-made for tourists. Perfect sand beaches and incredibly lush green mountains made us want to move in. Langkawi is at the northern end of the Malacca Straits, out of the murky water, where the seawater is crystal clear.

A few resorts had caught on to how nice this place was and had built along the beaches. There is a local legend that said Langkawi was cursed for seven generations by the Princess Mahsuri who had been wrongly accused of adultery and killed. The locals said that anyone who tried to open a resort or store failed until the seven-generation curse ended.

Anyway, the regatta ended at Langkawi, and what a feast the five star Pelangi Resort put on. It was beyond description. To just say that everyone ate and drank too much would probably be the understatement of the year.

While hanging around Langkawi, we didn't get to visit all 104 islands, but we did get to the small island with the Tasik Dayang Bunting - Lake of the Pregnant Maiden. Apparently there are lots of legends around this place. This legend said "Barren women can become fertile bathing or drinking the water." The lake was big enough to sail Shadowfax on (if we could have gotten her there), and we enjoyed playing in all that rare freshwater. As for the legend, it sounded pretty dangerous to us and we didn't want anything to do with it.

Just before leaving Langkawi we had a talk with the Raja Muda (Prince) of Selanga who had a yacht in the race (and

who the Raja Muda Sailing Regatta was named after).
While talking with a couple of friends at the Pelangi Resort,
we noticed the Raja in a t-shirt walking alone down a path.
We thought why not wander over and see what he was up
to. It turned out that the Raja was just your ordinary kind of
guy, except, of course, that he was a very rich prince. He
loved most things western and had even invested in a Hard
Rock Café in his capitol city. He told us that anything
western in Malaysia would be a hit. He said a friend of his
who opened a Harley Davidson Motorcycle dealership sold
70 bikes in his first three months of operation. After telling
us all this, the Raja told us that he was tired of being a rich
prince, and if we would kidnap him he would write the
ransom note to his father - the Sultan. This sounded like an
exciting idea, but we were sure the death penalty would
come at the end of an adventure like that. Oh well, the grass
is always greener....

Next stop, Thailand! We only had to sail 30 miles north
and what a change. The Thailand culture was completely
different from anything else we had been around. Even the
alphabet was different. We always tried to learn a little of
the language in every country we visited, and we could tell
right away that Thailand was going to be a tough one to
figure out.

Chapter 27

The Kingdom of Thailand is 198,455 square miles in size with a population of approximately 57 million (8 million lived in the capitol city of Bangkok). The country has Burma (also known as Myanmar) to the north, Leos and Cambodia to the east, and Malaysia to the south. Studies have shown that people have lived in the area since before 4,000 BC. Today the religion is 90 percent Buddhist. The most important fact was the water was crystal clear, and lobsters lived in the reefs. Priorities.

One of our first stops in Thailand was the island Ko Rok Nok. The island was said to be owned by a princess, and nothing could be built on it without her permission. The only structures on the heavily wooded shore were a few tents and one wooden hut. A very scenic place. We enjoyed swimming around the clear water and checking out the reefs, but the place sure was crowded for a tiny deserted island. Fourteen yachts that were in the regatta had also stopped at Ko Rok Nok, so the best idea would be to put together a beach party. Gretchen organized the party and 28 yachties showed up for a fantastic potluck dinner. We had enough food for at least 50 people, even chocolate cake. The party lasted for five days, but then we figured it was probably time to move on.

We dragged ourselves away from Ko Rok Nok with more than a slight hangover, and sailed on to "Funky Town." The real name of this Funky Town is the island of Ko Phi Phi Don, a real tourist spot. Bars, shops and restaurants lined the very narrow walkway that ran the length of the island. The sights, sounds and smells along this walkway were almost tangible. The island itself is one sheer cliff dropping straight off into the clear blue water. At least one cruise ship a day visited P.P. (the local nickname). What a cool place. Lots and lots of backpackers and hippies who were still living the lifestyle of the 60's. We could fit right in.

Just a mere 25-mile sail to the west put us on Phuket Island (pronounced Poo-ket, not the other way). Phuket is the largest island in Thailand and has a population of 168,000. What a wild place. Over 70 percent of the island is mountainous, and resorts lined the wide sand beaches. Definitely a place to put the motorcycle ashore.

It didn't take us long after arriving in Phuket before we started talking about staying for a while. Clear water, inexpensive prices and friendly people. That adds up to a pretty nice place. Even our friends on other boats - the ones who talked us into going up the Red Sea with them instead of around South Africa - had decided to stay for a while. The problem was the timing. Because of the weather-window for sailing up the Red Sea, if we didn't leave this season we would have to wait for almost a year. Too long, since there wouldn't be any yachts to sell t-shirts to until the next sailing season.

This was another port like Singapore where everyone seemed to have other things on their minds besides t-shirts. The next passage, for most boats, was to cross the Indian Ocean and people were more into provisions and repairs then buying a dozen or so t-shirts. At one point we had counted our last $75.00 for the fifth time trying to figure out how we were going to provision to make it across the Indian Ocean.

From what we could figure, we needed $600.00 for food, fuel, provisions and to repair the autopilot. The angel of sailors decided to watch over us and just before Christmas luck knocked on our hull, and our problem was solved.

Gretchen and I were just hanging around the boat when a well-dressed young man came over in a dinghy and asked us if we would be interested in a little work. He said that other yachties in the anchorage told him that we might be willing to take some people on a sail charter. Our new friend worked at a place called Southeast Asia Yacht Charters and apparently they had over-booked for the Christmas holidays and needed someone to help them out.

He said that if we would be so kind as to take a one-night charter for two people, he would give us 500 American dollars. No problem, mate. We told him we would take all those he wanted to give us. Five hundred bucks to sail snorkel and party. We were sure we could handle that.

The charter turned out to be lots of fun. A young British couple arrived, and we sailed them to the island of Ko Racha Hyai. An enchanting little island only a few hours' sail from Phuket. When we arrived there was quite a bit of tourist activity from all the large tour boats, and as I was about to apologize for taking our guests to such a crowded place, Mark, our charter guest, mentioned how quiet and peaceful the place was. Everything is relative I guess.

When we arrived back at Phuket and dropped off our guests, we went to the charter company to pick up our money and to see what the chances were of getting another couple to take sailing. True to their word we were handed $500, but as far as getting another charter we were told, "Don't call us, we'll call you." That was a short Thailand sail charter career, but with $500.00 in our pocket we couldn't help but smile.

When it rains it pours. We arrived back at our secure anchorage to find that a few people had been looking for us. With Christmas coming people started thinking of presents, and what's better than t-shirts with a picture of your boat on them.

We took every order we could as we weren't sure when we would be able to make more money after leaving Thailand. The next six countries we were to visit were political disasters, so we needed every penny we could get. The hardest thing about sailing around the world, at least for us, was wondering where our next buck would come from.

In between all this sailing and t-shirt work, we took some time to check out the countryside. Our little 125cc motorcycle wasn't big enough to take on any long-range touring, so one day we rented a larger bike. We're still not sure how big it was, but I think it was a 750cc. It's hard to tell because all the numbers had been filed off every bike the rental company had. It was better not to think about why.

It's true that Thailand had some major political problems of its own, but we didn't let that stop us from looking around. Off we went on this mystery bike, and I've gotta say we had a terrific time. We went through a couple of roadblocks, but we were never hassled. A friend of ours had also rented one of these mystery bikes, and we road for hours checking out dozens of Buddhist Temples along the way.

One temple was carved into a huge cave, complete with monkeys swinging through the limestone formations. A 30-foot-tall Buddha statue that was carved into the stone a thousand or so years before kept watch on the cave entrance.

Thailand's culture is one of the most fascinating that we'd seen. It seemed like every lake and mountain was covered with a legend or curse. We probably should have stayed for a year, but with our money situation we couldn't see any way to pull it off. This would be just another place that we would vow to visit again.

There is a story about how we met Knut, our biking buddy, and, in fact, he had agreed to make the passage to our next destination, Sri Lanka, with us. Three years earlier, when we were sailing around French Polynesia we met Knut. He was the first navigator aboard the sailing cruise ship Windsong - a computerized tall ship that sailed a weekly route from Tahiti to Bora Bora. Remember? This was the ship that broke all its dishes during cyclone Penny. We said goodbye to Knut in Bora Bora... sure that we would never see him again.

So there we were, anchored in Thailand and watching the number-one rated cruise ship in the world, Sea Born Spirit, anchor. And you guessed it. Knut had a new job as the chief navigator aboard this elite ship (432 feet and 106 staterooms of 600 square feet each). At up to $10,000 per week, I'm sure it was quite a ride.

Knut worked aboard for three months on, and three months off. Since he was entering his off time, we invited him to join the cruise ship Shadowfax as we rolled across the Indian Ocean. Why he would agree to sailing on a small boat after three months on Sea Born Spirit is a mystery to me, but he jumped at the chance. I was sure he was a qualified navigator, even though when he came out to Shadowfax he said, "What's that?" as he pointed to the steering vane on the back of the boat.

I'm probably making too long a story out of this because as it turned out, he couldn't come. Knut called Sea Born Spirit's home office in Norway to tell them what he was doing, and they had already booked him into a terrorist school in England for the following two weeks - not how to be one, but how to spot one.

I had already figured out how much extra sleep I was going to get with Knut aboard, so I was a little disappointed. I was sure he would have taught me lots of things I didn't know about navigation to keep me busy for most of the trip. At least he got to visit for a few days before he had to leave for England.

On Christmas day a storm blasted through with winds of over fifty knots, but we still managed to have a turkey dinner aboard a local sailboat. Shadowfax was anchored nearby so we could keep an eye on her as the winds blew, and the boat we had dinner on couldn't seem to stay put. After every course, we had to help re-anchor the boat. The strong winds kept trying to drag her out into the open ocean. No worries about dragging onto any rocks, we could drag for about 2,000 miles before hitting land.

The next day we heard about a couple of people who were returning to their anchored boat after a party on the beach Christmas night. They never made it. Maybe their outboard quit. Maybe their oars broke. We'll never know. Even after an extensive search, no one ever found a trace of them.

They were blown out to sea in a 12-foot dinghy. Even a simple thing we took for granted – like a dinghy ride of a couple hundred feet – could turn deadly. A sobering incident.

New Year's Eve rolled around, and we were still in Thailand. We were anchored in the Pa Tong Bay on the west side of Phuket along with three U.S. Warships. The U.S. ships were on leave, so most of the bars were jammed. Jet skis and parasailors totally filled the bay. This bay was one busy place. What a party atmosphere. When night came, the dozens of resorts along the shore tried to outdo each other in the fireworks department. What a New Year's celebration! Every spot on the beach was filled with fires, light-shows and rockets taking off. These people definitely took their fireworks seriously. It was a four-hour fireworks grand finale.

Gretchen and I spent the next few days loading the boat with food, water and fuel for the next passage. We also found someone who claimed he could fix our autopilot.

This autopilot was becoming a pain and a quest to get repaired. Whenever we had to motor, or if we were in winds of less than five knots, we depended on it. Hand-steering was the only alternative when there wasn't enough wind for the windvane, and as I've said before, that could get old fast. Picture yourself steering in an ocean swell at midnight and you have to hold a steady course or the boat will roll like crazy if the seas hit the side of the boat. Or maybe you are in heavy shipping traffic. Now add to that a desperate need to go to the head! Or maybe you just want to make yourself a cup of coffee. If the other person on the boat has just gone to sleep after a two-and-a-half-hour shift, you really don't want to wake that person up and rob his or her precious sleep. In a heavy sea, it's hard enough to get to sleep in the first place. With only two people on a long passage – or even a rough short passage – an autopilot is a must.

The guy we found in Thailand who said he could fix the autopilot was a sailor like us, and he kept himself busy by fixing everybody's everything - radars, sat-navs, radios, and yes, autopilots. Everyone we spoke with said he knew what he was doing, and since no repair shops in Thailand wanted anything to do with it, I took the autopilot over to his boat for him to check out.

After bringing it back to him four more times, Gandolf – our autopilot's name – seemed to be working again. We tested it out on a few short sails around Phuket, and we were back in business with our battery powered crewmember apparently happy and working. Our upcoming passage was over 1,000 miles to the country of Sri Lanka, and we didn't want to hand steer for any part of it.

With a fair weather forecast we headed west into the Indian Ocean for the first time. The winds were 10 to 20 knots on the beam, and the wind vane was happily steering the boat without a problem. The weather for the passage was just about perfect all the way. Gretchen told me that at one time the seas did get a little large, and we were surfing down the waves at around 10 knots, but I slept through the whole thing. Lucky me.

We caught a three-foot mahi mahi on the third day, but that was the only fish we caught on the seven-day passage. Five or six hooks were straightened out, and we lost two complete lures. I guess the Indian Ocean fish were a little too large for us.

What a great trip. Nothing exciting happened. We didn't see any ships, and porpoise played in our bow wave every sunset. Boring trips are safe. We sailed with a full jib, a shortened mainsail, and never took the cover off the mizzen. Gretchen and I each read six books, and the cat slept for the whole passage, except for a few times he got up to eat the flying fish off the deck. Unfortunately, the one time we tried to use the electric autopilot it decided to be broken again.

When we sailed from Thailand we thought we would be alone since most of our friends were staying there for the season, but that wasn't the case. Just a couple of hours out we heard another boat on the VHF radio saying goodbye to their friends in Thailand. It appeared that we weren't the only one heading west. We called them on the radio to say hello and report our position.

Our new friends were on the 38-foot sloop Tethys, an American boat from Seattle, with three women sailing around the world. We didn't know them, and it was just a coincidence that we left Thailand at the same time. Needless to say, by the time we arrived in Sri Lanka, after talking to them on the ham radio all the time, we were great friends.

Chapter 28

Sri Lanka - formally called Ceylon - is positioned just to the south of India and is shaped like a giant teardrop. Sri Lanka is 25,332 square miles in size and has a population of about 15 million. The southern part is very mountainous with the highest mountain being over a mile high (Mt. Piduruthalagala at 8,281 feet).

In 1505, the Portuguese arrived and ruled most of the land. In 1640 the Dutch threw out the Portuguese and ruled the same area. In 1802 the British gave the Dutch the boot and claimed Sri Lanka (Ceylon at the time) as a full Crown colony. In 1948, Sri Lanka won its independence and there went the British. What a mess.

After being in the country for couple weeks, we found most locals we met wished the British were still in charge. Sri Lanka was in a civil war, and with a population density of about 200 people per square kilometer, they could use help.

As for us, we probably had one of the most profitable businesses in Sri Lanka. From the moment we sailed into Galle Harbor we were busy screening t-shirts and sewing courtesy flags. It seems Sri Lanka is at a crossroads as far as sailors were concerned. At one point the small harbor was jammed full with 50 boats that would be sailing off in different directions. There were yachts from Turkey, Russia, Spain, and South Africa... to name just a few. They were heading toward Chagos, the Red Sea, India, South Africa or Thailand. We put on our silk-screen hats and started passing out brochures.

Since many of the boats in the harbor were heading to the Red Sea, we decided to do a spec shirt for people who didn't know what they wanted. It said "RED SEA '93" in red ink, and had a map of the Red Sea in blue with all the countries outlined and named. It even had some kind of wind god in the corner blowing wind toward the south in gale force against the direction of travel... the way we were told it would. By the time we got to the Mediterranean we had sold hundreds of these shirts.

We had 200 blank t-shirts aboard when we reached Sri Lanka, and we went through them quickly. I was busy cutting the screens for the different designs that people wanted, so Gretchen took on the job of "t-shirt acquisition." After traveling all over Sri Lanka looking for blank t-shirts, she finally had to tape $500 to her stomach and get on a train headed for Colombo, the capital of the country.

With Sri Lanka embroiled in a civil war, and the average income of the locals being about $1.00 U. S per day, Gretchen and I were a little nervous about her taking off alone. She ended up traveling around the capital with a salesman for a local t-shirt company. He drove her to all his competitors to show her that his prices were the best deal. He was right, and she ended up buying the shirts from him... nice shirts too. To get back to the boat Gretchen had to buy four seats on an old bus - one for her and three for the shirts - and finally returned after dark. A pretty brave and amazing thing to do.

Even though the country was having such a hard time politically, we still managed to have a good time and meet some nice people. We were invited to dinner by one local family who lived near the anchorage and we were treated like honored guests. We entered the family's small two-room wooden home and were introduced to the seven people who lived there.

When the time came to eat, we were seated at a small table loaded with food. The only other person at the table was the grandfather. Everyone else just stood behind us to watch us eat. I'm sure there was at least a week's worth of their food on the table. This family didn't want anything from us except our friendship and company, which proves that no matter how poor and war-torn a country is, the people can still be as friendly and generous as anywhere in the world.

Back in the anchorage we were going like crazy trying to fill everybody's order. One day, toward the end of our stay, we woke up and decided we were working too hard and we should throw a party. We thought maybe we should come up with a reason for the party, so Bud's birthday seemed like a good reason.

Bud was the name we finally attached to the cat. He had another name when he was given to us, but he didn't seem to mind the change - he never looked at us no matter what we called him. We had no idea when his real birthday was, but we didn't think he would care if we just made one up. We called everyone in the anchorage on the VHF radio to spread the news - thinking that twenty or thirty people might show up. All the yachties must have needed a party because at one point during the night I counted over sixty people on Shadowfax. We had over forty dinghies tied to our boat, with a stream of people coming and going. About halfway through the night a sailor from Spain was checking out Shadowfax's engine room. He called me over to point out a steady flow of water coming in through one of our thru-hull fittings. We were so weighted down with people that our bilge pump exhaust fitting was underwater and back-flushing into our bilge. That's a lot of people! I shut off the through-hull and went back to the party. I wasn't about to cancel the party just because of a little thing like sinking.

Just about everyone brought something, and we even had a birthday cake made out of a can of cat food to give Buddy. One family said if it was a birthday party for a human, they probably wouldn't have come. The cat thing intrigued everyone. All in all, the party was a huge success, and nothing important was broken. The next day we added up the empties - forty liters of rum punch, twenty liters of beer, and two liters of arak (the local hooch) were consumed. The cat hid in the aft cabin all night.

We all made new friends that night of the party, and it was our way of thanking people for ordering t-shirts, and more importantly, giving us their money.

We took all the money we made and turned it into more useful things, like food, fuel and repairs. Cash is worthless 1,000 miles from shore. One of the nicer things about stocking up in Sri Lanka was the fact that we could buy a couple pounds of fresh roasted cashew nuts for just a couple of dollars. Great stuff! We could eat them like popcorn. Sri Lanka grows tons of cashews and we wanted to take enough to last for months. A bag of cashews fit in perfectly with a midnight watch and Jimmy Buffett music.

One of my usual, and nasty, jobs was an oil change for the main Perkins motor and the Onan generator. I tried to do this whenever I had the chance, and since the old oil wasn't all that old, I usually passed it along to one of the locals so they could use it in their car or tractor. Our old oil was usually in much demand in poor countries.

When I dinghied to shore, the first person I found seemed to want it pretty bad. He was an elderly man sitting at the edge of the water and I tried to explain to him what I had. Because of the language barrier I had to open one of the two plastic containers, show him the oil, and then point to a car that was nearby. The man was all excited and kept nodding and smiling as I tried to explain what I was giving him. Finally, I was sure I had filled him in on what to do with the oil, and we both smiled as I started heading back to the boat. About halfway out to the boat I looked back and saw him emptying the five quarts of oil into the harbor. All he wanted was the plastic containers! This poor guy probably thought putting the oil in the harbor was the best way to get rid of it. It wasn't that he didn't care about the ecology of the world, it probably wasn't something he ever thought about. Unfortunately we found many situations like this throughout the world.

Back to our annoying electric autopilot problem. We couldn't find anyone to fix the autopilot in Sri Lanka, so I ripped the thing apart myself and replaced a handful of integrated circuits – called ICs – which seemed to get the thing going again. This thing always seemed to work great in an anchorage. The pilot charts, which predicted wind patterns around the world, showed that we should have good winds all the way to the Red Sea. I didn't think we would need the electric autopilot, but it's better to prepare for everything.

Our stay in Sri Lanka stretched into just three days short of a month and we finally had to "just say no" to a few t-shirt and flag orders and sail away. It's nice to be popular, but it was getting ridiculous. Our weather window for the Red Sea was getting shorter and shorter, and we had to get going.

We sailed out of the small harbor with stormy skies and a fair weather prediction. Southeasterly winds pushed us along for the first day with nothing going wrong and everything in working order. Nancy, Patti and Sue on Tethys sailed from Sri Lanka the same day that we did, but their destination was the Maldive Islands 400 miles to the south. Our destination was the country of Yemen, 2,200 miles to the west... maybe. Talk about flexible. After the first day at sea we still weren't sure where we were going.

If the wind stayed fair from the southeast, we would continue on to Yemen. If it didn't we would hook a left and head to the Maldives. Twice a day we would talk to Tethys on the ham radio, which didn't help our Yemen plans. We enjoyed traveling with them, and they kept urging us on to the Maldives.

Day two and the wind shifted. At least we think it shifted. There wasn't really enough of it to tell. We tacked Shadowfax to the northwest trying to keep heading slightly west, and it wasn't until we were 50 miles south of India that we noticed we were moving backwards. The current was on our bow at two knots, and our speed through the water was about 1 ½ knots. Well, you do the math. It comes out to "backwards."

We started the motor, flipped on the autopilot and headed south toward Tethys and the Maldives. The Maldive Islands didn't sound too bad anyway - famous scuba diving, warm clear water, and even a Club Med. I was sure we could handle it.

The third day out, not only was the wind gone, the seas were gone too. What an eerie feeling being on such a huge ocean that was so calm and flat. So much for the pilot chart's wind prediction. We motored along all that night and the autopilot was happily working. A flying fish landed in Gretchen's lap during her 3:00 a.m. watch, which she didn't care for very much, but Buddy the cat thought it was the best thing to happen since his birthday cake.

Day four of the trip and we caught two mahi mahi on a lure Gretchen made from cutting a red balloon into strips. I would fillet large fish in our cockpit since it was the safest place, but the first thing we had to do was kill the fish so it wouldn't flop around and smash into things. Hitting our future dinner on the head with a hammer would make a bloody mess, so we learned a better way of doing it. We would take a tablespoon of vodka and put it into one of its gills. I don't know exactly what this does, but it sure kills a large fish quickly.

On day five the autopilot died again. We still had no wind, but now we had to steer constantly. What a drag. We changed our shifts to two hours each instead of three. After a full day of this, you really want to have a break. Getting all your sleep in two-hour chunks is tough, and two hours at the wheel is also about all you can stand. The key to steering on a long passage has got to be music. Stick in some earphones and hope rock and roll will keep you awake for a couple of hours. The Maldives never sounded so good.

The Maldive Islands are so low that we didn't see them until we were just a couple of miles off the island of Male, the capital of the Maldives. It was a welcome sight.

Chapter 29

The 1,190 tiny Maldive Islands cover an area of 115 square miles. The southernmost island is on the equator, and from there the island chain stretches north 480 miles to the latitude of 8 degrees north. The total population is 198,000, with 54,000 living on the capital island of Male. The highest point on any of the islands was only 20 feet above sea level. Global warming scientists predict these islands will be the first victims of the future rise of ocean waters.

The first settlers probably came from India, or Sri Lanka, around 500 B.C. When we arrived, only 202 of the islands were inhabited and foreigners were never allowed to visit most of them. Fifty-nine of the islands had resorts on them, and the Maldivians had learned the value of the tourist dollar. As many as 114,000 tourists visited the islands each year, with 90% of them coming to scuba dive.

As Shadowfax sailed into the lee of Male Island, our first chore was to clear in through customs, health and immigration. It shouldn't have been much of a problem, except there was no place to anchor. Just off the island the sea dropped straight off to a couple hundred feet... too deep for Shadowfax to anchor safely. As we motored in circles waiting for someone to come out to the boat, we could tell that nothing was going to happen very fast. The reason was Ramadan.

Ramadan is a religious event that last for about a month. The religion in the Maldives is Sunni Islam, and no other religions are allowed by law. During Ramadan, no one is allowed to eat, drink, smoke or have sex from sunrise to sunset. As for the customs and immigration offices, they were open all day - tourists and ships still arrived - but they worked at an incredibly slow pace.

So there we were, sailing back and forth and wondering how to get cleared when an anchored container ship from Denmark, called Arktis Sky, had pity on us and called us on the VHF radio. They offered their stern for us to tie to. They knew all about Ramadan and how tough that made life for visitors.

As we tied to the stern of Arktis Sky we noticed they were putting up flags, balloons and banners. We thought this was awfully nice of them to do just for us. After Shadowfax was secure we climbed aboard the huge ship and learned, not really a surprise, that the decorations weren't for us. Arktis Sky was something like a delivery truck for Male. They would make constant round trips from Singapore, bringing Male most of the food they needed. A few companies on Male were run by Yanks and Aussies, and they always looked forward to the return of Arktis Sky and her crew. Their return not only meant food for the island, it also meant party time for westerners. We saw steaks, fresh vegetables, ice cream and more beer than we had seen in many countries. When they insisted we stay, I can't remember which of us said yes first, but it was fast and instantaneous.

The captain of the ship also arranged for a semi-speedy check-in through customs for us, and then it was time for a party. About fifty westerners hired boats to get out to the ship, and everybody had a great time. We met lots of new friends who all seemed to hate working on Male, but since we hadn't even be ashore yet, we just ate ice cream and listened.

We stayed tied to the ship overnight and were invited back aboard in the morning for breakfast. After our first full night's sleep in a while (dreaming of steering) and a huge breakfast, we were shown their collection of 100s of the latest videos. They also pointed us toward their hot showers and full-sized washer and dryer. To us this ship could have been the QE2. Tethys had arrived earlier and went to anchor at an island close by, and while it's true that we wanted to sail over to where they were, we called them on the radio and explained the breakfast and hot shower situation. Being true yachties, they understood completely.

Before we knew it, three days, seven movies and eight loads of laundry had passed, and we were still tied to the stern of Arktis Sky. Captain Erling should receive a medal for the way he treated us poor little yachties. His chief engineer, Frank, even arranged for a local helicopter electrician to have a look at our autopilot.

This sounded hopeful, but the electrician worked for hours and hours on our poor autopilot but couldn't get it to work. Intermittent problems are always the toughest to solve because when you think it's fixed, it's not. Since he couldn't get it working, the electrician wouldn't allow us to pay him a cent. What we did do was have him over for a big dinner of steak and potatoes. He ate a little of it to be polite, but since he was a local Maldivian, he wasn't used to that kind of food. We felt bad, so we invited him over again for a huge plate of rice. He went back for seconds.

It was somewhere during this attempted autopilot repair that we were hit by a tanker. The story starts with Shadowfax still hanging off the stern of Arktis Sky, the electrician and me were aboard Shadowfax, and Gretchen was aboard Arktis Sky.

The electrician and I had our heads down in the engine room working on the autopilot, and I decided to take a break and came topside. I noticed a tanker upwind from us start its motor and begin raising anchor. No big deal... lots of tankers were coming and going all the time. I went back to what I was doing in the engine room. Meanwhile, the tanker's engines stopped – for good – and it started to drift down on Arktis Sky and Shadowfax in a strong current. The captain never sounded the danger signal on his horn, and I guess he didn't feel he had enough room to drop his anchor again.

I heard some yelling from Arktis so I went up to the cockpit. I knew we were in serious trouble. The good news is that the tanker cleared Arktis Sky's stern by a couple of inches. The bad news is that we were trailing about fifty feet from Arktis' stern and right in the tanker's path. Gretchen was in the galley of Arktis and saw this huge ship go past a window, and then she ran out on deck. She said later that the worst part for her was not being able to do anything but watch. I don't think anyone wants to see their boat run down by a 600-foot tanker.

Luckily, at least one of us (me) was aboard and able to do something. What that something was, was to get the engine started – fast – grab a knife and run to the bow and cut the line tied to Arktis – fast – run back to the helm –fast – throw Shadowfax into reverse and put the throttle to full speed. The tanker hit our bow when I was just throwing it in reverse. It wasn't a nice sound. Sort of a snap-crunch sort of thing. I threw the boat into reverse as the tanker pushed us back. At least we were no longer tied to Arktis Sky and Shadowfax was able to roll with the punch and was pushed backwards. Since the tanker came between Shadowfax and Arktis Sky, nobody aboard Arktis - including Gretchen - knew the fate of Shadowfax (or me). Scary day.

Shadowfax is a tough old gal, so no serious structural damage took place: a squashed bow rail, a bent anchor, some cosmetic hull damage, and rust from the ship made a mess of our jib sail. We were lucky that's all that happened because the captain of the tanker said he wouldn't take any responsibility for any of it. Captain Erling of the Arktis told us that since it was a Maldivian tanker, we may be the ones to go to jail if we pressed it.

We couldn't believe this was true, so we decided to give it a try. That was our best plow anchor and we couldn't afford a new one. Captain Erling, along with his crew, signed a witness report, wished us luck, and waved as we dinghied to shore.

Male is like a desert atoll with tourist shops lining the streets. Actually, it was a deserted desert island because of Ramadan, but we were told a few shops would open after sunset.

We went to the owner of the tanker company, and then to the tanker's agent. The agent raised the tanker captain on his radio, and after a few minutes conversation in Arabic, the agent told us that we must have drifted into the tanker, and we had better be more careful in the future. The harbor master agreed with the ship's agent.

At least we didn't go to jail. Shadowfax was going to have to live with her punch in the nose. We didn't lose the boat, and she could still sail, so no real harm was done. The only thing we did get out of it was a great story. Later I was able to take the anchor ashore and pound it back into a shape that resembled an anchor.

The time came to leave our friends on Arktis Sky, and the least we could do was pass out Shadowfax t-shirts to everyone. With all our laundry done, and our fill of movies, we untied from their stern and made our way five miles to the tiny atoll named Farukolufushi - a real mouth full to say. Tethys and a couple of other yachts were already enjoying the snorkeling and scuba diving.

The small entrance pass led us by dozens of reefs until it opened into a crystal-clear lagoon. The only building on the small island was a Club Med that offered us their windsurfers and Hobie Cats when not in use by their guests. The nice people in this world definitely outnumber the no-so-nice... like certain tanker captains.

We had everyone in the anchorage over for a small party – all of them had been to the cat party in Sri Lanka – and we spread the word, "No t-shirt or flag orders!" We relaxed for a few days... just swimming, diving and playing onshore. We kept putting off the long passage to the Red Sea by saying, "One more day." We were definitely late heading out that way. We thought we might be the last ones sailing up the Red Sea this season.

We cleared out of the Maldive Islands and pointed the bow west with brisk winds in the company of Tethys. Wow! What a trip. The best way to sum it up would be to say "slow." Twenty-one days at sea! Quite a few times we were grateful to reach a speed of 2 knots. Of course, a slow speed like this meant we had to hand-steer.

We were almost always in radio contact with Tethys, and I think it was the fifth day out that we decided to plot a course to meet up with them for "a day at the beach." Of course we really didn't have any beach, but it was so calm that we just left the boats and swam around for most of the day. Crystal-clear water three miles deep and not a shark in sight. We stayed for an entire day and it seemed like such a strange place to be. The weather was so clear, and the seas so flat, it was hard to believe we were in the middle of the Indian Ocean. We thought our mid-ocean party would be a once-in-a-lifetime thing, but we actually met again to swim three more times as the trip slowly progressed westward.

Traveling in the company of another yacht on a long passage like this has a few advantages. All across the Indian Ocean we were helping each other with all the little things that seem to self-destruct. Tethys burned out an alternator - we had a spare. Shadowfax needed a single-sideband radio - Tethys had a spare. Tethys needed diesel fuel - we had plenty. And so on, and so on, etc.

I mentioned earlier that Tethys was an all-woman crew: Nancy, captain: Patti, engineer: Susan, navigation & boat management. Between the three of them they could fix just about anything that broke. I guess I could say something about giving women credit for doing something like that, but in this day and age it's pretty obvious that a woman can do anything a man can do. Well, maybe not so obvious to the culture of the countries bordering the Red Sea.

Day 18 of this marathon no-wind passage brought us close to the island of Socotra off the coast of Somalia. Socotra must be a strange place to visit, not that we would. We were told in Singapore and Sri Lanka to stay well off Socotra Island. We were told the island was infested with pirates. We were also told that these pirates had 60-mile radar and speedboats. We'll never know because we gave the place an 80-mile berth.

Our last "day at the beach" stop with Tethys was at this 80-mile distance from Socotra. We had to launch our dinghy for the visit because swimming was out of the question. I'm not exaggerating to say we had 300 sharks swimming around the boats. Maybe these were the famous "Socotra Pirates." We couldn't figure out what they were up to, but even the cat seemed to sense they were trouble. He normally liked to watch porpoise and fish, but after one look at all the sharks he went below and didn't come back out.

One of the reasons for all the stops along our way was so we could take a little time off and rest. Out of the twenty days it took us to get to Yemen, we hand-steered for sixteen. Not an easy task, but I actually think we got used to it. After suffering through the first week we fell into a routine - sleep for two hours, steer for two hours, sleep for two hours, etc. Just the two of us in a small boat on a huge ocean, and we hardly ever saw each other. The next time around I'll try to have at least one complete autopilot for a spare. Steering is for other people.

Two days out from Yemen and the wind finally came up. We raised the spinnaker and made terrific time... at least until two in the morning when the wind built to just over 30 knots. Way too much for our spinnaker. I don't know how many of you have tried to get a spinnaker down in that kind of weather and in the dark, but, believe me, it's not much fun. Whenever something bad happens, it's at two in the morning... why is that?

So, after twenty-one days at sea and many gallons of diesel, we entered the city of Aden in the Peoples Republic of Yemen. Many years ago Aden was the second busiest port in the world, but when we were there it was a communist country and the port was a neglected ruin. At first glance the port looked busy with a couple dozen tankers and container ships at anchor. In reality, they were Iraq ships with no place to go since the (first) Gulf War. Yemen sided with Iraq during the war, so Aden became a parking lot for these homeless hulks.

Chapter 30

Yemen has an ancient history going back to the Romans who captured it in 24 B.C. In more recent history, Yemen was captured in 1538 by Turkey and didn't become independent until 1735. The city of Aden was attacked and captured by the British in 1839. Another country with a stormy past.

In 1986 there was an attempted overthrow of the communist government that was very bloody and very unsuccessful. Aden was blown to pieces. Upon our arrived it looked like Aden was blown up the previous week. I don't think anyone had changed a light bulb since 1986.

Before 1990, Yemen was actually two countries – north and south. When the two reunified it gave the country an area of 188,000 square miles and a population of about eight and a half million.

As Shadowfax coasted to a stop and dropped her anchor, we were just a short distance from where the USS Cole would be attacked by a suicide bomber a few years later. Just moments after dropping anchor we were boarded and told we were welcome in Yemen. But being a communist country we were given a 6:00p.m. curfew and told not to take any pictures. That sounded a little paranoid, but at least we were given relative freedom.

Along with the women of Tethys, we were able to replace the diesel we burned. The cost of diesel in Aden was 25 cents per imperial gallon. A fantastic price, but we had to work for it. This was something like a legal black market. We weren't supposed to get diesel this way, but the customs agent was the one who told us what to do, so that seemed to make it okay.

We had to get up at 5:00a.m. and dinghy a half-mile. Then we had to beach the dinghy in deep muck behind the gas station. We carried our empty cans up an incline and through the muck to the gas pumps on the street. Next step, wake up the gas attendant who slept in the office. There was a rock holding the door closed, but banging on the glass was enough to get him up... or at least the attendant's mother who slept next to him. Once the jugs were full, we had to figure out how much it would cost because they dealt with three different kinds of money. They used the old money from the north, the southern money, and change that seemed to be from another planet.

We carried the jugs back through the muck and into the dinghy. Then we had to dinghy through tar and oil covered waters to get back to our boats. The locals told us the harbor was covered in oil and tar because of a leak and not to worry about it because it was always like that. We did this same 5:00a.m. diesel run four mornings in a row. The reason it had to be so early in the morning was because that's the way those black market things seemed to work. Not a pleasant way to shop. Fairly confusing too, since everyone (Customs agent included) seemed to know about it.

During the days, after our diesel duty, we found lots of things to do. Together with the crew of Tethys we arranged for a tour of the local museum and a visit to what they called a "camel market." The museum was a large two-story building filled with artifacts thousands of years old just sitting out in the open. We started to call it the "touch and feel museum." One inscribed stone was in the shape of what you'd think Moses carried down from the mountains... and it was used to hold a door open. Nobody could tell us what anything was other than to say, "These stones over here are very old." I've gotta say that this was one of the most memorable museums we'd ever visited, and when we left we were all in agreement that, yes, all their stones were indeed old.

The camel market was a place where nomads rode their camels out of the desert and brought to market anything that they might have to sell. I've never seen so many camels in my life, and almost every one of them had a sword-carrying Arab sitting on its back. One guy was so proud of his camel that he stuck his whole arm into the camel's mouth to show us it didn't bite. He then insisted that I climb aboard to see what a comfortable fit it was. I climbed up to the cheers of a few dozen happy Arabs. I don't think any of them had ever seen this many Yanks in one place before. As for what they brought to market, we saw absolutely nothing for sale. I think it was more of an Arab hangout than a market. One bit of trivia that came out of our hanging out with them was that a camel can drink six gallons of water at one sitting – actually standing. We watched one drink out of an old bathtub they used for a trough. Amazing to watch... and noisy too.

Something else about this part of the world is the local dress. In your imagination you picture Arabs dressed in flowing white robes with turbans wrapped around their heads. Well, you got it exactly right! Just add leather belts with daggers hanging from them, or maybe three-foot swords strapped to their backs, and you've got the whole picture. The Arab women are a different story. They were almost completely covered in black from head to foot in the 100 degree heat. The only thing you could see were their eyes, and we were told never to make eye contact with the women. We were also told that we should never touch or speak to them. Women were the property of men, nothing more. The three women alone on Tethys, sailing around the world, confused the local men. This was not something the men would ever let Yemen women do.

Whenever Gretchen went out in this Arab world she had to try and dress the part by covering herself up as much as she could. One time she put on all black to see what it was like, and in the one hundred plus degree desert heat she didn't last an hour before going back to the boat to change. We tried to go with the flow wherever we went, but this was tough on visiting western women.

One afternoon while Gretchen and I were just walking around Aden, we passed a place called "The Sailors Club," which was written in English. Definitely worth checking out. We took a seat by ourselves in a room full of Arab men, but that didn't last long. The largest table with the most men invited us to join them. We're always up for a party, so we wandered on over. Introductions were made all the way around. We really had picked a great table to visit. Everyone spoke a little English so we weren't completely lost. One man was a reporter for the local communist newspaper, another man was a Palestinian who claimed to belong to the P.L.O., and another was a captain on one of the Iraqi ships that had been stuck in the harbor for the previous two years because of us Yanks. I could tell right off that this was going to be an interesting night – if we lived through it.

The table where we were sitting was covered in half-empty Russian Stolichnaya vodka bottles, and I commented right away on their good taste in spirits, although slightly confused since Islam forbids alcohol. I was then informed that Russia no longer dealt with Yemen, so all they had left were the empty Stolichnaya bottles which they filled with the local homemade hooch. Off to a bad start right away. We decided not to ask why they were drinking alcohol.

The next subject brought up was the t-shirt I was wearing. The reason they were so fascinated by my shirt was because it was the "Red Sea '93" silkscreen we were selling. I had put all the names of the countries on it, so right dead center on the top was Israel... not their favorite place. Our new P.L.O. buddy wanted to talk about why we had Israel on a t-shirt and wanted to know our opinion about the whole Arab-Israeli mess. Actually, he only wanted my opinion because Gretchen was a woman. I answered as well as any politician could. I confused them to the point that they had no idea what I said. This would not have been a good time for us to take a stand on any of the issues.

All in all, we had a great night trading stories, and then we all agreed we were lifelong friends no matter what our disagreements might be. It's a good thing that we decided to be friends, because it was somewhere around this point that they wanted to show off their guns. Under their flowing white robes every one of them had an automatic weapon. They told us that after the trouble in 1986, everybody carried a gun when they went out. Everyone except these fool Americans.

After getting totally plastered at the Sailors Club, we were escorted back to the dinghy by General Mohammad of the Immigration department. Pretty high ranking for a couple of yachties, but he had a point - we did break our 6p.m. curfew. At least we were brought back to the boat instead of to a Yemen prison. I've never seen a Yemen prison, but somehow I know I wouldn't like it.

Besides buying the fuel, we bought a few eggs and a couple of bottles of the local hooch in the fancy Stolie bottles, and that about finished our money. We had spent almost all of it on supplies back in Sri Lanka, and since we just hung around the Club Med in the Maldives spending money, we broke our own "poor" record of $12.00 in Singapore. We sailed from Yemen with a total of $7.00 U.S.

But more important than money, the boat was stocked with food, and we had about 200 blank t-shirts. We were as ready as we would ever be to face the next 900 miles of desert sailing. We would need a few hundred dollars to transit the Suez Canal, but we had the next 900 miles to earn it. Actually we would need more than that to pay for things like a trip to the pyramids, a trip to the temples and scuba diving the Sinai Peninsula. That's a lot of silk screening and we weren't sure where or when that would happen.

Shadowfax sailed from Yemen with a fair 15-knot wind and fond memories of our first middle-east country. The idea was just to sail twenty miles to an island called Ras Imran. All my log book says about the place is, "Good anchorage, beach perfect for kitty litter." What more could you want than that?

We anchored behind the island so we could get in the water and try to scrape the tar and oil from around the waterline of Shadowfax. Even the waterline on the dinghy was a disaster. I don't know what kind of leak made that mess in Aden's harbor, but it sure was a big one. Paint thinner and lots of elbow grease were all we could find that would get it off.

We left Imran for a two-night sail north into the Red Sea. A hundred or so miles sail and we came to Bab-el-Mandeb (Gates of Sorrow), which is a narrow pass marking the entrance to the Red Sea.

The season for the most favorable weather for sailing up the Red Sea is about five month's long, and during that period, besides us, there were over 250 other sailboats making this Red Sea trip. This flow of yachties every year must be a real shock to the nomads and other locals along the coastline. Quite a few boats wanted to head through quickly, but at least half planned to do it the way we did it... slow and easy.

The charts showed good anchorages most of the way, and we had the benefit of having 99% of the other boats ahead of us to radio back all the best Red Sea gossip, which usually included a rating of the anchorages. The general state of the Red Sea was to give us following winds for the first 200 or so miles, and then the wind was to turn and start howling against us.

The boats that were taking their time and "anchorage-hopping" up the coast, as we were, were getting up at daylight – 4:00 a.m. – and then motor/sailing until noon, which is when the wind usually started slamming into them.

Another fact about yachts sailing in the Red Sea was the way sailors flocked together. It would be impossible for all 250 boats to sail together, so people bunched up into little "families" of about four boats each. You get close to each other on a trip like this - two and a half months of no stores and no civilization, just desert and heat. We formed our little family right at the start of the passage without even realizing it.

We were still in the company of Tethys, but a boat named Azura and the boat Moonshiner also left Ras Imran the same day as we did. We were happy to have such good company. If you're going to day-sail and party for 900 miles, it's great to have nice people to do it with. Actually, one more boat joined our group. They were ahead of us, and we hadn't caught up with them yet. They were stuck in the nearby country of Djibouti trying to get their motor rebuilt. What a disaster that must have been.

We entered Bab-el-Mandeb and the Red Sea just at sunrise. What a strange feeling to enter this historic area and pass through the eerie and narrow "Gates of Sorrow." All night a steady 30 to 40 knots of wind blew us along, and at dawn a huge red sun rose over the coast of Yemen. The sunrises and sunsets all the way up the Red Sea were fabulous. I don't know if it had anything to do with the desert, but they sure were strange and beautiful.

As the sun rose, we were exhausted. Dealing with that much wind all night tends to wipe you out. We thought the wind would die down after we sailed through the narrowest part of Bab-el-Mandeb, but we were wrong. No such luck. We were about to enter some of the roughest weather we had seen since leaving Florida.

The wind was directly behind us and building to an incredible roar through the rigging. We kept reducing sail until all we had up was a handkerchief-size foresail. We were flying at speeds of up to 12 ½ knots! The seas were close together, square and huge. Our steering vane seemed to love this kind of weather, which meant at least we didn't have to steer. The waves were breaking across the stern of the boat, and the wind was up to more than 50 knots. Along with this wind, there was the strange fact that the sky was crystal clear, the sun was blasting and the barometer was steady. Strange weather.

After the first day we actually started to enjoy it. It was very noisy with all that wind and the water hissing by, but we would definitely rather have the boat steering itself through a gale than for us to have to steer through a calm.

The second day we headed toward an anchorage in the northern part of Yemen. The port of Mokha was hard to pick out from open sea in that kind of weather, but we just trusted our navigation and headed in when we thought the time was right. We closed in on land and finally came to a marked channel that led directly into the wind.

We weren't sure we could make it upwind into this harbor, but we started the motor, dropped the sail and turned straight into the wind. What a ride! The bow of the boat would crash into each wave and throw a couple of tons of water back to the cockpit. The channel was shallow and narrow, so all we could do was hang on and keep inching forward. Two and a half hours later we made it to the anchorage.

It felt great to drop the hook. All we wanted to do was have something to eat and crawl into the v-berth to sleep. First things first. We had to deal with the officials... at least we think they were officials. Five minutes after anchoring, a large steel boat headed out from shore and came straight at us. What these guys wanted to do was to give us a simple paper to fill out, but to do it they slammed their steel boat into the side of Shadowfax. Shadowfax sure was taking its share of knocks lately.

Scrapes ran down the side of our hull, but fortunately, no holes. The people in the boat were yelling at us in their language, and it's hard to say what they were yelling about. I think they were telling us not to slam the side of Shadowfax against the bow of their boat anymore. We just took the paper, filled it out and off they went back to wherever it was they came from.

The next morning we headed back out, and my log says, "Left with barely 30 knots of wind, a little gusty." The wind increased around noon, and we planned to be at anchor by the evening. In the middle of the Red Sea, at the southern end, is Great Hanish Island with a perfectly formed cove to anchor in. We pointed Shadowfax toward it. Great Hanish Island was either part of Yemen, Ethiopia or Eritrea, depending on who you asked. This island was a point of contention, or argument, or even war, but since there were no officials (or anybody) on shore, we didn't really care who owned it.

Gale force winds blew us along again at over 10 knots and we were at Hanish Island before we knew it. We also caught enough fish to fillet to keep us busy for most of the day. This was the start of our fishing fame.

We sailed into the cove on Hanish and found a nice surprise. Ten other boats were at anchor waiting out the high winds. There was a beautiful and deserted sand beach on shore, and we had lots of fish. The perfect formula for a beach party and fish fry. We knew most of the people on the boats from ports around the world, and we had no trouble pushing the ol' "Red Sea '93" t-shirts at the party. Capitalists to the end.

We rested and played at Great Hanish for a couple of days, and when the wind dropped down to 25 knots, we sailed out. Tethys and Azura traveled with us for the short sail to anchor for the night at Zuquar Island just 25 miles away. A good idea, but it didn't work. By the time we got there the wind had increased and there were breakers in our intended anchorage. We had no choice but to sail overnight to the next anchorage 120 miles away.

Winds of over 40 knots pushed us north through the night. My entry in the ship's log at sunset reads, "Wind SSE at 40, 10-foot swell, clear sky, SHIPS EVERYWHERE!!" All night we never had less than six tankers in sight! The Red Sea was one busy place. Any ships heading to the Mediterranean had to go either up the Red Sea, or go all the way around South Africa. Being such an incredible short cut, it's guaranteed that the Red Sea will always be busy. We just kept our eyes open and dodged around the ships that got too close.

Our next anchorage was almost as bad as the one with the breakers, but we managed to find a place to tuck in safely. Our only choice was to drop the anchor onto a 50-foot-deep rocky bottom. With strong winds and a deep anchorage like that, it's hard to feel secure. The wind would have blown us out into open water if the anchor let go, so at least we wouldn't run aground on shore. If we dragged anchor out into 10-foot swells, we probably would have awakened quickly.

Besides Tethys and Azura, we also had a local fishing boat in the anchorage with us. Their boat looked more like a dugout canoe. Twelve people were aboard this tiny craft, and one of them had malaria. They were fishing for their village and didn't intend to head back before they loaded up with as much fish as they could carry. Helen and Ty from the yacht Azura passed them a supply of malaria medicine, and there wasn't much more any of us could do. The man with malaria was lying in the bottom of the boat as they left to continue fishing. What a rough life for these people.

The next morning the winds were down to a mere 30 knots so we took off for our next destination – the uninhabited Harmil Island in the country of Eritrea. Eritrea and Ethiopia were in conflict (war) with each other, and who owned this deserted island was part of the dispute. We talked about the two countries being at war, but every country along the Red Sea seemed to have the same amount of tension. We had received word through the ham radio (maybe real, maybe not) that the Eritrean government would look the other way if any sailing yachts wanted to stop at one of their outlying islands. I guess they had bigger problems than worrying about a harmless little sailboat.

So there we were, safely anchored in Eritrea (Ethiopia?) on Easter morning defrosting a ten-pound turkey that we had kept frozen since Malaysia. This was just one of life's ironies. Eritrea for a turkey dinner! It sounds decadent, but along with the crew of Tethys and Ty and Helen from Azura, we ate the whole thing.

The island of Harmil is a great place as long as you like desert. Actually, desert seemed to be the only choice in this part of the world. Hundreds and hundreds of miles of sand! This has to be one of the hardest places in the world to live. I have no idea how they do it. Finding food would be a huge problem, and finding water seemed almost impossible. We were told that a few of the tribes in the area wouldn't eat fish because they considered it "dirty" food. As far as I could tell, fish was the only food around – and there seemed to be plenty.

We dragged two of our homemade lures behind us all the way to Harmil Island, and we were starting to count the fish we caught in feet instead of how many. We caught more than 60 feet of fish (more than 40 fish) since we sailed from the Maldives, and over 40 feet of that was caught in Ethiopian/Eritrea waters! We were passing out fish left and right. No one else seemed to be having our luck, and we don't really know what the reason was. Maybe it was the homemade lures, or maybe it was because the locals didn't fish very often.

We spent a few days hanging out on Harmil, and when the time came to leave, twelve other yachts were packed into the calm harbor. The ham radio had spread the word about how comfortable, calm and deserted the place was, so every boat in the area had sailed on over. With an average of two people per boat, this meant a sale of at least 24 "Red Sea '93" t-shirts. We knew we needed a few hundred dollars to get through the Suez Canal, and no one around us was safe until we earned it.

Next stop - Sudan. Our first anchorage was called Kor Nawarat and is located at the southern end of the country. There was nothing there but another deserted desert island, with the exception of two nomads sleeping on a sand dune next to their camels. We only planned to spend one night at anchor there, but the next morning we were greeted by our first sand storm.

Conditions in a sand storm are a lot like a snow blizzard, except it hurts to look into it. Shadowfax got her first sandblasting – unfortunately not her last. What a mess! Even with the boat all closed up sand still managed to get everywhere. Even in closed drawers, lockers and even inside our air-tight microwave. We figured by the time Shadowfax got to the Mediterranean she would look like a floating sand dune.

After a couple days of sailing up the Sudanese coast, one of the boats that we were sailing with, Moonshiner, did what we all feared most: engine breakdown. With reefs everywhere and the fact that civilization was at least 1,000 miles away, this was the worst place to have anything like that happen. Shadowfax to the rescue! We threw Moonshiner a line and towed them whenever they had to weave through the reefs or get into a tight anchorage. Luckily the wind blew strong enough where they didn't need a tow other than through a few dangerous areas.

Of course, it would be possible to sail up the middle of the Red Sea without stopping, but I wouldn't wish that on any small sailboat. From this point north, the wind pattern switches 180 degrees and blows right on the bow at over 30 knots. Our routine was to leave anchorages at sunrise (4:00a.m.) when the wind was light and then try to be at anchor again by noon when the wind really started to howl. At least there were no problems finding anchorages. The west coast of the Red Sea has hundreds of great anchorages – called a Marsa – tucked in behind the reefs.

Chapter 31

We finally made it to the port of Suakin where we could clear into Sudan.

Sudan is the largest country in Africa with a total area of 967,494 square miles and a population of over 28 million. Sudan is bordered by Egypt, Libya, Chad, The Central African Republic, Zaire, Uganda, Kenya and Ethiopia. The country has more than 300 different tribes that speak over 100 different languages. The major religion is Islam.

Sudan was once known as The Land of Cush, source of gold, ivory, and slaves. Over the centuries the country has been conquered by Egypt, the Romans and the British. In 1956 Sudan proclaimed its independence.

Today there are so many groups with different interests, and with no real economy (average income $400.00 per year), the country doesn't have much of a chance for a stable government. A civil war has been raging for many years, and the future looks grim. It is reported that over 500,000 civilians have been killed since the war began.

So there we were, towing Moonshiner into Suakin, and hoping Sudan's feelings for Americans on that particular day were good. Suakin is a city of ruin that looks like a small nuclear bomb had exploded right on top of it. The place is in such a state that no one should live there - but people do. A hundred or so years ago Suakin was a slave-trading port, but when Port Sudan was opened fifty miles to the north, almost everyone in Suakin moved there, leaving the place to disintegrate. The buildings are made from coral and mud, so the years have really taken a toll.

One of Suakin's legends is worth repeating. It seems at one time Queen Balgies, of the Kingdom of Yemen, sent seven virgins as a gift to King Solomon in Jerusalem. While in route a great storm pushed their ship into Suakin. When the ship finally arrived in Jerusalem, the virgins were virgins no more. They were all pregnant! They claimed a demon named Ginn made them pregnant while they were in Suakin. Sure, I believe it. Fifty bucks says Captain Ginn was driving the boat.

As soon as we dropped anchor four officials came out to board us. We were given permission to stay for a week. However, every time we went ashore we had to go to their office to pick up a letter giving us permission to do whatever we planned to do. A curfew of 6:00 p.m. was also imposed.

We were all able to get water, which we badly needed. As long as I live I'll never forget the water delivery. Picture in your mind a huge city that looks like the Roman ruins with six donkeys walking along the main road towing two-wheel carts holding containers of water (one 50-gallon drum per donkey). The donkeys were led by turban-covered Arabs with swords strapped to their sides. I guess I was naïve thinking it would come by truck. You may want to know where the water came from... well, so did we and we never found out. I think sailors must be tough as far as diets go because we ate the strange foods and drank the water in every country (I think we could digest uranium), so we filled our tanks and were grateful to get it. Cost for 300 gallons of water, plus delivery by donkey - $3.00.

Sudan was also where I started being a rent-a-husband for the three women aboard Tethys. All the way up the Red Sea it was dangerous for a woman to go out alone, so they would ask me if I would mind going out with them and pretend we were married. This worked, but usually by the time we left a harbor a few of the locals would think I had four wives. I remember telling one of them that was why I had to leave the States.

Sudan was a good place to barter for what we needed at the local open market. Gretchen was the queen of trading, and managed to score a 200-year-old sword off the back of a camel-riding Arab. What a score! It had an inscribed blade with a silver handle. If it could talk, I'm sure we could hear some fantastic stories. The cost of the sword was an old jean jacket, a few t-shirts, and a couple of perfume samples.

For whatever food and vegetables we could find, Gretchen traded more perfume samples, which she had the smarts to collect for just such an occasion. The men never thought about giving the perfume to their wives. They started pouring it over themselves and even the camels. By the end of the day the market had the smell of a J.C. Penny cosmetics counter and a camel farm all mixed together. A smell even the open sewers couldn't overpower.

A few other yachts were in the anchorage and one night we decided to go to a small restaurant about 10 miles away. Two old pickup trucks were hired to get us there, and arrangements (bribes) were made so we could break our 6:00 p.m. curfew.

The ride to the restaurant was fast and bumpy and included a flat tire along the way. The meal was even faster than the ride. As soon we got there and sat down, we were informed we were in big trouble. Apparently, one of the people in the restaurant was an official who was upset that we were out past our curfew, and he thought maybe we should go to jail. I guess he wasn't in on any of the bribe money. It was finally smoothed over to the point that if we promised to eat at warp speed and get out of there, we wouldn't be arrested. The food wasn't bad, but with a Sudanese jail on our minds, we couldn't really enjoy it.

A couple of other things happened before we left Suakin - Moonshiner was repaired without needing to order parts, and our refrigeration compressor blew up and definitely needed parts. Of all the places in the world to break it had to pick the damn desert. It's true that most of the yachts sailing around the world's oceans don't seem to have refrigeration, but on the other hand, we always had lots of company for cold drinks. I think I learned just about everything there is to know about refrigeration repair on a sailboat. Between the fridge and the freezer I spent more time keeping them working than either the main motor or the generator. But this time there was no chance to get it fixed until Cyprus – about 900 miles away.

From Suakin we fought our way north past dozens of uncharted reefs and through thousands of jellyfish the size of manhole covers. Sailing along the coast during the daytime was fairly easy because the water was so clear that we could see the reefs a mile ahead. Most of the reefs on the chart didn't seem to exist, and most of the reefs in the water weren't on the charts, so it's a good thing we could see them.

One of our more memorable stops was the reef-enclosed lagoon called Sha'ab Rumi, one of the most famous Red Sea diving destinations. Sha'ab Rumi was made famous when Jacques Cousteau set up an underwater habitat so he could run experiments. Today the frame from the habitat, and a shark cage, are still in place. Believe it or not, the whole of the Red Sea is a much sought after, scuba diving haven. The waters are so clear, and the reefs so plentiful and unharmed, that this has to be one of the most enchanting places in the world to dive.

As Shadowfax entered the 30-foot-wide entrance to the lagoon, the first thing we saw was a half-dozen charter dive boats in the 50 to 100-foot range. Still being on the hunt for money, we dropped anchor and started working on a Sha'ab Rumi dive t-shirt. All those charterers aboard those boats probably thought they were safe from spending any money way out in the middle of nowhere.

Most of the charter boats had Americans aboard who worked in Saudi Arabia and were out on a short vacation. When we hopped in our little dinghy and went visiting dive boats to show off our cool "Dive Sha'ab Rumi" shirt design, we made a quick $300.

After we got our work out of the way we were able to dive on the reef, and it was spectacular. We dove down and came up under the old Cousteau habitat. Once inside we were able to take our regulators out of our mouths and breathe the air inside the dome-shaped structure. It must have been quite an experience to live underwater like that for an extended period of time. The coral formations outside the windows (in their backyard), along with all the colorful reef fish and sharks would be like watching a National Geographic special on TV.

After a five-day stay at Sha'ab Rumi we sailed out to continue our flight north. Each day the wind was against us at up to 30 knots, so we were happy when a high-pressure system moved over us and brought light winds with it. The wind was still against us, but it had dropped to only 10 to 15 knots.

We headed out for an overnight sail north to a place called Marsa Halaib, very near the Egyptian border. We didn't know it at the time, but later we heard on the Voice of America radio station that Halaib was a terrorist training camp. Looking back on it I guess it's sometimes good to be clueless, but on the other hand... Geez!

As soon as we had the anchor down a small boat with a deck gun (easily the length of the boat) came out with eight locals aboard. They crashed into the side of Shadowfax with a big bang and immediately started yelling in a Sudanese dialect. I think they were either apologizing for slamming into us or demanding to know why we were there. Their English was almost nonexistent, but "papers please" seems to be a universal request, and we handed over the boat's papers along with our passports.

We tried to explain that we just wanted to dive on the reef and visit their village while waiting for another break in the wind. After a little more screaming we were welcomed to their village - we think - and they zipped away.

The village was more like a military base. No women, children, or shops could be seen, but there were lots of guns. Nothing so unusual there. Guns, along with water pipes, seemed to be part of the way of life in this part of the world. Gretchen managed to find a few loaves of bread to bring back to the boat, but it was horrible. More like furry Frisbees.

Our second day there we were greeted by an Egyptian army helicopter flying at ground level taking pictures of everything - including us naïve Americans waving to them. We had read that this was a hotly contested border where both countries claimed ownership, but we thought these countries were friendly with each other. Again we were being naïve. What we heard later on the Voice of America was that the U.S. wanted to put Sudan on the list of terrorist supporting countries. They said the terrorists who had been killing tourists in Egypt were being trained in places like Halaib. The V.O.A. also said Egypt had had enough of Sudan, and they intended to take Halaib, along with the rest of the contested border, back "One way or another." Three weeks later another sailboat sailed into Halaib and they were welcomed to Egypt, not Sudan. I guess Egypt had kept its promise to take Halaib back.

All that terrorist stuff didn't seem to affect our stay, and we managed to have an enjoyable time. The people were friendly... for Sudanese terrorists. While we were anchored at Halaib a guard was posted on the sand dune near our boat for the entire time - just in case we were American C.I.A. with an incredibly good disguise in an incredibly slow boat.

Next stop Egypt, where nothing happens without a bribe, and fist fights between taxi drivers for your fare were commonplace. What an interesting culture.

Chapter 32

Egypt has an area of 386,659 square miles and is located in the northeast corner of Africa. To the east, across the Sinai Peninsula, is Israel, to the south is Sudan, and to the west, Libya. The population is somewhere around 42 million and the main religion is, of course, Islam.

About 5,000 years ago a king named Menes unified upper and lower Egypt, and from then on there was a long list of kings and queens. Huge stone cities and incredible pyramids were constructed at the cost of thousands of lives. The complex temple of Karnak was built on the Nile River in the city of Thebes (Luxor today). Thebes prospered for about 250 years, and this is the location of dozens of deep tombs cut hundreds of feet deep into limestone. Kings, queens, nobles, generals, and just about everybody else of significance was buried in one of the elaborate tombs. Fifty centuries later, we cleared into Egypt at the port of Hurghada.

To clear into the country we were searched by one of the officials - actually an army officer - for almost an hour. What he wanted he called, "girly magazines." He wanted anything that might show bathing suits or bra ads. Even a Sears catalog would do. This is called pornography in Egypt, but he wanted them for personal use... not to arrest us. We didn't have anything to make him happy, so we just paid him baksheesh (we called it a bribe, Egyptians called it a tip) and got rid of him.

We were warned long before we made it to Egypt that we would need cigarettes to pass out as baksheesh, or we would never make it through Egypt and the Suez Canal. Only packs of Marlboros were acceptable. One couple we met took a syringe out of their medical kit and injected saltwater into the sealed packs before passing them out as bribes. We didn't want to do anything extreme like that. It would make life harder for future yachts, so we just paid baksheesh in money, cigarettes, or t-shirts.

We thought Hurghada would be a convenient place to leave the boat and take a trip to Luxor to visit the famous temples and tombs, so we looked the chart over to find a safe anchorage. At this particular time tourists were being killed in Egypt, but we figured it would be crazy to sail all this way and not check the place out. If we took local transportation, instead of a tour bus, we thought maybe we could blend in with the locals. Fat chance, but we anchored the boat and set out to explore.

We arrived at the local bus stop at 6:00 a.m. to try and find the right bus for this five-hour trip to Luxor (cost $3.00). It seems we weren't alone. About a hundred other people holding luggage, chickens and swords were also waiting. There was also a nice little guy - I guess you could call him the bus monitor - who was walking back and forth holding a shotgun. In broken English he informed us that things usually got a little rough when the bus arrived and the doors opened, and maybe we might want to stand back. Gretchen did just that, but I really wanted us to get seats on the bus, so I joined the rush when the bus doors opened.

I'm not very good in a riot situation. I didn't get within ten yards of the door. As it turned out, I didn't have to. After everyone was onboard (chickens, people, swords), the guy with the gun climbed on and "appropriated" us a couple of seats. We felt a little guilty, but even the people on the bus wanted us to have the seats. Not everyone in Egypt was a baksheesh-demanding bully.

As we approached the Nile something happened to the desert. It went away to be replaced by green everything - trees, plants, grass. What a difference! I was about ready to hug a tree and kiss a bush. Week after week of looking at nothing but desert sand gets a little old and is hard on your eyes. The Nile area might be a bit polluted, but it sure was beautiful to us.

Once in Luxor we found a $7.00 per night hotel we'd been told about. We expected a dive, but the place was clean and comfortable. The hotel was run by a guy named

Muhammad Ali and had air conditioned rooms with a breakfast of fruit and coffee included in the price. What a deal! We crawled up the stairs, turned on the air, and tried to recuperate from the bus ride.

After we felt human again we threw ourselves on donkeys on the western side of the Nile River and rode to The Valley of the Kings. The Nile is an impressive river, and we could just picture Kings in their elaborate boats sailing along the shoreline. Hundreds of boats, called feluccas, were sailing along the river's edge loaded down with Egyptians just like they must have done thousands of years ago.

We bounced along on donkeys until we were once again out of the fertile Nile area and back in the desert. Donkeys sure can run faster than I ever thought a donkey could go. We must have looked ridiculous.

We made it to the Valley of the Kings, and we saw so many tombs that they all blurred together. Of course, the one that stuck in our minds the most was the smallest and least decorated tomb of King Tutankhamen (King Tut). I'm sure you've heard of that guy. The tomb was discovered in 1922 and was packed to the ceiling with gold, jewelry, beds, boats and food. Quite a find!

After roasting for the day on donkeys we headed back to the motel to recuperate. The desert sure gets hot.

That night we went to a light show at the Temple of Karnak in Luxor and found it loud and colorful, but interesting and a little hokey. The history was the interesting part, but the presentation was the hokey part.

We managed to fit all the touristy things into the visit and then it was back to Shadowfax. We had run into a few other yachties while touring Luxor, so we all split a taxi and were spared the bus ride back. So much for blending in.

Back at anchor aboard Shadowfax we were greeted by another sandstorm. This one was as bad as you can possibly imagine. If you could stand the pain of looking into it, you could barely see the bow of the boat from the cockpit. We would only go outside if we put on our dive masks first. We didn't want our eyes sandblasted. Even with the boat entirely closed up, the sand still managed to again get into every drawer and locker. What a mess! After the many sandblastings of the Red Sea, Shadowfax was in tough shape. We put a paint job on the "to do" list for when (or if) we ever got real jobs again.

While we were hanging around cleaning sand out of the bilge and waiting for the weather to calm, we took a day off and went to visit American soil. Actually American steel. Warship 47, or better known as the U.S.S. Guided Missile Frigate Nicholas. So many Americans in one place. What a treat! The ship was in port for a little R&R.

We were invited aboard by an ensign who visited Shadowfax a few days earlier. Once aboard they let us shop in the ship's store where we could buy American products we hadn't seen in years – like chocolate chip cookies. A great time, and I think they enjoyed trying to fill us in on the past five years of news we'd missed. And it's only right to mention the chocolate chip cookies again....

This was after the first Gulf War, and before Operation Iraqi Freedom. Their job was to search every ship heading toward Iraq to see if they were delivering anything against the U.N. embargo that had been in place since the first Gulf War. While we were on board we were given a fantastic cheeseburger lunch (sliders), and a tour of the ship. Needless to say, it definitely was impressive. These sailors and soldiers were even more impressive than the ship.

When we entered the C.I.C. (Command Information Center) we saw huge banks of computers and monitors everywhere. A couple of dozen young guys were watching different screens, but the majority of them were in the far corner all huddled together. I wandered over to see what they were doing, and I found them watching the largest computer screen I'd ever seen with an intense look that could only mean war. Sure enough... that's what it was. A video game where they were taking turns taking on alien invaders on a 3-D screen. What a great set-up and it was great to see them enjoying themselves.

When the weather calmed we made plans to leave the port of Hurghada and continue on with a small change in course – east across the Red Sea, instead of north. We also had a new crew member with us for the trip.

Sue from the yacht Tethys wanted to come with us because we were planning to sail part way up the Sinai Peninsula to do a little scuba diving. We told her she could stay with us until we caught up with Tethys at the country of Cyprus in the Mediterranean. The Red Sea had been fabulous in the diving department, and we were told that Sharm el-Sheikh was the best there was. Possibly the best on the planet.

Well, we haven't been everywhere on the planet, but this place was the best diving we'd ever seen. Day dives, night dives, wreck dives, we couldn't get enough. One of the boats we were traveling to Sharm el-Sheikh with, Intermission, had an air-compressor aboard to fill our scuba tanks and we were in heaven. We wrote in "air-compressor" on that wish list of ours.

I'll never forget one of the dives when we were circling a reef at a depth of around 150 feet, and we spotted a huge school of barracuda. There had to be thousands of them, and they were swimming in a tight circle like a tornado. Apparently they will do this before attacking and eating a school of fish caught in the center of the tornado. The sun was shining down and reflecting off their skins like a million mirrors. Truly incredible.

Another of our dives was on a wreck called the Thistlegorm. Thistlegorm is a World War Two supply ship still fully intact. It had just been discovered in about 100 feet of water. On deck and below deck we saw armored tanks, dozens of motorcycles, torpedoes, bombs and even a locomotive train engine. As you can imagine, we tended to swim very carefully around so much unexploded ammunition. Fish of all kinds swam in and around the ship.

I supposed the Thistlegorm had been their home since it sank 50 years earlier. As we looked the ship over it looked like a bomb had hit it dead center on the forward deck and broken its back, sending it straight to the bottom. I'm sure a few unlucky people went along with it. What a fascinating dive! The Red Sea lived up to its reputation as one of the world's best places to dive.

Sleeping in the desert anchorages of the Red Sea was always a little on the hot side, but in the Sinai it was like an oven. The wind blew off the desert at such a temperature that we had to close the boat up at night. It sounds crazy, but it's true. If we had the hatch over our bunk open, it was like standing inches away from an open pizza oven with a fan behind it. This is one hot place!

The next leg of the trip was the toughest 200 miles we had ever sailed. The Gulf of Suez is a narrow little waterway where all the wind in the world funnels and screeches right at you. We would leave early in the morning and go as far as we could before the wind hit its peak in the afternoons. Some days we made it five miles, and one day we lost five miles. Tough going.

The waves in this area were also a different shape that any we'd seen before. They looked a lot like the front bucket on a bulldozer. Our bow would hit one of the bigger ones, and so much water would crash over us that it was funny - well, maybe not so funny at the time. Water came pouring through closed hatches that had never leaked before. Some waves would swallow the bow of Shadowfax and make her look like a submarine that was getting ready to dive. We're talking rough.

The two other boats we were sailing with both broke their forestays (wire from the top of the mast to the bow) within days of each other. Luckily neither mast came crashing down on the deck. In order to help them repair the forestays we first sailed into a calm anchorage. We then got out our hacksaws and cut pieces of anchor chain to either splice together or replace the forestays. The whole Red Sea was a lesson in jerry-rigging repairs. New parts were hundreds of miles away and impossible to have delivered.

We finally managed to bang our way up the entrance to the Suez Canal, which leads to the Mediterranean Sea. When we approached the entrance lots of small boats rushed out to greet us. They had Egyptians aboard and they wanted to convince us that they were the best agent for us to get through the canal. An agent is mandatory to get you through the Suez Canal, and this is where the baksheesh (bribes) really starts to flow. The actual cost of the canal transit was $120.00, but much more had to be paid out.

Back in Hurghada, aboard the Guided Missile Frigate Nicholas, I had asked the crew what it took for them to get through the canal. They told me they had to pass out cartons of cigarettes and dozens of ship's hats. When I asked a cruise ship captain what they did, I was told they had to give cases of cartons of cigarettes and lots of baksheesh money. I was told if baksheesh wasn't paid, your canal transit would be "bogged down" in paperwork forever. The U.S.A. had given Egypt 2.5 billion dollars that year in aid, and our ships were protecting its shore. Something wasn't right. The fact that we worked our tails off trying to earn the money to get through the canal, while also sailing against gale winds, made it tougher for us to give it away for bribes.

Anyway, we picked a guy who called himself "Prince of the Red Sea" as our agent and proceeded to tie to the pilings at a small building that was called the Suez Yacht Club. It's not much of a yacht club, but at least we had a place to dock for a few days. This time we planned to leave the boat for a trip into Cairo, Giza and the pyramids.

A few things stick in my mind about the trip to Cairo. One was the constant bomb searches we went through at the Cairo Museum, the pyramids, the hotels and even the local Pizza Hut Restaurant. I'm glad they did it, but it keeps you looking over your shoulder for terrorists all the time.

When we made it to the pyramids we looked around for a cheap motel that wasn't a real pit. We could find "cheap," but we had to settle for a "pit." What a difference from Luxor. We stayed at the cheapest place we could find - $25.00 a night. What a dump.

To check out the pyramids we rented a couple of beautiful Arabian horses. Riding at an incredible speed through the desert heading toward those huge pyramids was an amazing feeling. Those horses were bred for the desert, and they seemed to love it. We couldn't slow them down. They had two speeds - stopped and full bore. I think this is the best way to experience the pyramids, but you also have the option of camels, or just plain walking.

The Cairo museum lived up to its fame with the golden contents of Tut's Tomb along with a couple hundred mummies tucked in the corners. The museum appeared to be falling apart with construction going on to keep the walls in place. Plaster and wood was falling on a few of the exhibits, but no one seemed to care very much. Even with the museum in disrepair, you still couldn't help but consider it one of the best in the world. Thousands and thousands of years of history filled every square inch of the place. A must-see if you find yourself in that part of the world.

Again, back to the boat to recuperate and get ready for the next part of the trip - the canal transit. The Suez Canal has a lot of history that goes along with it. The canal is the third longest major ship channel in the world at 100 miles (the first two are in the old U.S.S.R. territory). The Suez was first started around 610 B.C. by Pharaoh Necho, but after about 10,000 people died, he quit digging. The canal was completed just over a century later by a Persian ruler who used the Nile Delta to save many miles of digging.

The canal, as we know it today, was started in 1859 and completed in 1869. During construction, 3,000 camels were used to bring drinking water to the workers. Sounds like a hard ten years for that construction crew. In 1967, after the

Six Days War, the canal was closed for almost eight years until Egyptian President Sadat had it reopened.

The morning of our canal trip an Egyptian pilot came onboard for our transit. Having a baksheesh-taking pilot on board is mandatory, and we were glad that ours didn't bug us constantly for what he called "his gift."

The canal itself has no locks to raise and lower ships (like the Panama Canal) because the water in the Mediterranean and the Red Sea are about the same height. Both sides of the ditch are lined with desert sand dunes, military tanks and anti-aircraft guns. Also, signs demanding that no pictures be taken line both sides of the shore. Except for seeing all the military equipment along the way, it was just a motorboat trip up a straight ditch in the middle of the desert. I realize that it was quite a feat to construct, but after ten hours of motoring it became a little bleak.

Since we couldn't make it through the entire canal in one day, we stopped to anchor for the night halfway through in Lake Timsah (also known as Crocodile Lake) off the town of Ismaïlia. A pilot boat had to come out to pick up our pilot, and after a bribe was paid to our pilot, the pilot boat driver, the pilot boat line handlers and three of their friends, they left Shadowfax so we could recuperate (a lot of recuperating went on in Egypt), and get ready to do it again the next day.

At seven the next morning we again paid our baksheesh to the pilot boat driver and all his friends and we took on a different pilot for the second half of the trip. Ten more hours of motoring between anti-aircraft guns and tanks was only broken up by the one time we were made to pull over to a dock on the canal's edge so we could pass out packs of cigarettes to the local police who had their hands out.

Finally, the end of the canal. A pilot boat came out to get our pilot and collect his baksheesh. He wanted to give us another pilot for the last mile out to the exit marker, but by giving him the rest of our cigarettes we managed to convince him to forget it. The whole thing about having a pilot seemed a little silly anyway. They slept while we motored down a wide, straight, ditch. Nothing very difficult about that at all.

That's it. The Red Sea was history, and we were off to the Mediterranean. Lots of new countries, people and traditions to learn about. We had desert burnout, and we were looking forward to something different. We'd heard that in Cyprus there was even such a thing as a hose with unlimited running water... maybe even enough to wash off the boat. After three months in the desert, that sounded hard to believe.

The sail toward Cyprus was uneventful. Headwinds kept the going slow, but after the horrible winds in the Red Sea, it was a piece of cake. We wanted to "hook a right" and sail over to Israel, but we were cutting it close already if we wanted to slowly cruise through the Med and be out before the upcoming winter. We also still had Sue with us, and Tethys was waiting for her in Cyprus.

Chapter 33

The Republic of Cyprus is the third largest island in the Mediterranean and lies in the eastern end of the Sea. The island is 3,472 square miles in size and has a population of about 650,000.

The country is also divided almost in half with a border drawn from east to west. In 1974 Cyprus was attacked from the north by the Turkish Army and lost the whole northern half of their country. Barbed wire, 2,000 peacekeeping troops, and a minefield keep an unstable peace between the two areas. Needless to say, Cyprus and Turkey weren't very good friends when we dropped in for a visit. We found that everyone we talked to in the southern part were willing to do just about anything to get their country back. Since the Turkish Army was so strong they realized there wasn't much they could do, except hope Turkey didn't decide to take over their whole country.

We sailed into the port of Larnaca on the southeast coast of Cyprus and spent our first night tied to a dock since Australia - eleven countries earlier. As soon as we tied to the dock for our customs clear-in procedure, I could see what he had heard about the place was true. Just a few feet from where we were tied, there was a hose just lying on the pier, fully on, and spilling water onto the dock.

We'd been conserving water for so long that all we wanted to do was run over and shut the hose off. Such a simple thing as running water sure can be taken for granted. I think every person should have to make 200 gallons of freshwater last for three months. It sure does make you appreciate it a lot more.

Another plus about Cyprus was the fact that we could get things done. The refrigerator compressor had been broken since Sudan, and all it took to fix it was a hundred bucks, a couple of hours work and poof! Ice cubes again.

Even though our two weeks in Cyprus were filled with boat projects, we still managed to enjoy ourselves. Lots of yachts we'd followed up the Red Sea were also working on their boats. Quite a few were planning to leave their boats there and head back to their homes for a while.

This was the routine of almost everybody. Sail for six months and then return home to whatever life they had in the country they sailed from. They would then return after a few months, loaded with boat parts, supplies and whatever else they could get through customs. A nice way to travel, but on our budget, plane tickets back to the States was never possible.

Just before sailing from Cyprus we parted with the little blue motorcycle that we had been carrying and using since we bought it in New Zealand. We hated to sell it, but we knew we wouldn't be allowed to bring it back to the States with us. It would never pass the emission laws of America since it burned leaded fuel. Even if it did, we would have had to pay more in import duties than we paid for it. We sold it for enough to pay our dockage bill and to repair the refrigeration. The bike in exchange for ice cubes seemed like a terrific deal.

One thing about the Mediterranean Sea is that nothing is very far away. I don't think it would be possible to get lost even if you tried – at least compared to sailing on one of those huge oceans. When we left Cyprus, all we had to do was make it a mere 200 miles before we arrived in the next country - Turkey.

We were surprised how clear the Med waters were. Somehow we had the impression that the Mediterranean would be dirty and polluted, and we were pleasantly surprised. We could easily see the bottom in depths of up to fifty feet. Not bad. What was bad was the number of plastic shopping bags that were floating around. We were unlucky enough to get one sucked into one of our water intakes on the bottom of the boat. Lots of sailors (and local power-boaters) we talked to had a horror story about over-heating engines, or damaged propellers because of them. The locals we met called the garbage bags "Mediterranean Jellyfish."

Turkey is a huge country of 300,946 square miles and has a population of over 45 million people. It is bordered by Syria, Iraq, Iran, Bulgaria, the Black Sea, and the Mediterranean. The religion today is about 98 percent Muslim. Turkey has a long history of conquests and has many different cultures. The country was possibly settled in the 13th century.

Turkey is so huge, with so much of it being inland, that we had no chance of seeing anything but the southern coastline. We didn't know what to expect when we got there, but Turkey turned out to be one of our favorite places in the Mediterranean.

As soon as we sailed into Turkish waters we loved it. Cheap prices, beautiful anchorages and taverns called "tavernas" tucked into the mountainsides. Goats and donkeys always seemed to be running around the hills and grasslands. Even thirty miles before landfall we were hit with the heavy scent of pine trees. In just about every anchorage we saw an old castle or fort nearby to explore. A real picturesque place. One problem though - the crowds.

The Mediterranean has so many people and charter boats that there is no room to anchor the normal way. The way you have to anchor is called a "Med Moor." What you do is drop an anchor off your bow and then back up to shore and tie the stern of the boat to a tree or rock. This way an anchorage can hold ten times the usual amount of boats. Just like sardines in a can.

Picture this... we were in Turkey anchored in a small lagoon with steep cliffs on all sides and a small beach behind us. Goats covered the shore, and we were sandwiched in between two eighty-foot charter boats. We were trying to relax and enjoy the scenery when all of a sudden mobile phones on both sides of us start ringing. Wow! That's not what we were used to. We were sure that neither call was for us, so we didn't bother asking.

In spite of the crowds we still enjoyed the country. We sailed west along the southern coast of Turkey, stopping every night to squeeze in with the noisy local charter boats. There was always a fort or castle on shore that was worth investigating and the charterers didn't seem to leave their boats, so the shore was never very crowded.

We thought the crowds were bad in Turkey, but we had no idea what crowded meant until we sailed west into the Greek Islands.

My brother Neil and his wife Gail were flying in to the Island of Rhodes, so we cut our little vacation in Turkey short and sailed the thirty-five miles to Greece. The sail to Greece started out with light winds, but as time went on the meltemi filled in. The meltemi is what they name the strong kick-ass northwest wind in this part of the world. Apparently it's common and usually picks up to just over thirty knots by early afternoon. Every country in the Mediterranean had a different name for this wind. I thought it was a great thing to do. Somehow by naming the wind, it didn't seem so... windy.

We were crashing along through the seas on our way to Rhodes when Gretchen noticed a new boat noise. It sounded a lot like water sloshing around – probably because that's what it was. Shadowfax's bilges were filled with water. We were sinking!

Even though this was the first time this had happened, we'd thought about it enough to know what to do. We ran around examining all the through-hull fittings looking for anything that would make us take on water. After sailing two-thirds of the way around the world, sinking was definitely not on our agenda.

We checked everything we could think of and didn't find any possible way we could be taking on that much water. I turned on both our bilge pumps, and after the bilges were empty and the pumps shut off, I found the problem. One of the bilge pumps is supposed to come on by itself when bilge water raises a float switch to a point that turns the pump on. The float switch had quit working, and when this switch quit working, somehow water started to back-siphon up through the bilge pump exhaust port and into the boat. We were heeled over enough with the thirty knots of wind that the water was being forced back into the boat like a pressurized garden hose. At least Gretchen noticed something was wrong before it was too late.

Greece is another large country, but quite a bit of it is made up of islands scattered across the water in an area called the Aegean Sea. Islands are more our cup of tea.

Greece is 50,944 square miles in size with a population of just about a million people. From the crowds, I think there were that many tourists sailing around on charter boats. At least we could use the islands like stepping stones while sailing our way west.

We made it to Rhodes Island without any more disasters and found the main harbor to be the biggest madhouse of all. The harbor was well protected and appeared to be able to handle about 300 boats comfortably, but there were triple that number in there. Everyone was "Med Moored" with an anchor out and their sterns tied to the concrete wall. This would have been all right except the boats were three deep with one in front of the other.

Everyone's anchor line was crossed over everyone else's, and if the farthest boat back wanted to leave, all the boats in front had to raise anchor and get out of the way. Divers were kept working constantly to untangle anchors in the dirty harbor water as a constant flow of boats came and went.

I don't know how we managed to get Shadowfax secured, but somehow we did. We got the shoehorn out and squeezed in between a small sailboat and a huge sailboat. If my brother wasn't flying into Rhodes, we never would have stayed. Every day we were there we had to fend off "attacking yachts" that had drifted into us after hopelessly fouling their anchors.

We didn't want to leave the boat even to meet my brother at the airport, but we did. This is the story we heard when we returned to Shadowfax; a huge powerboat became hung up on our stern anchor while trying to leave. What he did was to give the boat more throttle until he cut through our anchor line. Once the anchor line was cut, he had to pull the line from his propeller. The people who told us this said that a few people on shore were yelling at him to come back and return the anchor. Unfortunately, he just threw the anchor back into the water and motored away. So much for our favorite (and only) stern anchor. I used up a whole scuba tank looking for it, but no luck. It was like trying to find your way through a pitch black room. I couldn't even see my hand in front of my face. I just wished we had put the anchor out that had all chain and no line. The chain would have won, and that powerboat joker would have needed a new propeller. My brother was probably getting the idea that all our sailing was this crazy.

Needless to say, we enjoyed sailing away from Rhodes Harbor. Rhodes has lots of things worth seeing, and it really is worth visiting... just don't bring your own boat.

The meltemi wind decided to take a few days off, so with Neil and his wife Gail aboard, we motored a short 18 miles to the northwest and anchored at the island of Symi. Amazingly, we were all by ourselves in the anchorage. This was a rare occurrence, and we made the most of it. The swimming was refreshing, and we let the cat off the boat and took him to the beach.

The cat didn't care all that much for the sheep that were running around, but when he tried jumping back into the dinghy, he liked it even less - he missed. I think this was the first time in his life that he fell in the water, and he didn't care for it one bit. He got back at us for letting him fall in the water by rolling around in the mud. We brought him back to the boat and his pride was definitely hurt.

Next stop... back to Turkey. We sailed north 27 miles to mainland Turkey and anchored at a place called Cape Krio. We were a little nervous because Krio wasn't a clearing in port, and we weren't sure if we would get in trouble by stopping for the night. We planned on clearing in at another port the next day, but we weren't sure how the Turkish government would feel about that. Since we had come from Greece, and they hardly tolerated anything to do with Greece, we were sure a heavy fine would be involved if we were caught stopping before clearing in first.

Well, nothing happened. We had a great night exploring an old castle on the shore and enjoying the calm anchorage. At least everyone except Gretchen. While climbing around on the castle she dislodged a huge rock that crashed down on her foot. Ouch! Her large toe swelled up and the nail cracked right down the middle. We put a little superglue along the cracked nail, bandaged up the toe, and gave her a pain killer. True yachtie first aid.

The next morning we took my brother, his wife and Gretchen's throbbing toe and sailed to the big city of Bodram, which is part of the Turkish mainland and seems to be where the land-based tourists went. Since we were playing tourist while we had company, we fit right in. The harbor was nothing but a large marina, so we had no choice but to pay for a slip and settle in for the night.

We were able to clear in at this port, which meant we didn't have to worry about fines, prison and vacation-destroying things like that. I took my brother with me when I went to the customs office so he could see how crazy it was to get through the paperwork of sailing. I should have known better than to tackle such a job. Gretchen usually conquered the bureaucrats, especially in Muslim countries where they weren't used to dealing with women. Usually they would take care of her right away just to get rid of her.

It was much different when I tried to take care of it. In Bodram I had to stand in four different lines, kill most of a whole day and fill out a stack of papers for customs, health, immigration, security and the port authority – all in different offices. At least my brother got to see how bureaucracy worked in other countries... like any registry of motor vehicles in the United States.

Bodrum was a fast, action-type place. Lots of bars, restaurants and streets as crowded as Disney World. We had a fun time trying to find the taverns with the loudest music. No shortage of choices in that department.

Just before pulling into the dock at Bodram our throttle cable had broken, so I had a chance to walk through a marine supply store. I think my mouth just hung open for the entire time I walked through the place. This was the first full-service marine store since Australia, and I wanted everything. I settled for a throttle cable and left before I spent everything we had. When I put the cable on the motor, it felt funny having a perfect replacement part. We had been jerry-rigging everything back together for so long it seemed like I was cheating.

My brother's vacation was ticking away, so after a couple of days in Bodram we sailed from the resort atmosphere of the city sixty miles west to the secluded Greek island of Astipalia. The island is shaped like a butterfly, and we found an enclosed lagoon about half-way up on the inside of the eastern wing. Only two other boats were anchored there, and right away we could tell we were going to like it. There was absolutely nothing on shore except for a herd of goats and an open-air tavern.

We decided to try out the tavern for dinner and we were surprised at how delicious the food was. Being a small island they had a captive audience, and the food was melt-in-your-mouth good. We ordered everything on the menu and ate it all. Fresh fish, rice, chicken and a few plates full of things we didn't recognize.

Friendly people and a great view of the water from the open porch. I'd tell you the name of the place, but I don't think it had one. If you want to get there, I think you have to take a ferry to the main town and then arrange for a donkey. Once you get to the lagoon, you can't miss it – it's right next to a herd of goats.

Next stop, Atlantis. At least that's what the guide books say. Currently called Santorini Island, they say it could have been the fabled lost continent of Atlantis. The island exploded in 1440 B.C. with a force three times greater than the eruption in 1883 of the volcano Krakatoa in Indonesia. The blast from Santorini completely flattened houses 160 miles away. The following tidal wave was 300 feet high! The destruction was incredible.

Santorini is still a very active volcano, and we kept that in mind as we sailed into the crater to find a place to anchor. The shoreline is a steep cliff with the town being at the very top. The only way up to civilization is by cable car, donkey, or on foot. As with most places like this, lots of legends surround everyday life. Vampires were said to walk the land at night along with ghostly apparitions that floated around the hillside.

With the day ending and a full moon climbing over the lost city of Atlantis, we dropped our anchor in forty feet of water and tied our stern to what the guidebook called, "The once hot lump of ash in the middle of the crater." With a setting like this we were sure we would get a chance to see a ghost or vampire hanging around. Unfortunately, the only ghostly apparitions we saw were dozens of tour ships and charter boats.

Their vacation over, Neil and Gail left on a ferry from Santorini that was heading to Athens. From there they would get on one of those big birds and fly home. It was hard to imagine being able to get back to the States that fast. We figured if we hurried, it would still take us three or four more months. Things sure happen a lot slower on ol' Shadowfax.

From Santorini we sailed south on an overnight sail to Crete, the largest of the Greek islands. We sailed into the main harbor of Iraklion on the northern shore and found nowhere to tie the boat – just a huge concrete wall extending the length of the harbor. We dropped anchor and tied the stern as best as we could to the wall... not feeling very safe about the situation. The 600-foot-long cruise ships across the harbor from us had to navigate past us, as well as the half-dozen other sailboats also tied along the wall. It appeared as though they would have plenty of room as long as nothing went wrong, but we understood how many things could go wrong with a ship. Getting hit by that ship in the Maldives kept coming to mind. Sure enough, at six in the morning something went wrong.

The boat tied next to us got the worst of it. What happened was that a large ferry boat backed out of its slip and came a little too close to us poor little sailboats. The ferry didn't hit any of us, but when the captain threw the boat into forward, he gave it way too much throttle.

The wash that was thrown from his propeller was like sailing into a twenty-knot current. Our anchor held, so all we got out of it was a rough ride. Our neighbor had a tougher time. The wash hit him full on his port side, which put tons of pressure on his keel. With his bow at anchor and his stern tied to the wall, his boat rolled as the pressure on his keel increased. The two people onboard were sleeping as their boat rolled to its side, and everything they owned crashed to the floor. When their keel was even with the water's surface, they stayed on their side until the ferry boat pulled out and took its wash with it. Maybe the ferry captain liked to do this to the yachts for fun. He should have known better.

There was a small marina at the far end of the harbor with no room for us, but we decided to get in there somehow. We were getting used to squeezing into places where a 46-foot boat didn't fit so we figured it was worth a try. After motoring in a half-dozen circles in the marina dockage area, we managed to get secured in a much better spot than we thought possible. Creative docking should be an Olympic sport.

The reason we were so intent on staying in Crete was because a couple of friends we had met in New Zealand were supposed to be coming there by cruise ship. It took us a couple of days to find them, and then we set out to explore

Crete and to see just how many Greek salads we could possibly eat.

Bill and Jane Perrin were from Canada, and we met them while they were on vacation in New Zealand. We'd kept in touch and we were excited to meet up in Crete. What a great island to get together with someone.

We rode in a rented car up into the mountains and then from one tip of the island to the other. There were lots of friendly people and no crowds the farther we traveled from the water. The scenery is spectacular and Crete is definitely worth checking out. And yes, we ate enough Greek salads to last us a lifetime.

In sailing nothing lasts forever, we said goodbye to our friends and after twelve days we sailed out and headed west. We wanted to exit the Mediterranean and sail south before winter settled in. Since it was already mid-September, we were, as usual, late. We still had lots of miles and countries between us and the Atlantic Ocean.

We stopped at the far western end of Crete at a placed called Suda Bay so we could load up on duty free diesel. Since we were leaving the country we were allowed to get the cheaper fuel, which we hoped would get us across the rest of the Mediterranean. We had read that fuel in Italy would be as much as $5.00 a gallon, so we wanted to fill up with duty-free while we could.

We didn't know until we arrived, but Suda Bay is a NATO base. Being a NATO base meant we didn't have to deal with tour boats or cruise ships when looking for a place to anchor. Actually, there was only one boat in the whole bay besides warships... our old friends the gals on Tethys. Since captain Nancy on Tethys had told us they were going to stop and sell their boat in Cyprus or Turkey, we were surprised to see them. We'd said goodbye to them at three locations already, but we thought it was a definite goodbye when we left them in Cyprus. Apparently they changed their minds and decided to complete their circumnavigation back to Seattle, Washington. Great news for us. We wanted someone to buddy-boat with across the Med, and who could be better than friends we knew so well. After surviving the Indian Ocean and all those Red Sea countries we were sure we could have a great time crossing one more ocean together.

After a couple of days at anchor and full fuel tanks, we took off for the country of Malta 500 miles to the west. The trip didn't start out very well and just after we left the bay a Greek warship screamed up to Tethys and sounded its alarm siren. We both tried to contact them on our radios, but no one we talked to could speak English. Finally someone came on the radio and yelled, "Go back! Go back! You are entering very dangerous waters!"

When someone from a big warship yells something like that, you tend to take them seriously. We immediately turned around and sailed back to the protected cove to try to figure out what was happening. It took an hour to contact someone who could explain it to us. We discovered that the area outside our harbor had been taken over by NATO for bombing and missile practice. We like a little excitement in our lives, but sailing directly into a bombing range might have been an overdose.

As soon as we received the "all clear" from the officials, and our heart rates returned to normal, we continued our way west. The sail to Malta started with fair winds and ended with unfair motoring. The trip was uneventful except for our many hitchhikers - sparrows everywhere. They landed all over the boat and slept aboard every night. We even had quite a few sparrows down below inside the boat. We had to be careful where we walked or sat or we would have had squished sparrows. They were perched inside the boat on fans, stairs and the floor. They even let us pick them up and move them if they were in our way. They must travel all over the Mediterranean by grabbing a lift from any passing boat or ship that looked good to them.

Chapter 34

As we approached Malta, we dragged out the guide book to see what to expect. Malta is a small island of 122 square miles with a population of about 350,000, and it seems Malta is most famous for being attacked by just about everyone. The reason is because of its strategic location in the Mediterranean. The most famous of these battles were two great sieges.

The first battle took place in the 16th century. After being thrown out of Rhodes Island, the Knights of St. John sailed to Malta and made it their new home. The 4,000 knights built a huge fortification (which still stands today) around the harbor entrance. In 1565, a large Turkish fleet of 138 ships filled with 38,000 men attacked the island. After fighting for an entire summer, this small band of knights managed to hold off the Turks. They killed two-thirds of the attacking Turkish troops.

The second great siege took place in 1941 during the Second World War when the Italians and Germans blitzed the island. Throughout 1942 Malta was bombed constantly and the Maltese were reduced to living in rubble. Again Malta prevailed, and after the war the islanders were collectively awarded the George Cross for their bravery.

We found modern-day Malta to be just that – modern. After an impressive entrance sailing past the gigantic castles and forts, we were greeted with a view of closely-packed, sand-colored buildings and a sea of TV antennas for miles in every direction. A perfect place for a cable TV salesman.

This was another place where we were a little nervous about clearing in. Most of the guide books we had aboard said that pets definitely would not be allowed in the country. They went on to say that they would immediately kill any animal brought into their country. This would make a bad day for our cat, Bud, if it were true. The reason we decided to stop at all was that one article we read claimed that this was no longer true, and we would be allowed a short stay. Besides, who in their right mind would kill a visitor's pet. That would be a horrible way to promote tourism.

We anchored right in front of the customs office in a well-protected harbor and launched the dinghy. We were ready to leave immediately if they said anything that even sounded like they wanted to fry our little fur ball.

Ironically, the cat actually saved us about fifty bucks. The articles we read were only slightly true, but they weren't as mean to pets as they once were. What they said was we could only stay for three days, and we would have to stay at anchor. Anyone who didn't have a pet was told it was mandatory for them to go to the marina, tie up and pay for dockage. Good kitty.

After clearing through customs we enjoyed walking through all the castles and churches. After sailing this far through the Mediterranean we could definitely call ourselves "connoisseurs of castles," and the ones in Malta were some of the most impressive.

We arrived at the gates of the largest castle, The Grand Masters Palace, just as they were closing. Gretchen, me and the crew of Tethys signed up for the castle tour and somehow ended up with a private tour. Sometimes it pays to be late.

All the hallways were lined with knights' armor and the walls covered with original 16th century paintings. Oddly enough, this place was hit with only one bomb during World War Two, and everything was very much intact. A great place to visit and investigate. Lots of history and an experienced guide definitely makes for a great tour.

Since winter was sneaking up on us we started watching the weather closely because of low pressure systems that were starting to develop out in the Atlantic. Most of them seemed to be moving our way.

From Malta we had to sail northwest and toward all that winter weather, so three days in Malta was just about enough. Besides, the weather report called for a favorable wind for our 570-mile jump to Spain. We hoped we could make it that far and get some miles behind us.

It didn't quite work that way. We sailed away in the company of Tethys and another yacht, Calliope. One day out of Malta we sailed right into a force-ten gale!

We were sailing up the Sicily Straits as a low pressure system decided to develop right over us. There were no safe ports to duck into, so all we could do was to put away most of our sail and ride the storm downwind. At least downwind was the direction we wanted to go. Shadowfax was surfing off the larger waves at over 12 knots with almost no sail up. What a ride! If it wasn't for the cold rain and the screeching noise of the wind, it probably would have been fun. As long as you are going in the same direction as the wind, it's easy to imagine how much worse it could be. All you have to do is look back at the huge seas and think about what it would be like if you had to punch through them.

That pitch-black night we flew along as the storm didn't seem to want to give up. We kept looking the chart over to try and find an acceptable anchorage and we noticed a little cove on the island of Favignana off the northwest coast of Sicily that looked safe and inviting.

We didn't plan on stopping in Italy, but after such a horrible night at sea we decided to head in. Any port in a storm and all that. The wind continued to increase, and when we rounded up behind Favignana and into protected waters, it felt wonderful. The harbor was a little on the small side, but we managed to get all three boats anchored comfortably... even if it was only for a couple of hours.

What happened next was that the wind shifted 180 degrees, and our calm protected anchorage became dangerous. We had to go to "Plan B." "Plan B" was to head for a tiny little marina that was nothing but a small square of plastic, floating docks. The marina could only hold about four or five small boats, and it was empty except for one police boat.

As soon as we got close to the docks a whole bunch of people materialized, and they all wanted to help us tie up. It's always a welcome sight to see friendly faces. Unfortunately for Tethys, after they finished "helping," their steering vane was broken off and a dropped line was wrapped around their propeller. Everyone who helped had good intentions, and we soon found that Italian hospitality didn't stop there.

Guiseppi, the owner of the marina, came down and presented us with a 10 liter jug of wine and an invitation to lunch. What a difference from fighting a full gale a couple of hours earlier. We drank a large portion of the wine and then trooped off with Guiseppi along the cobblestone streets past all the colorful shops of the town. It seemed like every building we passed had church-type bells that rang out every fifteen minutes. Almost every shop had someone sitting outside reading a newspaper, playing chess, or just watching the world go by. Favignana was like a storybook land.

The restaurant that Guiseppi took us to was small, but it didn't seem to lack customers. The place was crowded, and it wasn't long after we were seated that we figured out we were with someone pretty popular. Everyone who entered came over to greet and kiss Guiseppi. And I mean everyone – even the waiter. When the owner of the restaurant called him "Don Guiseppi" and kissed his ring, we just had to wonder....

From what we could tell, Guiseppi never ordered anything, but what came out of the kitchen was spectacular: shrimp pasta, anchovy pasta, sea urchin pasta, two platters of fish, a platter of calamari (squid) and a dozen bottles of wine to round it off.

The fact that none of us spoke Italian and Guiseppi spoke no English didn't slow anyone down. We used our own homemade sign language along with drawing on napkins to get a point across.

When we tried to find out our host's last name, he kept nodding and pointing to the wine bottles. We couldn't figure out what he was trying to tell us until we noticed that the wine bottles all had the same name on them. It turned out that he owned the winery, and his last name was on all the bottles. Do we pick the right friends or what?

We had a little work to do on the boats, and there couldn't have been a better place to be. Italian hospitality went on and on and on. Everyone we met was overly friendly and wanted to help. To this day I can't say the word Favignana without smiling.

The biggest project we had to do involved the line wrapped around Tethys' propeller. Nancy said the last time that happened the boat had to be hauled out of the water to repair it. The reason was that Tethys had a variable pitch propeller that changed the angles of the propeller blades for forward or reverse while the propeller kept turning in the same direction. Forward and reverse was all due to the pitch of the propeller blades. Even when the boat was in neutral the propeller would still spin. What this meant was that when a line wrapped around the propeller, all the little delicate parts could be squashed.

Since haulout facilities were nowhere to be found, Nancy and I spent a full day underwater carefully taking the thing apart and then trying to file the squished parts back into shape while we were still underwater. Very cold work, but the good news was that it worked. We managed somehow to get it back together while only dropping one small washer – never to be seen again. That's okay. We figured out how to get the spacing right so Tethys was good to go.

After a few more days at Favignana we had a farewell dinner for Guiseppi aboard the sailboat Calliope. Guiseppi showed up with a huge cake that had to be the biggest one the island had to offer. It's hard to leave hospitality like that. Guiseppi even learned a few English words that he kept saying over and over. He kept saying, "Free till Christmas," as he pointed to the dock, which, of course, turned out to be owned by him. A tempting offer, but winter was closing in and we wanted to get moving.

So off we sailed with the forecast calling for another gale to slam into us in about two days. The winds were light as we motor-sailed the 200 miles to the harbor of Carloforte on Pietro Island about six miles to the southwest of Sardinia. We liked Italy so much that another Italian port sound like a great idea. Especially since a gale was on the way.

This was another uneventful sail, and that's the way we like it. Boring is good. Calliope did add a little bit of excitement to the passage by getting an old fishing net wrapped around the propeller. At least Calliope had a normal propeller and they could just jumped in and cut the net away. With so much junk floating around in the Med I was surprised that this sort of thing didn't happen more often.

Carloforte is a much larger city than Favignana, and we didn't get the same small town attention. But that's okay, it just made Favignana all that more special.

Just a day after we anchored the promised gale rolled through. Even though it wasn't Favignana, we still liked it just fine. Sitting in port during a gale can only make you smile and realize just how good you have it. The wind rips through the rigging with a sound like a jet engine and the boat swings in a pleasant ark on the anchor. Add in a fresh Gretchen-baked pizza and a good book and it doesn't get much better.

We ended up staying at Carloforte for ten days as two more low pressure systems with storm force winds blew through. We could definitely see a trend starting. By looking at a weather map we could see one bad weather front after another coming across the Atlantic and entering the Med. It was sure to get worse as each week went by.

Once more we took our little caravan of sailboats and headed out with the promise of another gale about thirty hours away. We thought this should give us enough time to make it the 200 miles to the island of Menorca in Spain. This would be the last long, open passage that we absolutely had to make. From Menorca we could day-sail along the mainland coast of Spain if we had to.

We approached the entrance channel to Menorca at night and found it right where it was supposed to be. That GPS navigation computer really made life easier. Through most of the western half of the Mediterranean we never saw the sun or stars because of cloud cover and this made the sextant almost useless. Whenever the sun poked through I would still get a sun sight or two just to stay in practice.

The entrance channel at Menorca was a little on the narrow side, so we motored our way in at the slowest speed possible. Using our spotlight to find the channel markers, we turned down a side channel with ancient stone forts on both sides and kept going until we entered a small lagoon and dropped the hook. Tethys and Calliope followed us in, and we all managed to find a spot to wait for the next gale which was due anytime. When daylight came we couldn't believe how narrow the channel was that we entered. It was so narrow that two sailboats couldn't have passed each other. I guess sometimes it's better not to know. I remember Menorca as a great place with lots of tourists – and topless beaches full of topless women. Funny the things that stick in your memory....

Before we knew it five days had passed and two more low pressure gales. This Mediterranean was becoming a real pain to get through. We had to drag our hats, sweaters and long pants out of our storage lockers for the first time in years. Not liking cold weather was a given for us. We couldn't wait to get to the Atlantic and head south to more tropical weather.

We finally had a break in the weather and we headed out. We made it another 160 miles to Ibiza Island, just off the coast of mainland Spain. We were planning to wait for the next gale that had been forecast, but it never seemed to develop. A hole in the bad weather appeared, and we took off at four in the afternoon to see how far we could make it. The next nasty weather system was days away. Great news!

We sailed to the mainland of Spain and continued on with only one night's rest at the small port of Almeria. It felt great to get some miles behind us. It felt even greater when we crossed the zero degree longitude line and once again entered the western hemisphere. It had been a couple of years since we had been on this side of the line.

As we continued west along the coast of Spain we tried to stay as far inshore as possible because the ship traffic coming in through the Straits of Gibraltar. We could always see four or five ships motoring by in the distance. Unfortunately, our inshore route was where hundreds of fishing boats of all sizes were putting their nets. They had to weave their nets around us, and we had to try to avoid the nets they had already put down. I'm sure we were as much of a pain in the neck to them as they were to us.

Speaking of fishing, we dragged two fishing lines across the whole Mediterranean Sea and never hooked a thing. Tethys and Calliope had the same results. In fact, one day while we were listening to other sailors on the ham radio, we heard a report that someone had caught a fish off the coast of France. This was such an event that everyone listening on the radio wanted to know what kind of fish it was, what lure, what speed were they going, weather conditions and everything else about it. From what we could tell, this might have been the only fish caught in the Mediterranean that entire year.

After a few thousand years of the locals netting every size fish available, they're all gone. Over seventeen countries border on the Mediterranean, and they all want (and need) to fish its waters. It didn't appear that they had any central governing laws about exploiting or over-netting, so we weren't all that surprised to learn it was in danger of being fished out.

From thirty miles away the Rock of Gibraltar loomed out of the haze in front of us. A huge landmark in this round-the-world-trip. This meant that we only had one measly little ocean left to cross.

Chapter 35

The country of Gibraltar is only two-and-a-half miles long and a mile wide, but it has a population of about 30,000. Tourism is the main industry, and the famous 1,400-foot-tall "rock" is called one of the Pillars of Hercules marking the entrance to the Mediterranean - or in our case, the exit. "Gib" is also popular with passing sailboats. The customs office claimed that 5,000 sailing yachts a year stop in to rest, shop and recover.

The last twenty miles to Gibraltar took almost six hours for us to sail. The current entering from the Atlantic was something. We fought against it with a forward speed of about three knots and just had to wait for it to let up a little. On the up side, the strong current and slow speed gave us a good long look at the giant Rock of Gibraltar. What a landmark.

Finally we coasted into the main harbor and weaved our way past all the anchored ships until we dropped anchor just off the main airport. We didn't know it at the time, but every time a plane was to land someone had to go out on the runway and light off fireworks to scare the birds away. We had our own mini Fourth of July with every incoming plane.

We were excited about getting out in the Atlantic and heading south, but the weather wasn't about to let us out so quickly. The weather predictions called for storms, strong winds and high seas with not much time in between bad weather systems. We were hoping for a four-day period of fair weather for our escape. We weren't total wimps and we were prepared to leave in bad weather, we just didn't want to leave in a full gale. After making it this far we learned something - we suck at leaving a comfortable place.

At least Gibraltar had lots of things for us to do during our eighteen-day stay. The first of which was to head to the top of their famous rock. The huge limestone rock has over thirty miles of drivable road cut through it, but the cable car was the best way to get to the top. The view from that high up is spectacular as you look out over the water. To the south are the narrow Straits of Gibraltar, and to the west you could look over the harbor all the way to Spain.

Caves and tunnels are cut into the rock, and one of the largest and deepest is called St. Michael's Cave. The main chamber of this limestone formation has been converted into an auditorium for concerts, ballets and dramas. The acoustics in this place must be tremendous, and I wish we could have experienced a concert. You can explore this cavern all the way to the bottom of the rock where a subterranean lake extends for several miles.

What else you find at the top of the rock are a couple of hundred mean and professional pickpockets. These aren't what you would think of as your usual run-of-the-mill pickpockets. They are Gibraltar's Barbary apes. These apes are brave enough to run up to you and stick their hands in your pockets as they look for food. We saw a tour bus drive by, and one of the larger apes jumped right in the open driver's window. There are lots of stories and legends about how the apes got there, but the truth is that the British garrison brought them over from Africa as pets, and then they just took over the Rock.

One of the oddest things about Gibraltar was their legal smuggling operation. The large, modern marina was full of beautiful sailing yachts on one side, and small, fast jet black speedboats on the other side. These tiny powerboats had twin 200 HP outboard engines on them, and they could almost break the sound barrier.

What they were smuggling was cigarettes. They would buy them cheap in Gibraltar and then shoot the short distance across the harbor to off-load them in Spain. It was so obvious what they were doing that it was ridiculous. It seems smuggling was okay with the Gibraltar government, but not with the Spanish government. These guys would zip across the harbor all night long. Because of this we came awfully close to dying.

Gretchen and I were in the dinghy heading out to the anchorage after dark one night when out of nowhere one of these smuggling boats came flying around a corner and missed us by inches. The spray from the boat washed over us, and I don't think anyone on the boat had any idea we were there. Scary stuff! The smugglers didn't have any lights on, and they didn't watch for anything that might be in their way. They could have been arrested by the Spanish police for smuggling until they got safely back into Gibraltar's port, so they just went at full speed until they made it.

By the time the weather broke enough for us to sail out, we were freezing. We could see our breath in the air all day long. At night we crawled under every blanket we owned. We were ready to get out of there and head south.

It looked like we would have about five days of fair weather as we sailed out into the Straits of Gibraltar. Man, what a nasty place. We left at the right time for us to miss the worst of the incoming tide, but unfortunately that put us in that mess at night. At one point we had 26 large tankers or container ships within an eight-mile range on our radar screen. It felt like they were all heading right at us. What a crazy night.

Even after we finally entered the Atlantic, one last ship altered course and appeared to try to run us down. We shined our spotlight on our sails and hull, but nothing seemed to work. I finally just turned the boat and ran from him at a right angle to his course – running away is one of my favorite sailing tactics.

Once safely out in the Atlantic we were able to head in a southerly direction for the Canary Islands and warmer weather. The first part of the trip was stormy with waterspout-type weather. On top of that it was cold and the seas were huge, but at least no full gales were forecast to hit us.

The second half of the 600-mile trip was even more exciting. The stormy weather cleared, but the wind increased to over forty knots. What a ride! No bad weather, just lots of wind.

The Atlantic shallows up about seventy miles from the African coast (just about where we were) and the seas get stupid. By "stupid" I mean fifteen to twenty feet high with every fourth or fifth wave breaking over the boat.

We reefed the mainsail to its smallest size and flew no other sail. It may have been rough, but by reducing the sail that much we sailed smoothly and somewhere in the middle of the comfort scale. The windvane did all the steering, so what could be better? We would take turns suffering through our cold watches and then run down to the berth, crawl under ten blankets and sleep until our next watch three hours away.

Just about the time the weather started to warm up the Canary Islands came into view.

The Canary Islands are an autonomous region of Spain. There are seven major islands and many smaller islands. The closest Canary Island to the coast of Africa is only seventy miles away. The islands are mostly volcanic with the volcano still being active.

The name Canary Islands is a little deceiving. In 60 B.C., King Juba from Morocco discovered large dogs living on the islands, so the name Insulae Canium (The Island of Dogs) exists today as Islas Canarias. By coincidence, canaries fly all over the island too, so I guess you could look at the name either way.

In 1492 Christopher Columbus put in at the Canaries for repairs before setting out on his way to the New World. He also stopped again on his future voyages. In modern times tourism is the main industry, although coffee, dates, bananas, sugar, avocados and grapes are heavily exported.

We anchored safely on the east side of Lanzarote Island, cleared through customs and slept for twenty-four hours. With just two people keeping twenty-four-hour watches day after day, you really get wiped out. We probably could have slept for forty-eight hours if we put our minds to it. As soon as we got back to Florida, we were going to need a vacation. Sounds silly, huh? Take five years off, sail around the world, come home and take a vacation.

The Canary Islands are located at about 28 degrees north latitude, which means that by the time we dropped anchor on Lanzarote Island we were almost warm. I say almost because after being so cold for so long, it was going to take us a while to thaw. The Canaries were definitely warmer but not hot. We would have been more comfortable in the tropics, and 28 degrees north wasn't exactly in the tropics. We had to sail south to around 23 degrees for that. No matter what the weather, we were always happy to stop and check out a new place.

We only planned on staying in the islands for a short time before heading out to cross the Atlantic (how many times have I said that), but it would be fifteen days before we finally got on our way. Sadly, it was a time to say goodbye to everyone we had been sailing with. The Canary Islands are a popular jump-off spot for crossing the Atlantic, and at least a hundred yachts were gathered there preparing to make the crossing. We met many of them at one time or another during the almost five years we'd been out, and this would be the last anchorage together with any of them.

Most of the other boats planned to sail to Barbados on the other side of the Atlantic, and we planned to stay a little farther north and make landfall in the American Virgin Islands.

As usual, in this subculture of sailing gypsies, one party after another was held. Even though we would all be able to keep in touch along the way by ham radio, we still wanted to say our goodbyes in person. It was great to talk over our memories and laugh about all the strange situations we managed to get ourselves into and out of.

After sailing west through the Canaries we made our last stop at the island of Tenerife to fill up on food, fuel (duty free) and water. Since Thanksgiving was rolling around we thought a turkey dinner would be in order so we stuck a frozen turkey in our freezer. One more reason for staying at the Canary Islands for so long was because the Atlantic hurricane season didn't officially end until the last day of November, and we didn't want to end our circumnavigation by sailing into a late-forming hurricane.

We enjoyed the Canary Islands, but the time came when we couldn't put off our departure any longer. We raised anchor and sailed out into our last ocean passage.

Since Tenerife is the highest point in Spain (ironic since it was almost a thousand miles from the real Spain), we could see its snow-covered mountain peak for an entire day. Nothing to do but put the island behind our stern, put out the fishing lines, cross our fingers and head west. With a pod of pilot whales leading the way, we raised all our working sails and settled down for a 2,705 mile trip.

Chapter 36

Maybe now would be a good time to talk about seasickness. After meeting hundreds of sailors around the world, it was surprising to hear how many people suffered from it. I didn't think we ever met a crew where no one onboard got seasick. This fact always made it a conversation item. I'm one of the lucky people who never had to deal with seasickness, but I was always interested in why so many people were afflicted with it, what they did about it, and why the sailed at all when they knew they would end up being sick.

When the topic of a conversation turned to seasickness, the first thing mentioned was usually drugs. In this day and age there are literally dozens of different drugs to take to help deal with seasickness, and the one thing everyone seemed to agree on was there is no all-out best drug. Sailors could only tell which one worked best for them. Some sailors used acupressure bands on their wrists, while others stuck time-release pads behind their ear (probably the strongest medication). Sailors from other countries came up with even more drugs which couldn't be bought in the States. The list of options seemed endless.

Unfortunately for Gretchen, she was among this group of intrepid sailors who had to go by trial and error while searching for the "perfect drug." If you think about it, this has to be a horrible way to see if something works. You have to go out into rough waters and then just hope you picked a drug that worked for you. If it didn't, you were stuck being sick for five or six hours until you could try something else.

Gretchen had to self-regulate the amount she needed - more for rougher weather and less for calmer weather. Most drugs seemed to have side effects, like drowsiness or even slight hallucinations. Usually after a few days at sea Gretchen would be able to stop taking it all together. I know it was hard enough for me to get up for nighttime watches without having the extra burden of being wiped out by some drug. Gretchen and all the seasick sailors out there deserver medals.

Anyway, what every seasick person agreed on was that sailing was still worth it. Maybe all cruisers are adventure junkies. Traveling to new countries in all parts of the world always outweighed any objection. What other way can you travel to almost any country in the world and always have your house with you? The challenge of ocean passages added enough adventure for the hardest core adventurer. If you want to go sailing, and you think you can't because of seasickness, think again. Check it out with a doctor, see which drugs you should try, then go for it. Thousands of sailors can't be wrong.

Back to the passage - our Atlantic passage turned out to be a little bit of everything. The trade winds for the first part of the trip pushed us along nicely, and I thought we had it made. We sailed southwest until we reached about twenty degrees north latitude and then headed west. The best trade winds are usually farther south than that, but since we were going to make landfall on the Virgin Islands, which are at about eighteen degrees north, we decided to continue this route as long as the trade winds lasted. We figured we could always head farther south if we had to. Since our sails were more patches and stitches than sail, we also sailed a lot more conservatively (slower) than we wanted to.

What all this "staying north" and "conservative sailing" meant was that we had the longest passage we had ever made. Even though it was shorter in miles than the Pacific, it still took us longer - twenty-six days to be exact (that's 104 watches each). That's a long time at sea!

The trade winds decided to leave us just over halfway, and the weather started to change. In fact, the weather did everything. We had headwinds, beam winds and no winds. We tried heading a little farther south and had no luck searching for better winds. At seventeen degrees north, we just pointed the boat west and hoped for better winds somewhere up ahead.

We tried every sail combination possible, but just kept plodding slowly along. One day with the wind and seas against us, we only made 88 miles to the west. Not very productive for ol' Shadowfax. Ah well, at least we were heading in the right direction.

At one point the spinnaker halyard broke, and I decided I wanted to go up the mast to see what I could do about it. I waited a couple of days until one of those eerie calm periods came along and decided to give it a try. When Gretchen had winched me up to the top of the mast, I was reminded what happens to a calm day once you get to the top. Any little sea swell that comes along gets exaggerated a hundred times, and it's like being on the worst (or best) roller coaster you can imagine. Probably not the safest place to be either. Once the halyard was rerun through the pulley, I came down as fast as I could and hoped no more lines were ready to break.

After the longest passage of our lives, St Johns Island in the American Virgin Islands appeared through the haze. As usual, we were exhausted. We motored up to the entrance channel at five in the morning and waited until sunrise. What we could see of the channel entrance lights looked completely different than what was on the chart. We figured it would be safer to stay out until we could see the channel.

The Virgin Islands are a group of seven islands which are located to the west of Puerto Rico. Four islands are claimed by the British, and three are claimed by the United States. The U.S. Virgins, along with most of the Caribbean Sea, have an economy that runs mainly on tourist dollars. The main U.S. island of St. Thomas is always busy, crowded and hectic, so we decided to make our landfall at the smaller, less crowded St. John Island.

As usual, a little daylight made life - and entrance passes - a lot easier. We motored in, dropped the hook and went to sleep. We had wanted to make landfall by Christmas, and we made it a day early. A Christmas Eve nap was in order.

We didn't give ourselves much rest before heading out again. After a good nap - more like a short coma - a Christmas dinner at a local restaurant, and seeing the first American football game on T.V. that we had seen in years, we prepared to leave. The day after Christmas we found ourselves back at sea again and heading west.

The plan was to head straight for Key West, 950 miles away. It sounded like we were so close to home, but on the other hand, 950 miles was 950 miles. That's a long passage.

Fair winds and a steady barometer stayed with us for the first three days. What a great sail! We had the mainsail out to one side and the jib poled out on the other side. With the steering vane doing the steering, we didn't have to touch anything for days. That's perfect sailing.

Somehow we knew it wouldn't last. It never does. Anytime you are at sea for days and days you're bound to have changes in the weather. We actually passed through one warm front and two cold fronts before we made it to the Florida Keys.

The first cold front brought rain squalls, lightning and the U.S. Coast Guard. It was past midnight and we were sailing just north of Haiti when a Coast Guard cutter called us on channel 16 on the V.H.F. radio. We knew what was going to happen after the radio contact.

"Captain, we plan to put a small boarding party aboard for an inspection. Please maintain course and speed." Since we were in a small gale with eight-foot seas, I asked if maybe it would be a bit safer for his boarding party if I slowed down or at least turned into the seas. The answer was something like, "Probably, but we don't want to inconvenience you or slow your progress." Nice thought. They must be afraid of taxpayers complaining to their Congressman. We voluntarily slowed down.

Out of the darkness a huge inflatable boat crashed into Shadowfax, and five people crawled aboard. That was one dangerous operation. They actually had to crash into us twice to get everybody aboard. They all had float jackets on along with bullet proof vests, guns and briefcases. They made it aboard with only a couple of cuts and bruises. They seemed used to smashing themselves into boats.

We all went below to get to know each other. We were wondering if they were friendly, and they were wondering if we were Columbia's best smugglers.

Our question was answered first. They were all friendly and polite... four men and one woman just doing a tough job. While they were looking the boat over, one of the guys had me take up one of the floorboards so he could "check the bilge for water," as he put it. I thought that was awfully nice of him. After sailing around the world, here was this stranger apparently interested in whether we were sinking or not. I told him I would be interested in that too, so we both took a look. Somehow I think while I was looking for water, he was really looking for drugs.

By the time they got around to checking our safety equipment the atmosphere was friendly. They were pretty sure that we were "clean" as far as smuggling went. All our safety gear was looked over, and when the officer in charge asked us for our "Garbage Management Report," I had no idea what it was... never mind if I had one.

I was told it was a written list of what we do with our garbage. The first thing that came to my mind was back in Sri Lanka when the locals fought over it. I guess I was supposed to write that down. How about when that guy dumped my oil into the harbor because he wanted the plastic containers? Maybe my garbage management report could be riveting reading after all.

When they told me that this management report was a relatively new law, I tried to explain that we had been "out of town" for the past few years and hadn't heard of it. I also said I would start one right away now that I knew what it was. He was very polite, but "sorry, you will be notified by mail of what the fine will be" summed up his answer. Bureaucracy hit us smack in the face six-hundred miles before we even reached the coast. Oh well, the officials were lots tougher back in Egypt.

After a two hour search, the time came to send the Coast Guard home. I slowed the boat and headed into the wind and everybody smiled. They seemed to like that a lot. When it's that rough they should make boats slow down. Safety and all that. I wonder how they board a large ship underway? It must get a bit scary for our Coast Guard.

Over the next two days we were contacted by two more Coast Guard Cutters, buzzed by a Navy jet skimming across the water about twenty feet away, as well as the quietest helicopter I've ever seen. I just looked up and saw it hovering a couple of hundred yards away staring at us. After a brief radio contact, it streaked away. The U.S. sure seemed to have an effective force field around its perimeter. We had the same attention years earlier when we were trying to leave the country.

The next part of the trip put us just north of Cuba on New Year's Eve. We had never been at sea over a New Year's holiday before. There was no one to invite over and no way to celebrate. I came off watch at midnight while Gretchen went on watch. A kiss, a hug, and a glass of wine about covered it. It was a dark night with nasty weather, so we figured we could wait and have a real party once we made it all the way back to Captiva Island. Maybe a dozen parties.

New Year's Day brought clear weather and a thirty-five-foot sperm whale to visit. This whale must have thought it was a porpoise. It was all alone and just seemed to want to play with Shadowfax. He (she?) would dive under our bow and then pop up on the other side over and over again. One time he bumped into Shadowfax's side and gave us a good jolt. We didn't care for that very much. We didn't mind if he wanted to be friends with Shadowfax, but hands, er, fins, off. Too many boats have been sunk by whales for us not to take it seriously when this huge animal decided to crash into us.

We slowed the boat a little, hoping this would discourage him. He stayed with us for the next few hours, but he didn't' hit us again. Maybe he just wasn't paying attention and hit us by mistake. Maybe he didn't' enjoy it any more than we did. He finally just ducked under our bow one last time and disappeared. Maybe he found his lunch swimming around down there somewhere.

As we approached the Gulf Stream, the weather reports on the ham radio started giving gale warnings because of an approaching frontal system. That Gulf Stream always seemed to give us trouble. The stream sure can be one rough hunk of water when the wind picks up.

Sure enough, as soon as we entered the stream, the worst weather of the nine-day trip hit. The wind stood the seas straight up. One of the stronger rain squalls came along and slammed into us with winds strong enough to put a good-size rip in our poor old mainsail.

Without the mainsail, sailing into the wind, like we were, would be impossible. Gretchen went up on deck to try and sew it back together, but after using every limb to hang on to the boat there was no way that she could sew. Taking the sail off to sew it was also out of the question. It was much too rough. For us to get into the Florida Keys before dark would only be possible if we came up with some way to get the mainsail back in use.

The people at North Sails, or any of the other large sail-making companies, would cringe at what we came up with. We stapled it back together with a regular office stapler. Seventy-nine staples (Gretchen counted). The strangest part was that it worked great. We raised the sail, headed into the wind and continued on to the Florida Keys.

Next problem, the jib sail decided to blow out. King Neptune was making us earn every foot of the last twenty miles back to the States. The jib didn't just get a rip in it, it shredded along the entire foot of the sail. Instead of the office stapler, I took our sharpest scissors up on the bow and just started cutting. By the time I finished, our poor jib looked terrible, but it would work. I cut out a one-foot strip all along the foot of the sail. Messy, but effective.

Once all our sails were again up and flying, Gretchen said something that caught my attention. She said, "You know, this storm is pretty bad. Huge seas, lightning and gale force winds. How come it's no big deal? Have we gotten used to this or what?" She was right! We were used to sailing - gales, whales, pirates, reefs and whatever else sailing had to offer.

What we were terrified of was coming home. Even calling someplace "home" didn't seem right. Home was aboard Shadowfax. It didn't matter where the boat was, that was home. What started as a trip around the world turned into a lifestyle that felt completely normal. We were sure we didn't want that to change. We couldn't see how we could ever fit into the old rut of life ashore again. We had become sea gypsies!

But even sailing around the world ends sometime and just at dusk we were weaving our way past thousands of floating crab-trap markers (the main reason we wanted to arrive in daylight) and into the Big Pine Key anchorage in the Florida Keys. We didn't have time to get to the clearing in port of Key West, so we just dropped the hook, feeling like we had accomplished something. Exhausted, as usual after a passage, but smiling constantly.

Chapter 37

Bright and early the next morning we raised anchor and headed the short distance to the most southeastern point of the United States, Key West. We anchored in the large anchorage off the main town and waited for someone to come out to clear us in. One of the other sailboats in the anchorage saw our yellow quarantine flag flying from our spreaders and yelled over to us that we would be there for years if we waited for someone to come out. We were told that we had to go ashore and call customs on the phone.

We dinghied ashore, found a pay phone and called the U.S. Customs Office in Key West. We were told by the lady that answered, "No, don't call us here. Go to the grey customs phone a couple of blocks away and call from there."

Off we went to find this "grey phone." It was all by itself against a brick wall, and it was just like we were told... grey. It seemed like a strange way to clear in, but we approached this funny looking phone box and Gretchen picked it up. It rang directly into the customs office in Miami where another lady asked us a whole pile of questions - one of which was to name every place we'd been. We were then told to stand by while they relayed all this information back to the Key West Customs Office. We were one block from the Key West Customs Office and relaying information to them through Miami. Makes perfect sense to me. This was before 9/11 so hopefully they are a bit more attentive to who sails in these days.

After a short wait we were told to write down our six digit clearance number and to enjoy America. That was it! No visits by customs, immigration, health, security or agriculture. Of all the places in the world, we expected a lot of bureaucracy from the States. On the other hand, we were very happy we didn't' have to deal with more people, more questions, and another search of Shadowfax.

After a day of wandering around our first port in the States, there was nothing left to do but raise anchor and continue back to our point of beginning. The one-hundred mile sail into the Gulf of Mexico was uneventful and calm - a good chance to get the boat cleaned up for our arrival. At least on the inside. When we left the States, Shadowfax's hull looked clean and shiny. You could even see yourself in its shine. Not now. After all the sand storms of the Red Sea, Shadowfax looked like she had been through a war or two.

We arrived at Redfish Pass on the north end of Captiva Island just at daybreak. I wasn't sure we wanted to try using this entrance. The pass didn't look quite the same as when we left. The most important difference was the absence of an entrance marker. Redfish Pass was known as a "local knowledge" entrance with constantly shifting sandbars. It was a flat calm morning, so I figured why not give it a try.

Gretchen had all our flags from the countries we had visited, along with our signal flags, ready to raise. I told her to wait until we got through the entrance because I would hate to run aground while all those flags were attracting attention to us. It would be embarrassing enough without the flags.

No problem, mate. We never had less than thirteen feet under us. Plenty of water to spare. We rounded up on the bay side of Captiva Island and into the waters that I knew like the back of my hand. Gretchen raised the flags just seconds before we screeched to a halt on a sandbar that wasn't there five years earlier. The first thing I thought to say was, "You better take those flags down."

This was the first time we had been aground since we left! Honest! Gretchen summed it up best when she said, "The rest of the world is deep." Ah well, we were only aground for about twenty minutes, but we knew we were home. Florida, the home of the sandbar.

We hit the horn as we passed our good friends at Jensen's Marina and we coasted up to the dock at 'Tween Waters Marina on Captiva Island where we untied the lines four years and nine months earlier. With our flags flying and horns blaring we officially finished our circumnavigation. The feeling is hard to explain. Happy, sad, excited... everything at once. A crowd of friends waited on the dock at 'Tween Waters to take our lines and that was that. The total was 31,768 nautical miles (36,768 statute), and a world full of new friends. An incredible trip, and I highly recommend it to anyone who has had thoughts of sailing over the horizon.

The "official list" of countries we sailed to is, Belize, Guatemala, Honduras, Panama, Galapagos, French Polynesia, Cook Islands, American Samoa, Kingdom of Tonga, New Zealand, Fiji, Vanuatu, New Caledonia, Australia, Indonesia, Singapore, Malaysia, Thailand, Sri Lanka, Maldive Islands, Yemen, Ethiopia, Sudan, Egypt, Cyprus, Turkey, Greece, Malta, Italy, Spain, Gibraltar, Canary Islands and the Virgin Islands.

Once the thrill of being back started to wear off, the next step was almost more difficult than passage-making. We had to completely start life over again. We needed a place to keep Shadowfax, a car, a phone, an address and worst of all, land-based jobs. Arab terrorists were nothing compared to this.

The funny thing about it was that within a couple of months of being back we had a clear goal in mind – to sail out again! We had given ourselves two years to get Shadowfax back in shape. We must be nuts, but we liked floating around out there. After all, look at the places we missed. You may only live once, but it might be possible to go around twice.

Photos can be found at
www.LifeAtFiveKnots.com